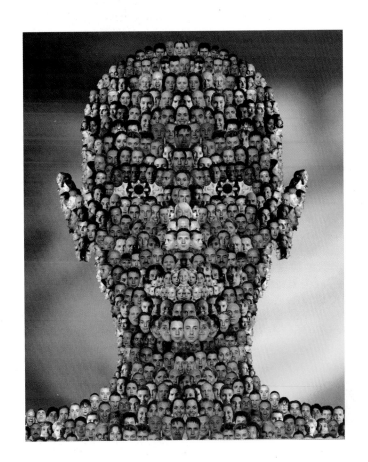

INSPIRATIONS

ORIGINAL LYRICS AND THE STORIES BEHIND THE GREATEST SONGS EVER WRITTEN

In aid of Norwood Ravenswood and Nordoff-Robbins Music Therapy

Sanctuary

ACKNOWLEDGMENTS

THE HITS UNDER THE HAMMER COMMITTEE
David Glick, Harriette Goldsmith, Ronnie Harris, Steven Howard,
Andrew Miller, Richard Rosenberg and Richard Shipman
would like to thank the following for their help in bringing this
book to fruition:

ASCAP, BASCA, BMI, MCPS, MPA, PRS, Les Allen, Penny Braybrooke, Eileen Buss, Peter Compton, Jane Curtis, Deloitte & Touche, Amanda Denning, Eatons Solicitors, Ruth Graham, John Grayson, Harris & Trotter, Diane Hempsall, HG Events, David Houghton, Jeff Hudson, Paul Judge and Barbara Freshwater at Fox Studios, the late Barry Lazell, Eddy Leviten, Andrew Miller Promotions, Mike Miller, Charlotte Murphy, Michelle Knight, Michael Randolfi, Mike Read, Richman Management, John Rifkin, Gary Schwartz, Sedley Richard Laurence Voulters, Tim Smith, David Stark, Storm Thorgerson, Caryn Tomlinson, Richard Tomlinson-Hare, Tim Trevan, Zomba Music Publishers, together with all the music publishers, artist managers, music industry accountants, lawyers and record companies who have helped.

Finally and most importantly, we are most grateful to all the songwriters who have
donated their time and talents to our cause.

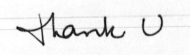

Design by: David Houghton
Cover image: courtesy Storm Thorgerson
Text by: Michael Randolfi, Mike Read and David Stark
Printed by: SFERA International, Milan
Photography by: Les Allen with Charlotte Murphy at Fox Studios
Published by: Sanctuary Publishing, Sanctuary House, 45-53 Sinclair Road, London W14 0NS
www.sanctuarypublishing.com
Copyright: Hits Under The Hammer, 1999

ISBN: 1 86074 300 5

INTRODUCTION

EVERY PROJECT STARTS WITH AN IDEA.

Some ideas start with a question. For us it was a question, born out of a bike ride across the Sinai Peninsula in the Middle East, organised to raise money for Norwood Ravenswood.

One of the 80 riders, Steven Howard, wondered how he could raise more significant sums for the charity than a sponsored bike ride across hundreds of miles of desert. Sitting around the campfire that evening he broached the subject with three of his fellow cyclists – David Glick, Ronnie Harris and Richard Rosenberg – and, based on everyone's links with the music business, the idea of holding a music-related event emerged.

The discussion continued on our return to London where it was finally decided to hold an auction of hit songwriters' original lyric sheets. Such an auction had a number of advantages: it would focus on songwriting for which most artists like to be recognised first and foremost; donations need not demand too much effort on the part of the songwriters and artists; bidding for something as unique as an original lyric would be something that both the serious collector and the ordinary fan could relate to; and the whole concept ought to capture the imagination of the media. Everyone would be a winner – but especially the charity.

Having agreed the concept, the way forward was obvious. Through our various contacts within the music industry the committee members – Steven, Ronnie Harris, David Glick, Andrew Miller, Richard Rosenberg, Richard Shipman and co-ordinator Harriette Goldsmith – would ask the stars to sign and donate for auction the original lyrics or score for a famous song they had composed. If the originals were not available, then they would be asked to write out the lyrics in their own handwriting, possibly on an interesting object which related to the song itself.

With the scale of the project so ambitious, we contacted Nordoff-Robbins, the large and well-connected music-related charity, for support. They loved the idea and the 'Hits Under The Hammer' project was born. Next the search began for an auctioneer. Sotheby's, with their reputation in the sale of pop memorabilia, were approached. They agreed not only to participate but also waived their commission.

Meanwhile, Steven Howard, a music publisher by trade, drew up a list of some 400 songs that were immediately recognisable, significant to the development of pop music and had stood the test of time. With these targets set the long process began of begging for donations.

While the music industry is one of the most actively charitable of all business sectors, artists are frequently imposed upon to give of their time and money and we were concerned that we might meet with 'charity fatigue'. However, in reality, the response was immediately favourable. Direct personal requests to Mark Knopfler and Andrew Gold resulted in the first donations – the original manuscript of 'Your Latest Trick' torn out of Mark's lyric book (a full size diary, the words written on the page for 8 March 1984) and Andrew's lyrics for 'Thank You For Being A Friend' handwritten on parchment. Roger Greenaway, as composer and Senior Vice President of ASCAP (an American society which looks after the performance rights of songwriters), donated the lyrics for 'I'd Like To Teach The World To Sing' and wrote a letter of recommendation for the project to all his personal contacts. These included Bryan Adams, who rang to say that he would donate a computer print-out of the lyrics for 'All For Love' – his Number One duet with Sting and Rod Stewart from the soundtrack for Disney's *The Three Musketeers*. The print-out had been used in the studio, and had annotations in different coloured inks noting changes made during the recording. Bryan had signed it and got Sting, Rod Stewart, Michael Kamen (who wrote the score) and Mutt Lange (Bryan's co-writer and the song's producer) to add their signatures.

Bryan's generosity was nearly in vain, however, when it came to shipping the score. Because of the piece's value we had arranged to collect it by hand. But the envelope – which bore no address, simply a name – was accidentally put into the mail along with all the other correspondence from his office that day. On hearing of the loss, Bryan went down to the sorting office himself, explained the situation, described the envelope and waited until it was found!

The first few donations were crucial in convincing other artists that the project was worthy of their participation, nudging the doubters into making their own donations. With these in hand, it was time to blitz everyone's contacts, however tenuous.

The profile and credibility of the public launch was of paramount importance and there seemed

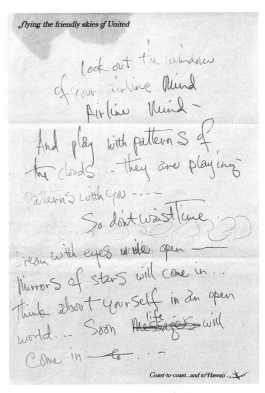

Original Jimi Hendrix lyrics which raised £12,500 for Hits Under The Hammer

no better place than the January 1998 MIDEM, in Cannes – the music industry's equivalent of the Cannes Film Festival. Nanette Rigg, the Director General of British Music Rights, had suggested the Government's support might add a certain credibility, so when it was announced that Secretary Of State For Culture, Media And Sport, Chris Smith, would be visiting the Best Of British stand, British Music Rights invited us to meet up with him. Such a high profile meeting was the perfect photo opportunity and reinforced the Government's explicit backing for the venture. Tony Blair had been embracing the music industry since his victory in the 1997 election, and had encouraged leading pop artists to be associated with the Government, most famously inviting Noel Gallagher to 10 Downing Street.

The first press coverage appeared in *Music Week*, the industry's weekly trade journal, which was soon followed by a three-page photo spread in *Q* magazine which also showed some of the items already donated.

A further boost for the campaign came in April 1998. In February, Peter Cunnah and Jamie Petrie had donated the original working lyrics for 'Things Can Only Get Better' – the song that the Labour Party had adopted as their theme tune in the 1997 UK general election. Tony Blair, through Chris Smith, agreed to get the entire Labour Cabinet to sign this item too. In fact, the Prime Minister even posed for photographs as he handed over the signed lyrics in Downing Street on 23 April and a formal endorsement from Tony Blair for the project was given in July.

NORDOFF-ROBBINS MUSIC THERAPY

NORDOFF-ROBBINS MUSIC THERAPY

THERE ARE MANY DIFFERENT APPROACHES TO MUSIC therapy. Nordoff-Robbins use a creative approach where therapeutic changes are worked for within music itself. Therapists create a very personal environment which is developed, built on a relationship of trust and respect, where the clients/children are valued for what they can do, and are encouraged to express themselves within the language of music.

From this starting point, client and therapist work together towards overcoming the limitations imposed by the child's disturbance or special needs, and strive towards realising their potential within the limits of that handicapping condition or disability.

Music is an intrinsic part of all of us: pulse and rhythm are found in our heartbeat, our breathing; melody is created in our laughing, crying, screaming, singing; the whole range of our emotions is held within the structures of harmony, and of musical style and idiom. These intimate connections with music remain despite handicap or illness and are not dependent on a musical training or background.

Because of this, music therapy has helped children and adults with a wide range of needs, arising from such varied causes as learning difficulties and handicaps, mental and physical illnesses and physical and sexual abuse, amongst others.

HUTH's Harriette Goldsmith, Steven Howard and Andrew Miller witness Tony Blair signing 'Things Can Only Get Better'

Liam Howlett from The Prodigy, Phil Collins and Roger Greenaway added theirs. Adam White from *Billboard* brought the power of the international music press and industry bodies. By this stage, the project could not have been more heavily or widely endorsed.

The last logistical problem was to find a venue for the auction and we have Robert Earl to thank for the solution. During a conversation at Nordoff-Robbins' Silver Clef lunch – one of the charity's biggest fundraising events – Robert offered not only the use of his newly opened restaurant, Sound Republic in Leicester Square, but included in his donation food and drinks for the press launch and the auction night itself.

By now, items were rolling in: the lyrics to 'MacArthur Park' written on a cake box by Jimmy Webb; the original working lyrics of 'Three Lions' signed not only by Frank Skinner, David Baddiel and Ian Broudie, but the entire England football squad on the eve of the World Cup.

Ironically, the number of donations was becoming a problem. In fact, the response in general was so overwhelming we decided to postpone the auction from the originally intended date of Autumn 1998 to March 1999.

Sotheby's advised that they would only be able to get through about 50-60 items in one evening, but it was clear that Hits Under the Hammer would have far more than that. Around this time, we heard about a company called Interactive Collector which conducted auctions over the internet. We approached them with the idea of setting up an internet catalogue to auction those items that Sotheby's did not pick up in their 50-60 lots. This alternative auction would take place over a two-week period, culminating a week after the Sotheby's auction.

With the items for auction now almost all in, the auctioneers selected, and venues for the auctions agreed, it was time to start putting together the printed auction catalogue and, of course, to seek sponsors of the design and printing. Deloitte & Touche agreed to sponsor the catalogue and Virgin Megastores offered to distribute it through their stores. Designed and printed free of charge by Noem Design and Manor Park Press, the catalogue featured Tony Blair's endorsement as a foreword. Yet, even that contribution was trumped. Sir Evelyn de Rothschild, of Norwood Ravenswood, wrote to

Hugh Grant with the lyrics for 'Love Is All Around' handwritten by Reg Presley

the Queen, as their Patron, asking for her support. In November 1998, he received her letter of endorsement, which naturally took pride of place in the catalogue.

Once the catalogue was ready, all that remained was to ensure publicity for the auction and for this we had the help of Darren Anderton of the England squad, who posed for photos with the framed lyrics to 'Three Lions', and Tom Jones, who posed for photographs with the lyrics to 'Delilah' as well as doing an interview with *OK* magazine, further donating his interview fee to Hits Under The Hammer. Coverage for the media launch on 11 February 1999 was extensive.

And still donations rolled in: Reg Presley wrote out the lyrics to 'Love Is All Around' on the back of an acoustic guitar, also signed by Hugh Grant, Duncan Kenworthy and Richard Curtis in recognition of the song's success as the theme to *Four Weddings And A Funeral*. The original script for *Notting Hill* with the lyrics for the theme tune by Boyzone written on it, and signed by Julia Roberts, was offered with two tickets to the world premier of the film. Errol Brown of Hot Chocolate sent in some silver boots on which he had written out the lyrics to 'You Sexy Thing'. Right Said Fred sent in the lyrics to 'I'm Too Sexy' on – what else? – a pink La Roca shirt. Eric Clapton sent in the lyrics to

Madness singer Suggs with the door for 'Our House' alongside its new owner, Emma 'Baby Spice' Bunton

Hot Chocolate's Errol Brown with the 'You Sexy Thing' boots he donated to Hits Under The Hammer

'Pilgrim', and Madonna the lyrics to 'Little Star'. Madness, wrote out 'Our House' on a wooden door. And, with only two days to go before the auction, George Michael sent in the original lyrics to 'Faith'.

Finally, the day of the auction came – 22 March 1999 – and the venue was filled with stars and key players in the music industry. All 60 items under Sotheby's hammer sold (Interactive Collector had 120 items under their virtual hammer) and most for well above the guide price printed in the catalogue. All told, some £300,000 was raised.

Steven, Ronnie, Richard and David had succeeded. They had raised significantly more money for charity than they could have in years of sponsored bike rides.

And the process continues. This book is part of the on-going fundraising. We hope you enjoy it. In any case, by buying this book, you are helping two very deserving charities, adding your effort to the many generous artists and volunteers who made Hits Under The Hammer such a huge success. Thank you.

The Hits Under The Hammer Committee

NORWOOD RAVENSWOOD

NORWOOD RAVENSWOOD'S MISSION IS TO BUILD A BETTER future for disadvantaged children, young adults and people of all ages with learning disabilities and to offer support to their families. The charity believes that people who are disadvantaged or have a disability have a right to be supported in pursuit of personal growth and development.

Norwood Ravenswood provides a 'one stop' family service looking after children as they grow up and, where necessary, offering on-going help through adulthood. This means local, accessible services where people can get the help they need by making just one telephone call.

A fully comprehensive range of caring services is offered including community services social work and counselling which encompasses a range of support services for children, dealing with abuse, financial hardship and family breakdown and provides services for people with disabilities and their families.

Ravenswood Village in Berkshire provides residential care for 179 children and adults. Group homes offer differing levels of support appropriate to each resident, while the Adolescent Unit provides accommodation for vulnerable teenagers who are unable to live at home. Education is developed through an independent school and a multi-disciplined education service, designed to help children achieve their potential. Fostering and adoption schemes are also run.

CONTENTS

A DESIGN FOR LIFE

MANIC STREET PREACHERS

COMPOSED BY **JAMES DEAN BRADFIELD/NICKY WIRE/SEAN MOORE**

IN FEBRUARY 1995, AT THE AGE OF 27, Manic Street Preachers frontman Richey Edwards disappeared. It's still not known whether he committed suicide, or simply vanished to start a new life, as many have done before. Despite their personal sadness, it left the group with a major dilemma: should they continue or disband? After talking with Edwards' parents they decided to carry on, with their blessing.

Written about "the pride of the working class struggle and the patronising attitudes of the bourgeoisie", 'A Design For Life' was the band's first song completed without Richey, and their first single without him. Remaining members James Dean Bradfield, Sean Moore and Nicky Wire drafted in keyboard player John Green to thicken up the group's sound, and it was this song which gave them the mental strength to continue and became a pivotal number in the renaissance of the group.

The single was recorded with the rest of the songs for the *Everything Must Go* album, at Chateau de la Rouge Motte in Normandy, France. 'Design For Life' was released as two CD singles on 1 and 2 April 1995 and as a live cassette single. Selling 93,000 copies in the first week, it soared to Number Two, selling more than all their other singles put together. James Bradfield admits, "When I woke up that Sunday morning and realised 'Design For Life' was Number Two, I felt the most relaxed I'd been for a year and three months." ▣

Handwritten lyrics by Nicky Wire

A Design For Life

LIBRARIES GAVE US POWER
THEN WORK CAME AND MADE US FREE
WHAT PRICE NOW
FOR A SHALLOW PIECE OF DIGNITY

I WISH I HAD A BOTTLE
RIGHT HERE IN MY PRETTY FACE
TO SHOW THE SCARS
TO SHOW FROM
WHERE I CAME

WE DON'T TALK ABOUT LOVE
WE ONLY WANT TO GET DRUNK
AND WE ARE NOT ALLOWED TO SPEND
AS WE ARE TOLD THAT THIS IS THE END

A DESIGN FOR LIFE - A DESIGN FOR LIFE
A DESIGN FOR LIFE

I WISH I HAD A BOTTLE
RIGHT HERE IN MY DIRTY FACE
TO SHOW THE SCARS
TO SHOW FROM WHERE I CAME

WE DON'T TALK ABOUT LOVE
WE ONLY WANT TO GET DRUNK
AND WE ARE NOT ALLOWED TO SPEND
AS WE ARE TOLD THAT THIS IS THE END

A DESIGN FOR LIFE - A DESIGN FOR LIFE
A DESIGN FOR LIFE

A GIRL LIKE YOU

I've never met a GYL before
Now just like in a song
From Days of Yore
Here y'come Knockin' on
my door
and I've . . .
So you give me just a taste
I want more
Now my hands are bleeding
and my knees are raw
'Cause now you got me
crawling on the floor
And I've never met

You made me acknowledge
the Devil in me hope to God
I'm talking metaphorically
Hope that I'm talking allegorically

A GIRL LIKE YOU

COMPOSED BY **EDWYN COLLINS**

EDWYN COLLINS BEGAN HIS CHART CAREER WITH SCOTTISH band Orange Juice, formed in the 1970s and featuring Collins, James Kirk (guitar/vocals), David McClymont (bass/synths) and Steven Daly (drums). Their recording career began on the small Postcard label before they signed to Polydor which led to nine UK hits including the Number Eight 'Rip It Up' in 1983.

Collins' non-OJ hits began a year later with 'Pale Blue Eyes' but it was to be ten years before a follow-up charted. Originally peaking at Number 42, 'A Girl Like You' stormed back into the charts the following summer when it reached Number Four.

The song was taken from the 1994 album *Gorgeous George*, the making of which wasn't exactly straightforward, as Collins admits. "In 1993, I bought a 1969 film console that had been used for dubbing things like *Time Bandits* and *Brazil*," he says. "I had it re-configured into a 24-channel rock 'n' roll desk, even though it didn't have pan pots and things. I produced an album for The Rocking Birds which had its teething problems and wasn't sonically the most perfect thing I've ever done but they became the guinea pigs for *Gorgeous George*. I found it an inspiring desk to work on, just as I've always favoured vintage guitars, and I felt confident it would, in a metaphysical way, help us in the recording of the album."

The band was a three-piece: Collins playing guitar and keyboards, with Paul Cook (ex-Sex Pistols) on drums and Claire Kenny on bass guitar. Collins' co-engineer, Sebastian Lewsley, played the "Eno role and also did some weird mono-synth things". The album was recorded over the summer of 1994 in a two-month period and 'A Girl Like You' was the second last number put down.

"The song was based around a Motown drum loop which Paul augmented," Collins recalls. "At last I could get my interpretation of the kind of Isley Brothers sound I loved. It's also influenced by a northern soul track called 'I'm On My Way' by Dean Parrish, which starts off with a great fuzz guitar, so I wanted to get this bona fide authentic kind of fuzz sound. The song is just three chords really, based on a drone that doesn't change. It started with the chorus idea effect before I had the title and then I improvised the other lines – a lot of them. I had the kind of two verses, all the bridges were improvised in the studio. The vibraphone part was just played by me and I'm not a very good keyboard player but one thing I have taught myself is the pentatonic scale so I had some sampled vibes, and played the first thing that came into my head. It was loosely based round the piano motif from, 'The Hunter Gets Captured By The Game' by Martha Reeves And The Vandellas.

"People gradually picked up on it, and it was actually Vic Goddard, who was doing backing vocals, who was the first one to say, 'This song could potentially be a Number One, it's fantastic' – although he didn't specify that it would be Number One in Belgium, Hong Kong

Handwritten lyrics by Edwyn Collins

and the Philippines! Lyrically it's kind of generic, and the line that everyone picks up on all over the world is 'too many protest singers, not enough protest songs'. By that, I meant there's ten songs called 'I've Never Met A Girl Like You Before' or 'A Girl Like You' which it is actually called. There's one by The Kinks, there's one by The Troggs, there's one by The Young Rascals and Foreigner. It's just a totally generic title."

When it finally came out, press reaction to the album was fairly non-committal, but crucially wasn't bad. "To a certain extent I relied on the press to sell my albums," Collins admits, "since being a kind of cult figure, I didn't expect to get any radio play. But then almost simultaneously, GLR and Steve Wright on Radio One started rotating it and it wasn't even a single yet. My record label, Setanta, at the time was a two-man operation based in a squat in Camberwell, and releasing singles is a very expensive process which could bankrupt a company of that size. So initially they had no real intention of releasing it but their hand was kind of forced the more Radio One kept playing it. Then all the independents started playing it and BBC local radio. It behaved very strangely, just like the old days, when 45s were on vinyl: it spent something like eight weeks in the Top Ten, but not in the *NME* indie charts because they wouldn't have it. But in the bona fide indie charts it was two or three months at Number One. In the airplay charts it was months at Number One, it was bizarre. It's become a perennial."

Fostering a perennial leads to the oddest of circumstances. "The weirdest thing was going along to Wembley Arena and seeing Rod Stewart and his band covering it," Collins admits. "In fact I got £500 from Rod because he did it on his whole world tour. It was also featured in the movie *Empire Records* starring Liv Tyler, which went straight to video, and was a flop, but they were using my song to sell the film and soundtrack album. Iggy Pop was also going to cover it before my version was released in America but then my version came out. I think he still might."

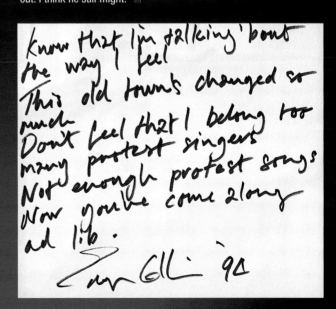

Handwritten lyrics by Hawk Wolinski:

'AIN'T NOBODY' HAWK WOLINSKI '83

V1 CAPTURED EFFORTLESSLY THAT'S WAY IT WAS
IT HAPPENED SO NATURALLY I DID NOT KNOW IT WAS LOVE
NEXT THING I FELT WAS YOU HOLDIN' ME CLOSE
WHAT WAS I GONNA DO I LET MYSELF GO
AND NOW WE FLY TO THE STARS
AND HOPE THIS NIGHT LASTS FOREVER

V2 I'VE BEEN WATCHIN' FOR YOU IT'S BEEN SO LONG
I KNEW JUST WHAT I WOULD DO WHEN I HEARD YOUR SONG
YOU FILL MY HEART WITH YOUR KISS YOU GAVE ME FREEDOM
YOU KNEW I'D NEVER RESIST I NEEDED SOMEONE
AND NOW WE FLY TO THE STARS
AND HOPE THIS NIGHT LASTS FOREVER

CHORUS: 1 AIN'T NOBODY LOVES ME BETTER
MAKES ME HAPPY GIVES ME PLEASURE
AIN'T NOBODY LOVES ME BETTER THAN YOU...

V3 I WAIT FOR NIGHT TIME TO BRING YOU TO ME
I CAN'T BELIEVE I'M THE ONE I WAS SO LONELY
I FEEL LIKE NO ONE COULD FEEL I MUST BE DREAMIN'
I WANT THIS DREAM TO BE REAL I NEED THIS FEELIN'
I MAKE MY WISH ON A STAR
AND HOPE THAT WE'LL LAST FOREVER

CHORUS: 2

BRIDGE FIRST YOU PUT YOUR ARMS AROUND ME
THEN YOU PUT YOUR CHARMS AROUND ME
WE'VE GOT A FEELIN' MOST WOULD TREASURE
A LOVE SO DEEP WE CANNOT MEASURE

VAMP CHORUS:

AIN'T NOBODY

CHAKA KHAN

COMPOSED BY **DAVID WOLINSKI**

BORN YVETTE MARIE STEVENSON IN GREAT LAKES, ILLINOIS
in 1953, she took the African name 'Chaka' which means 'fire'.
Chaka formed her first group, The Crystalettes, at the age of
eleven, working with Lyfe and The Babysitters after leaving school
in 1969. In 1972 she teamed up with Rufus, the group which had
evolved from The American Breed of 'Bend Me, Shape Me' fame.

The chart breakthrough for Chaka Khan and Rufus came through
'Ain't Nobody', a song written by group member David 'Hawk'
Wolinski and taken from the double album *Rufus And Chaka Live*
which contained three sides of live material, and one side of new
songs. The live section was recorded at their farewell concert at
the Savoy Theatre, New York in February 1982.

'Ain't Nobody' climbed to Number Eight in the UK in the spring of
1984, which resulted in Chaka Khan undertaking a short tour of
Britain. At the 26th annual Grammys, 'Ain't Nobody' won the
award for Best R&B Performance By A Duo Or Group With Vocal. ▨

Above: handwritten lyrics by Hawk Wolinski
Right: handwritten lyrics by Charlie Dore

AIN'T NO DOUBT

JIMMY NAIL

COMPOSED BY **DANNY SCHLOGGER/CHARLIE DORE/JIMMY NAIL/GUY PRATT**

IN THE MIDDLE OF JULY 1992, JIMMY NAIL'S RECORD 'AIN'T NO
Doubt' knocked Erasure's 'Abba-esque' off the UK Number One spot,
staying there for three weeks. Nail, whose acting career had taken off
after appearing in the highly successful TV series *Auf Wiedersehen
Pet*, began recording seriously in the mid Eighties, making his chart
debut with 'Love Don't Live Here Anymore', produced by Queen's
Roger Taylor, which reached Number Three in 1985.

'Ain't No Doubt' was written by British singer/songwriter/actress
Charlie Dore and Danny Schlogger. As a singer, Dore's biggest hit
was her 1979 classic, 'Pilot Of The Airwaves', which charted in
both Britain and America. As an actress she co-starred with
Jonathan Pryce in the award-winning film *The Ploughman's
Lunch*, and appeared in TV's *Hard Cases* and *South Of The Border*.
As a songwriter, her biggest hits include her own 'Pilot Of The
Airwaves, 'Strut' for Sheena Easton, 'Refuse To Dance' for Celine
Dion and Jimmy Nail's 'Ain't No Doubt'. ▨

ALL BABIES

SINEAD O'CONNOR

COMPOSED BY SINEAD O'CONNOR

SINEAD O'CONNOR, BORN IN GLENGEARY, EIRE in 1966, got her first musical break when she joined the group Ton Ton Macoute in 1985, the same year providing vocals for the soundtrack album of the film *Captive*. In 1988 the Number 17 hit 'Mandinka' launched her solo career, while her debut album, *The Lion And The Cobra* became a hit in Britain and the States. The following year she was nominated for Best Female Vocalist at the 31st Grammy awards at which she also performed 'Madinka'. 1990 saw the release of her second album, *I Do Not Want What I Haven't Got*, which went to Number One in Britain, America, and eleven other countries, largely thanks to its main single, her cover of Prince's 'Nothing Compares 2 U'. The song went to Number One on both sides of the Atlantic and hit the top in 18 other countries. Also in 1990 she performed in The Wall concert in Berlin and collected several awards.

Always outspoken and opinionated, whether about the music industry, politics or religion, Sinead has often alienated herself with the press, but remains a successful artist always prepared to do her bit for charity. 'All Babies' comes from her 1994 album *Universal Mother*, which reached Number 19 in the UK and Number 37 in the States. The album is full of "nakedly uncompromising material...stark lyrics that contrast with tranquil arrangements and melodies," she admits.

All babies are born saying god's name
over and over all born singing god's name
All babies are flown from the Universe
from there they're lifted by the hands of Angels
god gives them the Stars to use as Ladders
SHE HEARS their Calls
She is Mother and father

All babies are born into great pain
OVER and OVER all BORN OUT of great pain
All BABIES ARE CRYING
FOR noone REMEMBERS god's name

Sinéad O'Connor

'All Babies' lyrics painted by Sinead on a shelf from her son's bedroom

ALL FOR LOVE

STING, ROD STEWART AND BRYAN ADAMS

COMPOSED BY **ADAMS/KAMEN/LANGE**

UNTIL THE TIME THAT STING, ROD Stewart and Bryan Adams came together to record 'All For Love', their vocals had featured on no fewer than 109 UK hit singles alone. Rod Stewart made his chart debut in 1971, Sting, with The Police, in 1978 and Bryan Adams in 1985.

'All For Love', which reached Number Two in 1994, was from the 1993 Stephen Herek-directed film *The Three Musketeers*, starring, amongst others, Charlie Sheen, Kiefer Sutherland, Chris O'Donnell, Oliver Platt, Tim Curry and Rebecca de Mornay. There had already been three productions of the film during the 1930s, another in the Forties and a fifth in 1973. The original book had been written by the French author, Alexandre Dumas in 1844 as *Les Trois Mousquetaires* whose rallying cry was 'All for one and one for all', the song from the film giving this slogan a romantic spin. ▤

ALL FOR LOVE

Verse 1
When its love you give - I'll be a man of good faith
Then in love you'll live - I'll make a stand I won't break
I'll be the rock you can build on - Be there when your old
To have and to hold

Verse 2
When there's love inside - I swear I'll always be strong
Then there's a reason why - I'll prove to you we belong
I'll be the wall that protects you - From the wind and the rain
From the hurt and pain

chorus:
Lets make it...All for one and all for love
Let the one you hold be the one you want - the one you need
Cuz when it's all for one - it's one for all
When there's someone that should know - Then just let your feelin's show
And make it all for one - and all for love

Verse 3
When it's love you make - I'll be fire in your night
Then it's love you take - I will defend - I will fight
I'll be there when you need me - when honour's at stake
This vow I will make...

chorus:
That it's all for one and all for love
Let the one you hold be the one you want - the one you need
Cuz when it's all for one - it's one for all
When there's someone that should know - Then just let your feelin's show
And make it all for one - and all for love

Middle 8
Don't lay our love to rest - Cuz we can stand up to the test
We got everything - and more - than we had planned
More than the rivers that run the land
We've got it all in our hands

chorus:
Now it's all for one and all for love
Let the one you hold be the one you want - the one you need
Cuz when it's all for one - it's one for all
When there's someone that should know - Then just let your feelin's show
And make it all for one - and all for love

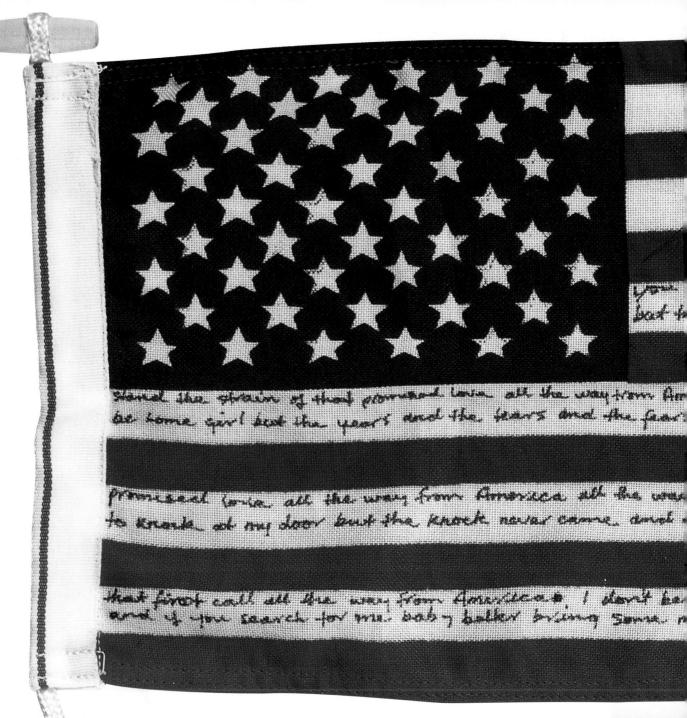

'Flag' lyrics handwritten by Joan Armatrading

ALL THE WAY FROM AMERICA

JOAN ARMATRADING

COMPOSED BY **JOAN ARMATRADING**

ALL THE WAY FROM AMERICA

BORN IN ST KITTS IN THE WEST INDIES, JOAN ARMATRADING moved to Birmingham, England in 1958, aged seven. After appearing in *Hair* and working with fellow West Indian Pam Nestar, Joan released her first album in 1972, the Gus Dudgeon-produced *Whatever's For Us*, also featuring Nestar.

In 1980 the album *Me Myself I* became her first US Top 40 album and put her back in the UK charts. The title track went to Number 21 with 'All The Way From America' being the next release. It still remains a popular song despite its rather lowly chart position of Number 54.

"The song seems to be a favourite when I perform live, especially in America," Armatrading explains. "At one point I used to open the show with it. I was in America before this song was written and I met a chap who I ended up spending quite a lot of time with," she recalls. "He was a lot keener on me than I was on him, and when I got back to England he kept phoning me, trying to get me to go out with him or to go back there. It was all just friends really for me, but I was touched that he was so bothered and that's where I got the idea from, him ringing constantly 'all the way from America'.

"I took artistic licence when I was writing it. Not everything mentioned in the song was said, obviously you mould the ideas to form the story and give it some depth. Another change was that it was written from the point of view of the woman wanting him, when in fact it was vice versa, but it just seemed to work better that way.

"The song was a single on the *Me Myself I* album which was produced by Richard Gottehrer, who also produced Blondie's first album. I had some great players on it, like Chris Spedding, Will Lees, Anton Figg and Paul Schaffer, who eventually formed the basis of the house band on *The David Letterman Show* on US TV. They all met playing on my album, which is nice to remember."

Joan's hit singles continue sporadically, but her albums are more consistent. In 1988 she performed at Nelson Mandela's 70th birthday concert.

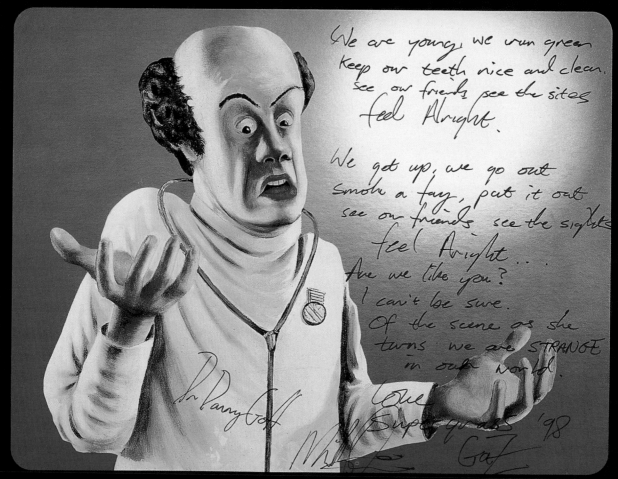

Handwritten lyrics by Gaz Coombes

ALRIGHT

SUPERGRASS

COMPOSED BY **DANIEL GOFFEY/GARETH COOMBES/MICKEY QUINN**

BASED AT WHEATLEY IN OXFORDSHIRE, DANNY GOFFEY AND GARETH 'Gaz' Coombes' first recording outfit was The Jennifers, whose debut single 'Just Got Back Today' came out in 1992. Other members were Andy Davies and Danny's brother Nick, who eventually went off in other directions, while Danny and Gaz briefly rehearsed with Tara Milton, before Mickey Quinn joined, and Milton went off to form The Nubiles.

By early 1994 they were performing as Theodore Supergrass, but had dropped the 'Theodore' by the time they released 'Caught By The Fuzz' in the August of that year.

The band's debut album, *I Should Coco*, released in May 1995 spawned their big hit 'Alright' which won the year's Best Contemporary Song category in the coveted Ivor Novello awards. ▤

ANOTHER BRICK IN THE WALL

PINK FLOYD

COMPOSED BY **ROGER WATERS**

ESSENTIALLY AN ALBUM BAND, THIS SONG, WHICH TOPPED THE singles chart on both sides of the Atlantic, was Pink Floyd's first single for over ten years.

Written by founder member Roger Waters, it was part of the concept album *The Wall*, mainly written by Waters. The single features a hastily gathered together children's chorus, which they were going to use in the background. Lead guitarist Dave Gilmour admitted, "We were going to put them in the background, but it was so good that we decided to let them do it themselves." Proving that, in the words of the song, they didn't "…need no education"!

While the misuse of the English language by children in the song upset educational authorities in the UK, the South African authorities banned it completely, after the young people of Soweto adopted it as their anthem.

In 1982, Alan Parker directed a movie version of *The Wall* starring Bob Geldof and, in 1990, Waters, with an all-star line-up, undertook a complete worldwide TV performance of the music on the site of the Berlin Wall (a piece of which, supplied by the German government, is pictured).

Handwritten lyrics by Roger Waters

Another Brick I.
"We don't need no education
We don't need no thought control
No dark sarcasm in the classroom
Teacher leave those kids alone

All in all it's just another brick in the Wall"

Roger Waters

"Copyright 1979 Pink Floyd Music Publishers Ltd"

AS TEARS GO BY

MARIANNE FAITHFULL

COMPOSED BY MICK JAGGER/KEITH RICHARDS

'AS TEARS GO BY' WAS WRITTEN BY MICK JAGGER AND KEITH RICHARDS, at the behest of the then manager of The Rolling Stones, Andrew Loog Oldham. The song almost certainly would never have been written were it not for a certain chain of events. A 17-year-old convent girl from Reading, Marianne Faithfull, the daughter of Eva Sacher-Masoch, the Baroness Erisso, was taken to the launch party of a new singer, Adrienne Posta. Marianne accompanied her boyfriend John Dunbar, but caught the eye of all the men in the room, including Mick Jagger and Oldham, the latter offering her an instant recording contract! Marianne remembers his somewhat unusual opening gambit as being: "Hey, would you like to make a record?"

The Lionel Bart song that he intended to record with her didn't suit her voice, so he turned to Jagger and Richards. "I told them, 'Marianne's a convent girl. I want a song with brick walls around it, and high windows, and no sex!'"

Originally titled 'As Time Goes By', it became 'As Tears Go By' and she recorded it in the studio, completely in the dark. "I was," she says, "embarrassed to be the centre of attention." Marianne sang an a cappella version in the Jean-Luc Goddard film *Made In The USA* in 1966, the same year The Rolling Stones (in reality Mick Jagger with an orchestra) recorded it in Italian as 'Con Le Mie Lacrime'. Marianne was the centre of attention again in April 1999, when she performed it as part of the tribute concert for Linda McCartney at the Royal Albert Hall.

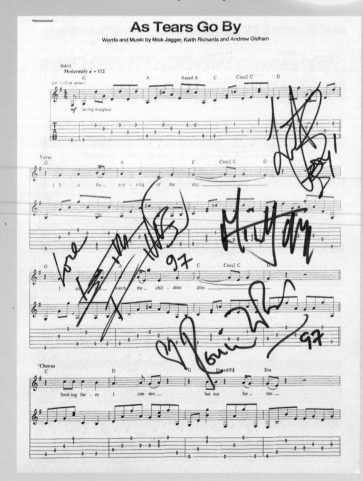

Sheet music signed by The Rolling Stones

Handwritten lyrics by Bryan Ferry

AVALON

ROXY MUSIC

COMPOSED BY BRYAN FERRY

'AVALON', FROM THE ALBUM OF THE SAME NAME, became Roxy Music's 15th British hit when it went to Number 13 in the summer of 1982. Produced by Rhett Davies, the album topped the British chart for three weeks, reaching Number 53 in the States.

"Avalon is part of the King Arthur legend, and it's a very romantic thing," Roxy's vocalist, Bryan Ferry, explains of the album title. "When King Arthur dies, the Queen ferries him off to Avalon, which is a sort of enchanted island. It's the ultimate romantic fantasy." Avalon is said to have been on the site of what is now Glastonbury. The album title gives it the appearance of being a concept album, but as Ferry confesses, "It wasn't. I often thought I should do an album where the songs are all bound together in the style of *West Side Story*, but it's always seemed like too much bother to do it that way."

A WHITER SHADE OF PALE

PROCOL HARUM

COMPOSED BY **KEITH REID/GARY BROOKER**

Handwritten lyrics by Keith Reid, including famous 'missing' third verse

THIS SONG BEGAN LIFE AS A LYRIC ONLY, WRITTEN BY A
20-year-old lad called Keith Reid. "One day I just sat down and did some writing, and then I put the words in an envelope and gave them to Gary Brooker (then still a member of Southend group The Paramounts). Then I didn't see him for six months except by chance, and he said, 'Oh, I've written some music to your words.' After that, I didn't see him for another six months."

Early in 1966, a year and a half before the song was released, Reid had shown the lyric to Moody Blues record producer Denny Cordell. "I told him the words were beautiful, but I could do nothing for him unless he had music," Cordell recalls. He also suggested that Reid got a group together, so Reid borrowed £100 from his publisher, David Platz, and a group was built around Brooker. The name Procol Harum, means 'beyond these things', although the correct spelling, in Latin is 'procul'.

For the melody, Brooker used the chord structure from Bach's 'Air On A G String', the second movement of his 'Suite In D', composed over 200 years earlier.

A Whiter Shade Of Pale
(inc "famous" missing third verse)

We skipped the light fandango
An turned cartwheels 'cross the floor
I was feeling kind of sea sick
but the crowd called out for more
The room was humming harder
as the ceiling flew away
When we called out for another drink
The waiter brought a tray
And so it was that later
as the miller told his tale
That her face at first just ghostly
turned a whiter shade of pale

She said "I'm home on shore leave"
though in truth we were at sea
so I took her by the looking glass
and forced her to agree
Saying "You must be the mermaid
who took Neptune for a ride"
but she smiled at me so sadly
that my anger straightway died
And so it was that later
as the miller told his tale
That her face at first just ghostly
turned a whiter shade of pale

She said "There is no reason
and the truth is plain to see"
But I wander'd through my playing cards
and would not let her be
One of sixteen vestal virgins
who were leaving for the coast
And although my eyes were open
they might've just as well been closed
And so it was that later
as the miller told his tale
That her face at first just ghostly
turned a whiter shade of pale

Keith Reid
his words
5-11-98

BABY DON'T CRY

INXS

COMPOSED BY **MICHAEL HUTCHENCE/ ANDREW FARRISS**

INXS, ORIGINALLY THE SYDNEY-BASED 'FARRISS BROTHERS', comprised Tim, Andrew and John Farriss alongside Michael Hutchence, Kirk Pengilly and Garry Beers. Formed in 1977 they built up a formidable live reputation before releasing their debut single in Australia in 1980. The group made their US chart debut in 1983 and their UK debut in 1986, going from strength to strength.

In 1991, the year that 'Baby Don't Cry' was written, INXS won Best International Group and Hutchence walked off with Best International Artist at the UK Brit awards. 'Bitter Tears' was in the charts at the time 'Baby Don't Cry' came to life.

Lead singer Hutchence was found hanging in his hotel room in 1997, a tragedy which the band has yet to come to terms with. However it was a happier time, for Andrew Farriss in particular, which prompted 'Baby Don't Cry'.

"The song was basically about the birth of my first daughter, Grace Elizabeth," Farriss recalls. "It was such a wonderful experience, it made me a much more positive happy person and I wanted to convey that. The lyrics talk of wanting to enjoy life and the moment, not looking for the bad but the positive. I wrote it in 1991, around about June because her birthday was the tenth. We now have two daughters and a son."

The track was recorded at Rhinoceros Studios in Sydney in 1991. Unusually INXS decided to record it live with a 64-piece orchestra. "That isn't something bands do much anymore," Farriss says. "We wanted to catch a certain vibe that we thought woudn't be achievable with overdubs.

"It reached Number 20 in the UK in September 1992, and that year we also played the Concert For Life benefit, raising A$600,000 for charity and performing the song for the first time live. We didn't perform it live very often, it would have been impossible to take a live orchestra on tour and that was one of the reasons we'd enjoyed it so much in the first place – tapes and technology just didn't seem the same. As far as I'm aware there are no other versions of it by anyone else, but I think it would make a great hip-hop cover."

'Baby Don't Cry' was written by Farriss and Michael Hutchence for the album *Welcome To Wherever You Are*. These days the memories of writing the song are inextricably linked with Farriss's memories of the late singer. "When Michael heard the song he was fascinated with the emotions that I was feeling towards having a child," Farriss recalls. "Having that song on the record became important to him because it was a step away from the more introspective stuff we were writing around that period. I remember he was very happy with his vocal – he was a lovely humorous guy who was great to work with and very talented."

Handwritten lyrics and signed guitar by
Andrew Farriss

BACK FOR GOOD

TAKE THAT

COMPOSED BY **GARY BARLOW**

TAKE THAT WERE FORMED IN THE SUMMER OF 1991 BY manager Nigel Martin-Smith, and despite their debut single meeting with little success, they persisted and gradually won over the record industry and the public. They had their first hit late in 1991, their first Top Ten record, 'It Only Takes A Minute', coming in the summer of 1992. It wasn't until their ninth single, though, that Take That topped the charts with 'Pray', soon repeating the achievement with 'Relight My Fire', this time featuring Lulu. More massive hits followed, and in 1995 their chart topping album *Nobody Else* yielded another three Number One hits, 'Sure', 'Forget' and what was to become their first big US hit, 'Back For Good'.

Robbie Williams left the group in July 1995, and after two more Number Ones, leader and songwriter Gary Barlow decided that the group had had its day. They disbanded in February 1996 breaking the hearts of a million teenage girls.

Take That created a new record by having eight singles go straight into the chart at Number One, and became the first act since The Beatles to have four consecutive Number One singles.

Handwritten 'T-shirt' lyrics by Gary Barlow

BACK TO LIFE

SOUL II SOUL

COMPOSED BY **BERESFORD ROMEO/CARON WHEELER/SIMON LAW/NELLEE HOOPER**

FOLLOWING A COUPLE OF SMALL HITS IN 1988, featuring vocalists Rose Windross and Do'reen respectively, Soul II Soul came good in the spring of the following year with the Top Ten hit 'Keep On Moving', before going all the way to Number One with their next single. 'Back To Life (However Do You Want Me)', featuring the vocals of Caron Wheeler, knocked Jason Donovan's 'Sealed With A Kiss' off the top UK spot, staying in pole position for four weeks.

Soul II Soul was founded by Jazzie B (Beresford Romeo) and Philip Harvey, the guys taking the group name from a soul album on the Stax label. By the time they had 'Back To Life' in the chart, the mainstays of the outfit were Jazzie and Nellee Hooper, with Wheeler on vocals and Hooper in the producer's seat. They also worked on remixes for Sinead O'Connor, Hooper eventually departing to become a successful producer. Soul II Soul continued to chart during the Nineties with vocalists Kym Mazelle and Kofi joining them for 'Missing You' and 'Move No Mountain' respectively.

Handwritten lyrics by Jazzie B

BAKER STREET

GERRY RAFFERTY

COMPOSED BY **GERRY RAFFERTY**

THE WRITER OF 'BAKER STREET', PAISLEY-BORN GERRY RAFFERTY HAD BEEN a member of mid Sixties outfit Fifth Column with fellow musician Joe Egan, recording for EMI. In 1968 Rafferty left to form The Humblebums with Billy Connolly, but after two excellent albums went solo briefly before teaming up again with Egan to form Stealer's Wheel. But ever restless, Rafferty left after making their first album, although was persuaded to rejoin after the single 'Stuck In The Middle With You' went to Number Six in the States, and Number Eight in Britain. After several line-ups, two more hit singles in the UK and the US and minor success in the States with the album *Ferguslie Park*, the outfit folded.

Rafferty re-emerged three years later, in 1978, with a solo album, *City To City*, which topped the US chart knocking the long-running *Saturday Night Fever* off the top, and eventually going platinum. The album yielded a song that was to become Rafferty's calling card – 'Baker Street'. Featuring the now legendary sax solo from Raf Ravenscroft, the song went to Number Two in the States, selling over a million copies in that country alone, and reaching a respectable Number Three in Britain, where the parent album went to Number Six. 'Baker Street' went gold, sold some five million copies around the world, and in a 1992 UK poll was voted the 22nd most popular single ever.

**Handwritten lyrics by
Gerry Rafferty**

BALLROOM BLITZ

THE SWEET

COMPOSED BY NICKY CHINN/MIKE CHAPMAN

EX-WAINWRIGHT'S GENTLEMEN

members Brian Connolly and Mick Tucker formed a new group, Sweetshop, during 1968 with Steve Priest and Frank Torpey. By 1970 Andy Scott had replaced Torpey and the group's name had been amended to 'The Sweet'. The outfit first charted with 'Funny Funny', written by Nicky Chinn and Mike Chapman, a partnership that would go on to supply many hits including a Number One ('Blockbuster') and five Number Twos – among them 'Ballroom Blitz'...

"I don't really remember how it was inspired, only that Mike and I were sitting in my flat as we did every day," Nicky Chinn recalls. "We met in the morning and went through song ideas. The title came first as it did with most of our songs, and the song developed from there. The original title suggestion was 'Bar Room Blitz', but lyrically 'Ballroom Blitz' sounded better. It was in the early Seventies and there were lots of Mecca and Top Rank dance halls around, so 'Ballroom Blitz' was really inspired by that kind of scene, live bands, packed out with kids.

"From early on we thought it was a great idea and since doing 'Blockbuster' and 'Hellraiser' with Sweet we found that we were getting bigger and more aggressive, not to mention alliterative with our titles. Shortly afterwards we made a little demo, played it to the guys in the band and the next thing was that we went in and made it.

"It was a very tongue in cheek song, especially Steve Priest's camp spoken part, as was all of our writing for Sweet. It was all about having fun and you could take it how you liked."

In the early 1970s Chinn and Chapman's work with various Glam Rock acts – The Sweet, Mud, Suzi Quatro and others in the Mickie Most stable – dominated the charts. "Back then we were on a roll," Chinn admits. "But I think the definitive Sweet record is definitely 'Ballroom Blitz'. It's also my favourite song too, and as close to perfection as a songwriter and producer can get, everything just came together. Phil Wainman was the producer as he had been on all the Sweet hits until 'The Sixteens'. He was the guy who found the band actually. He knew me and Mike and after we'd written 'Funny Funny' he said he knew just the people and that's how the band came to be. There was a big cover version which Tia Carrera did in *Wayne's World* which was great because the album went to Number One in America, but I think in general they are hard songs to cover because Sweet made the definitive record." In the UK the Carrera version reached Number Six in 1992.

To the writers' disappointment 'Ballroom Blitz' never reached the top spot in the UK. "The charts then were very different to now," Chinn reflects. "Records move around all over the place these days but back then we were the only one that went in at Number Two and never got higher, the reason being The Simon Park Orchestra and 'Eye Level' jumping at Number One for weeks. We stayed at Number Two for five weeks and shipped a huge amount of records but never reached the top slot. At the time it was really disappointing because we'd banked on a Number One hit. However it also went Top Five in America which was great for the band."

The Sweet continue today with various line-ups but always including some original members. Connolly, who'd been ill for some years, died in 1997. ▤

BEN

MICHAEL JACKSON

COMPOSED BY DON BLACK/WALTER SHARP

AS MICHAEL JACKSON'S LAST TAMLA

Motown hit in 1972, 'Ben' marked the end of one phase of the young singer's career. When he would return in the late Seventies it would be with *Off The Wall* and then *Thriller*, and superstar status would soon follow. But with 'Ben', as with 'Got To Be There', he showed a talent not yet spoiled by hype.

"Although 'Ben' was written about a rat (!) it is actually about friendship," the song's lyricist, Don Black explains. "Sometimes there's often a lot of opposition to these songs and there's a lot of struggling and trying to fight one's corner to get the songs recorded or into a movie. I got to know Michael Jackson quite well during that period and he actually painted a picture for my wife that I think is probably worth more than the song now – if only I could get my wife's name off it! However the song went to Number One, so I guess it was a fair trade."

'Ben' reached Number One in the States and Number Seven in the UK in 1972. ▤

Top left: handwritten lyrics by Nicky Chinn on Brian Connolly's famous 'Mickey Mouse' T-shirt

BLACK EYED BOY

TEXAS

COMPOSED BY **MCELHONE/SPITERI/HODGENS/CAMPBELL/HYND**

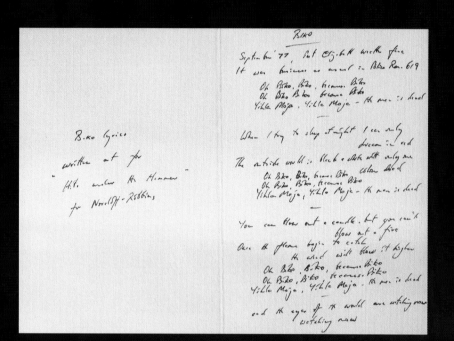

FROM GLASGOW, SCOTLAND IN 1986, TEXAS TOOK their name from the Wim Wenders-directed film Paris, Texas, for which Ry Cooder wrote the music. Formed by bass player John McElhone, a former member of Scottish bands Altered Images and Hipsway, the original line-up included Craig Armstrong and Stuart Kerr. More than a decade later, the line-up is more famously Sharleen Spiteri (guitar and vocals), Ally McErlaine (guitar), Richard Hynd (drums), Eddie Campbell (keyboards) and McElhone. First charting in 1989, Texas had 15 UK hit singles in the ensuing decade, including three Top Five singles, the second of which was 'Black Eyed Boy' in August 1997.

"I write songs usually because I find it hard to talk on a one to one basis," singer Spiteri reveals. "The best way to explain 'Black Eyed Boy' is about female heroism. It's very Sixties Motown influenced but it's also a love song. When we wrote it I was trying to think of a girl singing to a boy. He wants to throw it all in (as men so often do) because just a couple of things go wrong and the woman wants to make it better. So many women do, that's what the song's about – as a woman you'll dig very deep, go so far to try and make things better.

"Within the band, Johnny and I do most of the writing, but on this everyone was involved. We all sat down everyone bringing in bits and pieces and that was the result. Usually when you make an album, everybody says, 'Wow, this is the best thing we've made so far,' but for us we felt that we had to go in a different direction, we wanted the goosebumps back again and felt that if we didn't get it right this time it would all fall to pieces. We needed to prove it to ourselves because we knew that we could do it.

"I like to write from a personal point of view, not so much clever wordplay as real emotions, partly because I remember how much songs meant to me when I was growing up. Things were personal and I, like most people, really believed the song was for me. We wanted to achieve that with 'Black Eyed Boy'.

"When it came to recording I had Motown in mind, especially Diana Ross. I wanted to sing like her. The phrasing is very similar and the snare drum is like they used on a lot of Motown stuff. I think we achieved a really close result. Obviously the public thought so, as it won an Ivor Novello award as one of the top three PRS most performed songs of the year. I used to call my little boy Jack 'my black eyed boy' way before the song was written, so every time he hears it now he looks really proud and says, 'That's me!'"

BIKO
PETER GABRIEL

COMPOSED BY **PETER GABRIEL**

PETER GABRIEL ONCE SAID THAT HE IDENTIFIED WITH SOUTH African Civil Rights leader Steve Biko, as he was a "very able, articulate, and intelligent leader of youth". Gabriel confessed that he was "really shocked when I heard that he had been killed. I am not a political person, but this was just something that I wanted to write about. When I started getting into these South African rhythms it seemed appropriate. Then I did a lot of research on him, and the song was completed."

An active anti-apartheid campaigner, Biko was arrested in September 1977 and died six days later while in the custody of the South African police. He founded the South African Students Organisation in 1968, and was co-founder, in 1972, of The People's Black Convention. Biko's death led to Gabriel becoming permanently committed to the cause of human rights.

Peter Gabriel performed the song 'Biko' at the Reading Festival in 1979, and despite Ahmet Ertegun, the boss of Peter's US label disliking the song, and passing on the single and album, 'Biko' reached Number 38 in the UK in 1980, with a live version getting to Number 49 seven years later.

Handwritten lyrics by Peter Gabriel

Black eyed Boy

Chorus:-
Your black eyed soul
You should know

We should know
We're on our own
And we will find
Our own space in time

No I don't lack ambition
Can't you see what I hate
That its you who is sinking
locked behind Iron gates

Bridge:- We should know
You should know your falling into fiction
I could tell your on some foolish mission

Chorus:- Your black eyed soul
You should know.
That there's nowhere else to go
My Black eyed boy.
You will find
Your own space in time

You call me superstitious
Tie me up with your deceit
I could never be malicious
Though I seem so bittersweet

You should know
Your such a contradiction
I can see a
head to head collision

Bridge:- You should. know your on some foolish
telling who fiction
I could tell your on some foolish mission

BLUE CAFE

COMPOSED BY **CHRIS REA**

CHRIS REA, BORN IN MIDDLESBROUGH IN 1951, joined the group Magdalene in 1973 replacing David Coverdale who had been enlisted by Deep Purple. Despite the group's name change to The Beautiful Losers in 1975, Rea left two years later to sign to Magnet Records as a solo artist. Produced by Gus Dudgeon, his debut album was released in 1978, the title – *Whatever Happened To Benny Santini?* – referring to the name that Magnet had wanted him to adopt. The album went gold in the States while the single, 'Fool (If You Think It's Over)' peaked at Number Twelve there. The American success resulted in a big UK push which included an amazing 33 hit singles, most of which missed the Top Ten until the

arrival of 'The Road To Hell' (Number Two) and its chart topping parent album.

The 1998 single 'Square Peg, Round Hole' was taken from the album *Blue Café*, the origins of which began at 35,000 feet. "Blue Café started out on an aeroplane," Rea explains of the work in progress (pictured). "Showing the musical riff and drum beat is an idea added to the lyric sheet at a later date, on the way to an interview. The smudging is British Airways tea."

Rea has recently gravitated more towards film work, writing the soundtrack to *Soft Top Hard Shoulder* in 1993 and starring in Michael Winner's *Parting Shots* in 1999.

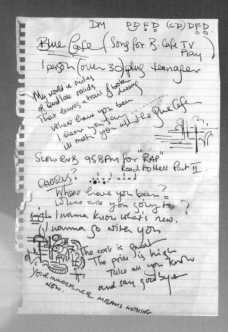

Working lyrics by Chris Rea

BLUE EYES

COMPOSED BY **ELTON JOHN/GARY OSBORNE**

HAVING PAID HIS DUES ALONGSIDE LONG John Baldry in Bluesology, Reg Dwight renamed himself, borrowing the 'John' from Baldry and the first name of bluesman Elton Dean. Elton John was to become one of the most successful artists in the world, winning dozens of awards, running out the best selling artist of the 1970s and becoming the first artist to enter the US album charts at Number One.

Having forged an historic relationship with lyricist Bernie Taupin, Elton began to experiment with other wordsmiths during the late Seventies/early Eighties. For the 1978 *A Single Man* album it was Gary Osborne who gave the words to the pianist's music.

"I was the sole lyricist on that album," he recalls, "and I shared the honours with other lyricists on Elton's next three albums, *21 At 33*, *The Fox* and *Jump Up*, which 'Blues Eyes' is on. Very often Elton would give me a tune that he was hot on. He's so prolific and so quick that he writes a tune in five or ten minutes – if it takes longer than ten, he'll say, 'Forget it.' When I heard this song I thought, 'Very nice, but that's going to be one of the ones he's least likely to record.' I thought 'Nobody Wins' was going to be Number One, and that 'Blue Eyes' was going nowhere.

"Elton was recording in Montserrat and I was

Handwritten lyrics by Gary Osborne

in Regents Park working on the lyrics, and every now and then I would get a phone call or a telex message asking, 'Have you done "Blue Eyes" yet?' I'd then telex back saying, 'Not yet, but I've just finished "Princess".' Then one day a tape arrived in the post containing a backing track for 'Blue Eyes', and I thought, 'My God, he's really going to record it!' Fortunately, it's short: it's only got two verses, and was one of the quickest things I ever did – two hours later I'd written it. Basically, the song simply has a guy saying in the first verse that his girl's eyes are like a

deep blue sea because she's sad that he's going away, while in the second verse she's got blue eyes like a clear blue sky, because she's happy that he's coming back.

"I asked Elton if I could change the title, and it was the one time when he said no. I felt there'd been a lot of songs about blue eyes which I didn't really want to duplicate.

"He had to take five stabs at the vocal. The first time he sounded too much like Dean Martin, because it is a corny song. On the second try he sounded like Elvis, and producer Chris Thomas would say, 'No, that's too much like so and so.' Eventually, on the fifth take, Elton said, 'If I don't get it this time, I'm not doing it again.' I was thinking, 'Blimey, you mean I've written it in spite of myself and he still might not do it...' But he did, and thank God he did, because people like it. I still don't know quite what appeals about the song, but it does. I like corny stuff, but it didn't really appeal to me at first. It does now, because it bought me a house!"

The house came courtesy of a Number Eight showing in the UK and Number Twelve in the USA in 1982, but for Elton it proved a minor success compared with his recording of 'Candle In The Wind 1997' which, as a tribute to Diana, Princess of Wales, became the world's best selling single. ▪

BORN FREE

MATT MONRO

COMPOSED BY **DON BLACK/JOHN BARRY**

Handwritten lyrics by Don Black

FOREVER ATTACHED TO THE MEMORY OF THE FILM WHICH GAVE IT ITS NAME, 'Born Free' has actually charted several times in several forms, thus proving the strength of the actual song. Matt Monro took the film soundtrack version into charts around the world, but Roger Williams, The Hesitations and even comedian Vic Reeves have all scored hits with the Don Black/John Barry composition. For Black in particular, writing the song was just another day in the office...

"Whenever there are hits, people expect incredible anecdotes to go along with them, but it's not always the case," he says. "More usually stuff is written as part of a brief and one becomes amazed at what happens with them. And when songs like that have such an impact it's also amazing what people expect of them. I've always been a great lover of words though, so being a lyricist, my job is really a labour of love, difficult though it can be sometimes.

"For example, with the theme song from the movie *Born Free*, the producer, Carl Foreman, didn't like the lyrics – he thought it should relate more directly to lions roaming in the wild. However, I preferred to make it more of a social comment and felt vindicated when the song (sung by Matt Monro) went on to win an Academy award, so the mix was right in the end."

Handwritten lyrics by Neil Sedaka

IN THE SUMMER OF 1962 'BREAKING UP IS HARD TO DO' climbed into the British Top Ten staying on the chart for 16 weeks. It made another appearance ten years later as part of a three-track maxi-single with 'Oh Carol' and 'Little Devil', reaching the Top 20 and remaining on the listings for 14 weeks. The latter release was in the wake of The Partridge Family, featuring David Cassidy, having had a Top Three record in the UK with 'Breaking Up…' a few months earlier. Neil Sedaka who had the original hit and co-wrote the song, is amazed at how the phrase came into common usage: "I've seen that phrase in print for the last 25 years, wherever I've looked. I've seen it in newspapers, in magazine articles; it has become a phrase that has just followed all over.

"It's a fictitious song, and I had to convince Howie [Greenfield] to write it. It was cute in the fact that it was a sad title but a happy tune, and I was always very partial to it."

Neil cut a slower version of the song in 1976, giving him the distinction of charting two different versions of the same song, 14 years apart.

There were other hit versions in America for The Happenings (1968), Lenny Welch (1970) and The Partridge Family (1972). Other artists who have recorded the Sedaka classic include The Four Seasons, Shelley Fabares, Brian Poole And The Tremeloes, The Carpenters, Sha Na Na and Johnny Preston.

BREAKING UP IS HARD TO DO

NEIL SEDAKA

COMPOSED BY **NEIL SEDAKA/HOWIE GREENFIELD**

Working lyrics by Bruce Dickinson

CAN I PLAY WITH MADNESS

IRON MAIDEN

COMPOSED BY **ADRIAN SMITH/BRUCE DICKINSON/STEVE HARRIS**

BETWEEN 1980 AND 1986, EAST LONDON HEAVY METAL OUTFIT Iron Maiden notched up 14 hit singles, although only one, 'Run To The Hills', had actually got into the Top Ten. They rectified this in 1988, when they swept back with a vengeance to have a string of Top Ten hits, the single 'Can I Play With Madness' being the torchbearer when it got as high as Number Three in the UK charts. Its parent album,

Seventh Son Of A Seventh Son, fared even better, topping the album chart in the UK.

Bruce Dickinson, as well as being Iron Maiden's frontman, was also ranked seventh in Great Britain in the fencing rankings, his club, Hemel Hempstead Fencing Club being the National Champions. ▣

CAN'T SMILE WITHOUT YOU

BARRY MANILOW

COMPOSED BY DAVID MARTIN/CHRIS ARNOLD/GEOFF MORROW

A JUILLIARD MUSIC STUDENT, BARRY MANILOW WORKED AS A jingles composer and arranger in the Sixties before accompanying Bette Midler in the early 1970s. It wasn't until early 1975 that his own recording career took off, 'Mandy' making Number One in the States and Number Eleven in Britain. A string of successful singles (including three American Number Ones) and albums and live appearances followed, establishing Manilow as a major musical force. A talented pianist he also writes a lot of his own songs, although not, ironically, 'I Write The Songs'. 'Can't Smile Without You', which was a worldwide hit in 1978, came from the pen of songwriter David Martin.

"Back in 1975, I was in town working with my partners Chris Arnold and Geoff Morrow at in our office in Green Street," Martin says. "On one particular day I went to Hampstead to pick my wife Debbie up from the family card shop that she ran, and when I walked in she handed me a plain blue card with a little badge on the top right hand corner with a tear coming down it. The card's message was simply 'can't smile without you', and I thought what a great idea for a title.

"So then we were driving back from Hampstead to our house in Harrow, which takes about 35 minutes, and by the time we got home the song was written, and that's basically where it started. I then recorded it myself and it came out on the DJM label, it had lots of airplay but it was never a hit. However, the record was later taken up by my publisher in America who pitched the song to a bunch of record companies over there. It got recorded by Engelbert Humperdinck and also by The Carpenters as B-side to 'Calling Occupants Of Interplanetary Craft'. Eventually Clive Davis, who was head of Arista (and still is) heard it and thought it was perfect for Barry Manilow. He took it to him and asked if he'd like to record it, but Barry was a bit reticent at first. Clive asked him if he would just do it as a favour, so he did and it went to Number One in the States.

"Amazingly, Manilow's original version was three and a half minutes long which included a tap-dance routine during the solo! When he brought it out of the studio he played it to a friend of his who was also a pretty well-known songwriter, and this guy said to him, 'Barry, I think you've lost the plot on this – this is a very commercial song.' So Manilow realised he should look at it more seriously, went back in the studio and put in the various key changes, and the rest is history."

Handwritten lyrics by
David Martin

CAST NO SHADOW

OASIS

COMPOSED BY **NOEL GALLAGHER**

NOEL GALLAGHER'S SONG 'CAST NO SHADOW' CAME FROM THE OASIS album *(What's The Story) Morning Glory* which spawned the singles 'Roll With It' and 'Wonderwall'. Originally to be called 'Flash In The Pan', the album was recorded at Dave Edmunds' Rockpile Studio in Gwent, during a five week spell in May and June 1995, and cut at Abbey Road Studios in London at the end of July.

Drummer Tom McCarroll was sacked prior to the making of the album, and new boy Alan White drafted in. White, the brother of Paul Weller's drummer Steve, was never auditioned. Noel Gallagher's opening words at their first meeting were apparently, "Right mate, you're in – you're not 30 stone, you look all right…do you want the job?" One of the first tracks White got to play on was 'Cast No Shadow', which Noel dedicated to "the genius of Richard Ashcroft", his friend, and leader of The Verve. ▨

Working lyrics by Noel Gallagher

COME ON EILEEN

DEXY'S MIDNIGHT RUNNERS

COMPOSED BY **KEVIN ROWLAND/JAMES PATTERSON/KEVIN ADAMS**

KEVIN ROWLAND AND AL ARCHER FORMED DEXY'S MIDNIGHT Runners after leaving Birmingham punk outfit The Killjoys and first charted with the mod/soul-orientated 'Dance Stance' in 1980. Their next single, 'Geno' – a tribute to Geno Washington – went to Number One in the UK, as the band was augmented by Style Councillor Mick Talbot, but their next chart topper went one better by reaching Number One in both the US (1983) and UK (1982). That song was 'Come On Eileen'.

"The idea came to me because I met this beautiful girl in Sweden in 1981 who came to see us," lead singer Rowland says. "She was really into our music, moved by it, so that was one idea. The reason it was 'Eileen' was because there was a song by Squeeze called 'Labelled With Love' that I really liked. It contained the lines 'drinks to remember I'm me and myself', but I thought it was 'Eileen and myself'. My sister put me right, although I still thought it was a lovely name and wanted to use it.

"We were going through a tough period songwise and wanted to do something that really cut through, so myself, Jim Patterson, Billy Adams and Micky Billingham came to the first songwriting session. We used to have regular sessions round my place. We'd get records out for inspiration about rhythms, and 'Concrete And Clay' was the starting point where we got this from. We adapted lots of bits of stuff like we always did and they'd end up very different. So, now we had the idea about Eileen and a musical starting point.

"When we used to write songs in those days we'd go into the rehearsal room and get the band to play what we had, usually a chord sequence that we'd play over and over, and put melodies over the top. We often wrote happy feeling songs, then we'd go away with a cassette to work on. Usually I'd go away and write the lyrics separately. We tried the chorus in every single key and as we were making the demo I got the idea to sing the 'too roo loo ay a' bit. As regards using the name Johnny Ray, I wasn't a fan but the words fitted well. I tend to write ideas down on scraps of paper and use them at different times. The 'beaten down eyes and sunken smoke dried faces' was written a year earlier when I lived in Smethwick in Birmingham; loads of factories around there smoking and stuff.

"The song was recorded as part of an album produced by Clive Langer and Alan Winstanley at Streetly Studios. Not a particularly happy process because the band was breaking up at the time. We weren't getting on, so most of the band came back just to do the work as sessions. It was more like a salvage operation really, to try and get something from our earlier work. Not all the tracks reached their full potential but 'Eileen' did – it was too good not to. I knew that because even then it stood out as potential single material.

"When it came out, everybody just latched onto the image, the feel and the hook. It became a bit of an anthem in a way. I'm not sure what the appeal was – we just did our best at that point. If I knew what it was I'd do it again." ▨

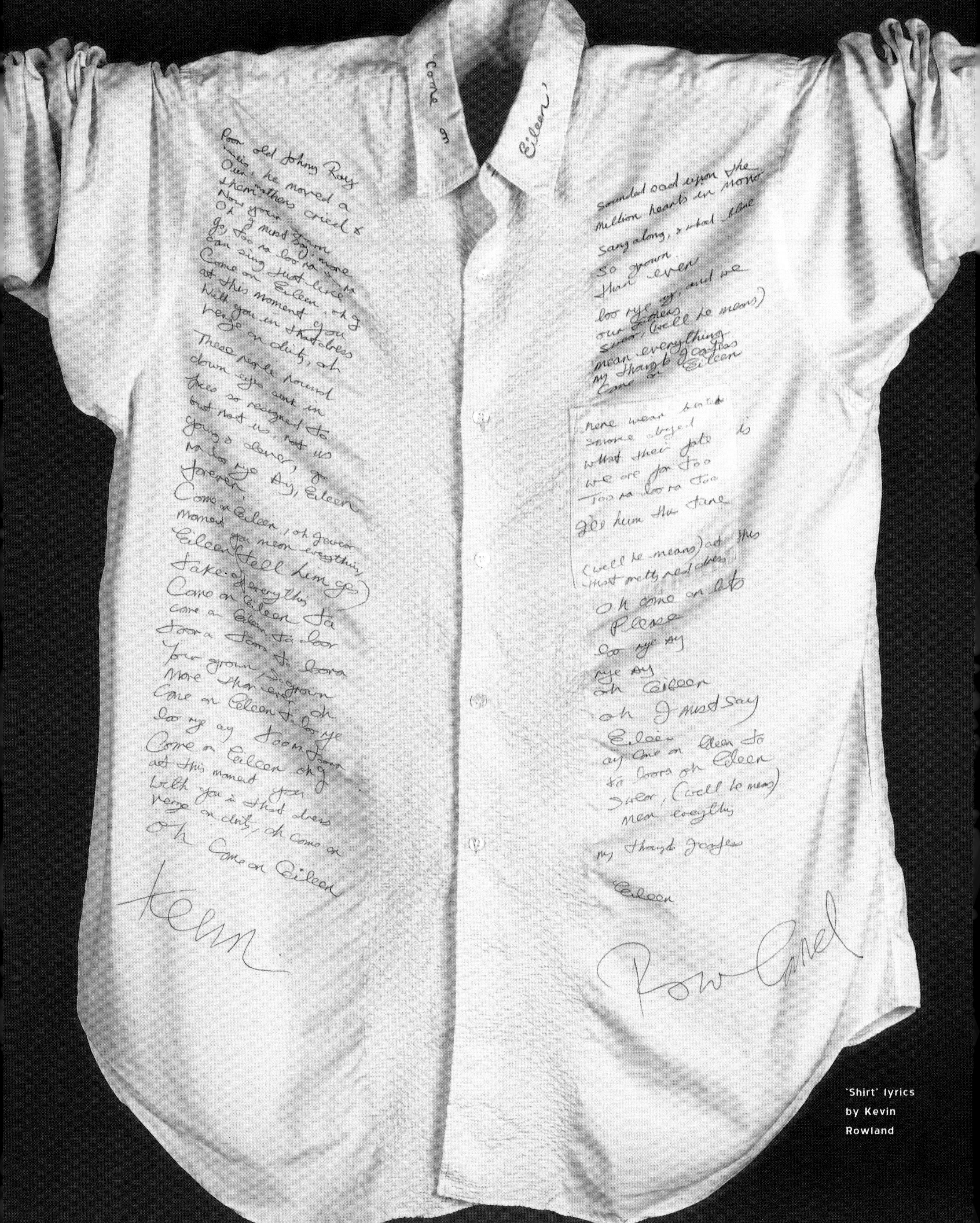

'Shirt' lyrics by Kevin Rowland

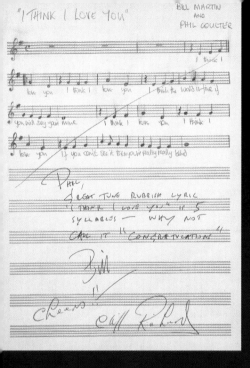

Working score for 'I Think I Love You' which became 'Congratulations'

CONGRATULATIONS

CLIFF RICHARD

COMPOSED BY **BILL MARTIN/PHIL COULTER**

CHARTWISE, CLIFF RICHARD IS NOW THE most successful UK artist of all time. With 89 Top 20 hits and 13 Number Ones Cliff has worked with a lot of songwriters, among them Bill Martin who, along with Phil Coulter, penned the Number One hit 'Congratulations' for Cliff to sing at the now much maligned Eurovision Song Contest.

"At the time of writing this in the 1960s, the contest was only twelve years old," Martin explains, "and it was an incredibly big deal to get your song in the finals, let alone win – which Phil and I had already done the year before with 'Puppet On A String'. We wrote a song specifically for Cliff Richard called 'My Magic Music Box', which we thought was great, but our publisher Jimmy Phillips said, 'Why don't you try another one.'

"We had the first song ready but to keep Jimmy happy, Phil started another song, which went 'I think I love you, I think I love you, I think the world was fine when you will say you're mine...' I thought that was awful: you can't say to anybody, 'I think I love you,' you've got to say, 'I love you' or 'I don't love you'. Phil said, 'I know it's not right, so help me out.' So I worked around the five syllables of 'I think I love you', and came up with 'Congratulations' and 'celebrations' and that was really my only contribution to the song. But having such a catchy title made all the difference. Then we entered it into Eurovision and the rest is history.

"'Congratulations' has become like a second national anthem, which has opened many doors for me. It's a great thrill because it's played at weddings, for the Queen, even when the British troops came back from the Falklands." ▊

COOL FOR CATS

SQUEEZE

COMPOSED BY **GLENN TILBROOK/CHRIS DIFFORD**

FORMED IN 1974 WHEN GLENN Tilbrook and Chris Difford met via an advertisement, Squeeze began recording in 1977 after Jools Holland and Gilson Lavis joined. Their debut effort, 'Packet Of Three' failed to penetrate the listings, but 'Take Me I'm Yours' reached the Top 20 in 1978 to give them the first of 23 UK hit singles. 'Cool For Cats' reached Number Two in 1979.

"I can remember the scenario as if it was today," Chris Difford says of the latter. "Glenn had a backing track that we'd recorded in a studio in London but we didn't have a lyric for it; it was the only song on the album that was unfinished. So I took the track back home that evening to work on ideas, and happened to be watching Benny Hill on TV. He was doing his normal stuff and his usual couple of songs, which I always thought were quite ridiculous. However, I was listening to the meter of one of the songs and thought it

might fit in with what would become 'Cool For Cats', and that's how it was written, sitting at the kitchen table in Greenwich. Like the Benny Hill numbers, each verse is really a little vignette about different situations. It was all to do with television of the time mentioning things like the Indians, *The Sweeney* and discos, it was all relevant for the Seventies. In a kind of way, it's almost like a rap thing of its day, but for south London as opposed to south Harlem.

"The next day I went into the studio, we stuck a mike up and I just sang it. Glenn came up with the idea of having the backing vocals singing 'cool for cats', but because we couldn't afford expensive backing singers we got our girlfriends in to sing the line, and in many ways they sold the song. We still do the song live and our audiences know all the words and usually sing all the backing vocals along with it." ▊

Handwritten lyrics by Chris Difford

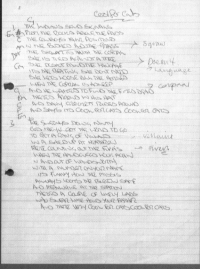

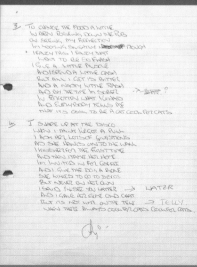

COUSIN KEVIN

THE WHO

COMPOSED BY **JOHN ENTWISTLE**

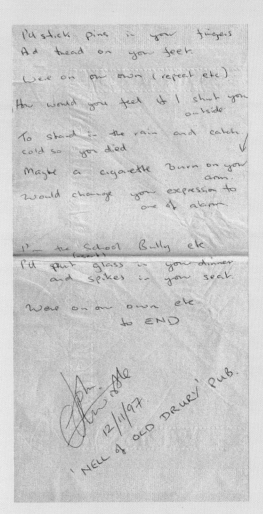

Handwritten lyrics by John Entwistle

ONE OF THE WORLD'S TOP ROCK BANDS,
The Who began life as The High Numbers before taking off in 1965 with 'I Can't Explain' and notching up 14 hit singles in the UK alone in the 1960s. A legendary live act, the band also became remembered for their 'concept' albums, most famously *Quadrophenia* and, in 1969, *Tommy*. *Tommy* has reappeared in many forms over the years, but although most of the credit goes to main songwriter Pete Townshend, bass player John Entwistle also contributed a couple of tracks.

"'Cousin Kevin' began when Pete Townshend and our manager Kit Lambert decided that there should be three nasty experiences for Tommy," Entwistle explains. "An acid trip, a homosexual encounter and a bullying encounter. Pete wrote 'Acid Queen' but felt that he couldn't write the other two, and discussed it with me in a hotel when we were on tour. I said I'd have a go at writing it and by the time I got back to the room I'd already got an idea to write about 'wicked Uncle Ernie'. That was the homosexual encounter, 'Fiddle About'. For the other song, I figured it might as well also be a relation of Tommy's and that's where the name 'Cousin Kevin' came from.

"I based him on the school bully that just happened to live across the street from me. Basically there were things he threatened to do to me. He never actually got round to doing any of them but when I got a bit bigger I beat the shit out of him!

"The song has quite a complicated melody and structure, probably because of my classical background. I wanted it to sound sinister, like a nutter playing 'Chopsticks'. I found that sort of riff very interesting and followed it through the first progression. It started off very peacefully and then got very nasty, just how I wanted it to – schizophrenic, as though he had an instant temper.

"Although some of the production on the *Tommy* album suffered a bit because we were always running late, I was pretty happy with the original recording of the song. Pete and I worked out some harmonies which really gelled and Pete later took over the orchestration for the film version in 1975. It took him ages to work out what the hell I was doing, he didn't realise how complicated it actually was!

"The *Tommy* film was pretty tough on Roger [Daltrey] because he had to act out all the worst bits of the lyrics! I went along to filming when he was being dragged up the stairs and they were pulling his hair out. He shouted out to me that I should have written gentler words to it, but then that would have defeated the object.

"I was quite happy with the interpretation in the stage musical. I saw the New York version but the guy kept changing his accent all the way through. And when Billy Idol did his version for our live shows in 1989 he was having a bit of trouble with the tune and asked to speak some of it. I didn't mind but it was rather ironic as I thought it was pretty melodic and ahead of its time. But then *Tommy* always got a lot of stick which we shared, but they blamed most of it on Townshend!"

THAT KINDA LOVIN' TURNS A MAN TO A SLAVE
THAT KINDA LOVIN' SENDS A MAN
RIGHT TO HIS GRAVE ...

I GO
CRAZY
CRAZY CRAZY
BABY I GO CRAZY
YOU TURN IT ON
THEN YOU'RE GONE
YEAH, YOU DRIVE ME
CRAZY CRAZY CRAZY
FOR YOU BABY
WHAT CAN I DO HONEY
I FEEL LIKE THE COLOR
BLUE ...

Steven Tyler
X

'Crazy' lyrics written on a straitjacket by Steven Tyler

CRAZY

AEROSMITH

COMPOSED BY **STEVEN TYLER/JOE PERRY/DESMOND CHILD**

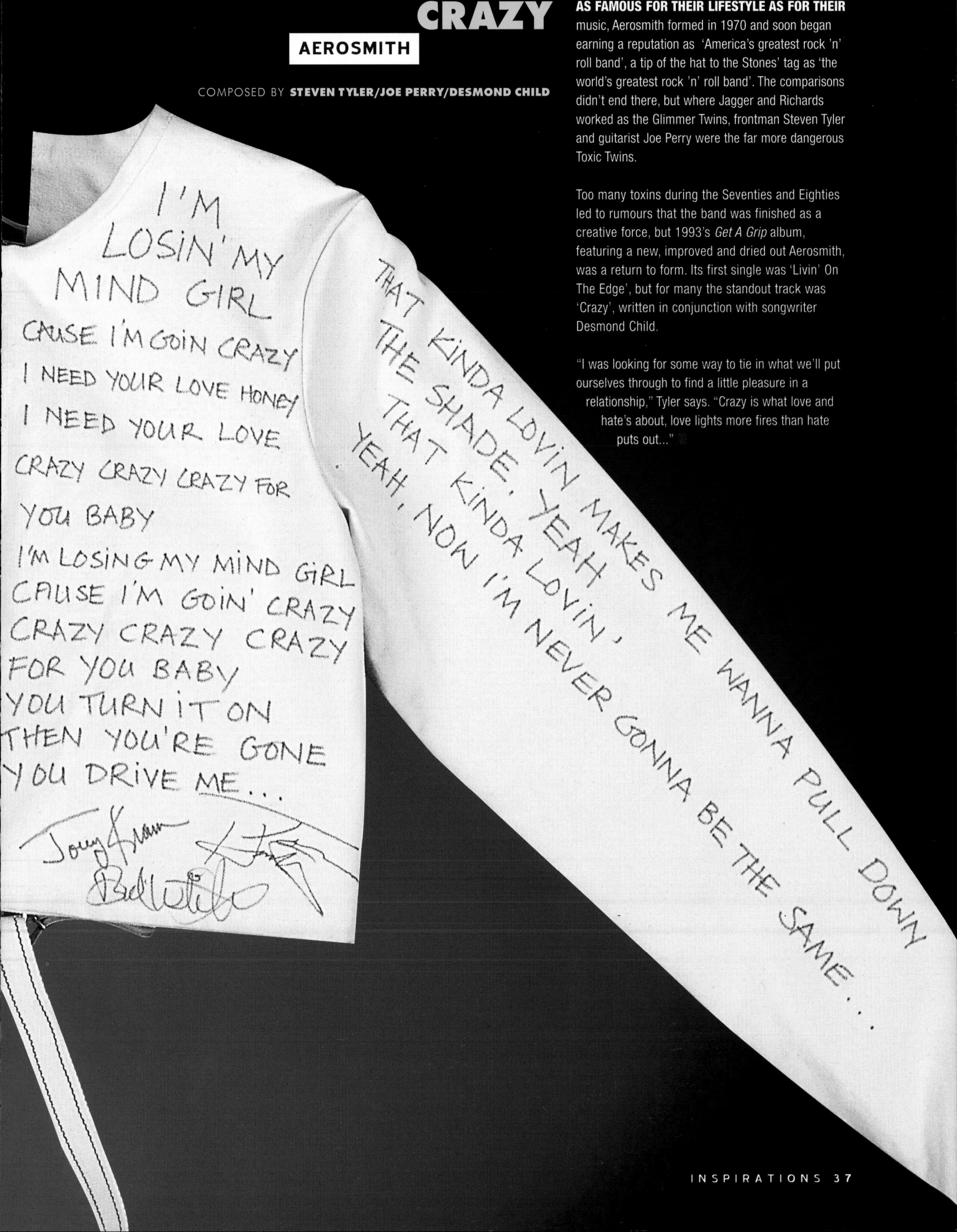

I'M LOSIN' MY MIND GIRL
CAUSE I'M GOIN CRAZY
I NEED YOUR LOVE HONEY
I NEED YOUR LOVE
CRAZY CRAZY CRAZY FOR
YOU BABY
I'M LOSING MY MIND GIRL
CAUSE I'M GOIN' CRAZY
CRAZY CRAZY CRAZY
FOR YOU BABY
YOU TURN IT ON
THEN YOU'RE GONE
YOU DRIVE ME...

THAT KINDA LOVIN MAKES ME WANNA PULL DOWN THE SHADE. YEAH THAT KINDA LOVIN, YEAH, NOW I'M NEVER GONNA BE THE SAME....

AS FAMOUS FOR THEIR LIFESTYLE AS FOR THEIR music, Aerosmith formed in 1970 and soon began earning a reputation as 'America's greatest rock 'n' roll band', a tip of the hat to the Stones' tag as 'the world's greatest rock 'n' roll band'. The comparisons didn't end there, but where Jagger and Richards worked as the Glimmer Twins, frontman Steven Tyler and guitarist Joe Perry were the far more dangerous Toxic Twins.

Too many toxins during the Seventies and Eighties led to rumours that the band was finished as a creative force, but 1993's *Get A Grip* album, featuring a new, improved and dried out Aerosmith, was a return to form. Its first single was 'Livin' On The Edge', but for many the standout track was 'Crazy', written in conjunction with songwriter Desmond Child.

"I was looking for some way to tie in what we'll put ourselves through to find a little pleasure in a relationship," Tyler says. "Crazy is what love and hate's about, love lights more fires than hate puts out..."

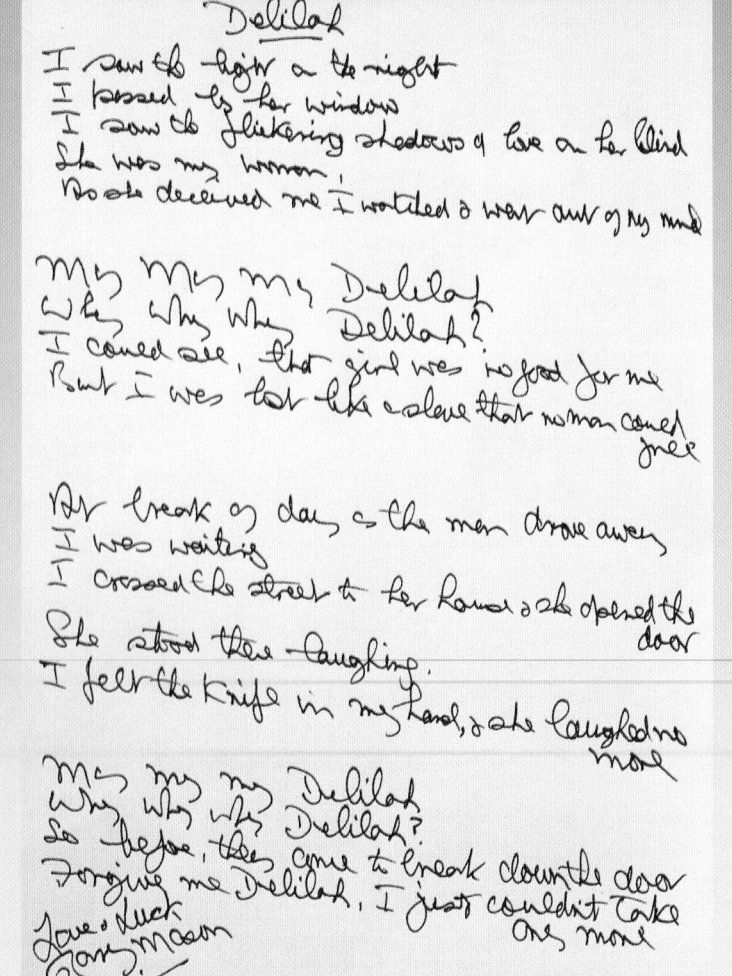

DELILAH

TOM JONES

COMPOSED BY **LES REED/BARRY MASON**

A GERMAN NUMBER ONE FOR PETER ALEXANDER AND A TOP TEN hit for The Alex Harvey Band in 1975 have done little to dowse the public's association of 'Delilah' with one man: Tom Jones. Born in Pontypridd, Wales as Thomas Woodward, 'Jones The Voice' began a massive run of hits on both sides of the Atlantic in 1965, reaching Number Two in the UK (15 in the States) three years later with just one of the songs that he has made his own – Barry Mason and Les Reed's 'Delilah'.

"The inspiration came from a woman I was once in love with in Blackpool," Barry Mason reveals. "I was really very hurt at the time because she'd gone off with someone else. The title came first, and it's definitely an evocative one. I was looking for a woman's name to use for this song about the great temptresses of history. Jezebel had already been used, so Delilah was the obvious other one that could capture people's imagination.

"Les Reed's arrangement stands up through time, I think it's fantastic. It's so good that people even sing the arrangement whenever it's played, they go 'la la la, Delilah'. They all sing the figures that Les wrote, which is the biggest tribute you can pay to an arranger. They now tell me it's the biggest karaoke song of all time, which is quite incredible.

"We had over 700 covers of it in the first couple of years in the Sixties, so there's probably a couple of thousand by now, in every country of the world. Wherever Les or I go it's a like musical passport, we've been incredibly fortunate and grateful that so many people can identify it. It seems to go hand in hand with having good times and being with good friends. Of course, Tom's version is still the definitive one, and he's performed it at some of the most fantastic places around the world. I must say that he gave me one of the biggest thrills of my life recently when he sang it at Wembley Stadium along with the London Welsh Choir, in front of a crowd of 80,000 at the England versus Wales rugby international. That was a high point for me and my family, and I was very, very proud indeed."

A somewhat lower point for Mason came in the toilets at the BBC Club not long after the record came out.

"I was in the toilets and a chap was standing next to me whistling 'Delilah'," he explains. "I'd never heard anyone whistling any of my songs before. Having recently come from Wigan to riches, as it were, I just couldn't believe it, and out of sheer joy and excitement I turned to him and said, 'Excuse me, but that's my song you're whistling!' He replied, 'I thought Les Reed wrote that one.' I said, 'Yes, but I wrote the words,' and he said, 'I'm not whistling the bloody words!'"

DIAMONDS ARE FOREVER

SHIRLEY BASSEY

COMPOSED BY DON BLACK/JOHN BARRY

SHIRLEY BASSEY WILL FOREVER BE ASSOCIATED WITH THE JAMES
Bond series of films, singing the title songs of three of them – 'Diamonds Are Forever', 'Moonraker' and 'Goldfinger' – and inspiring the singers of others. In 1972 she took 'Diamonds Are Forever' to Number 25 in the UK and 57 in the US, six years after fellow Welshman Tom Jones charted with the fourth Bond theme, 'Thunderball'. Both songs were written by the series' long-time composer John Barry and lyricist Don Black.

"With 'Diamonds Are Forever', Harry Saltzman the producer thought it was too sexy and provocative," Black recalls. "Lines like 'touch it, stroke it and undress it', for example. I argued that Shirley Bassey would expect something like that, besides which there are certain 'givens' with Bond collaborations – they always have to be threatening, mouthwatering, inviting and dangerous and risky and sexy. And in a way, difficult though the criteria is, it helps to work to a brief. Writing songs for movies you are at least working from a title, which helps."

Handwritten lyrics by Don Black

DIARY

BREAD

COMPOSED BY DAVID GATES

ALTHOUGH DAVID GATES, JAMES GRIFFIN, ROBB ROYER AND MIKE
Botts had all been recording, writing and performing for many years individually, they didn't come together as Bread, until 1968. The group, who ostensibly decided upon their name after being stuck in traffic behind a bread van, released their eponymous debut album in the autumn of 1968. Their second album was *On The Waters*, after the words of the Book of Ecclesiastes: if you "cast thy bread upon the waters…you shall find it after many days". After not too many days, the album gave them a Number One single in the States with 'Make It With You', the track reaching Number Five in Britain. Now firmly established, a string of hits followed, during which time Royer left to concentrate on writing, and was replaced by Larry Knechtel, a multi-instrumentalist who'd been one of Duane Eddy's Rebels, played bass on The Byrds 'Mr Tambourine Man' and piano on Simon And Garfunkel's 'Bridge Over Troubled Water'.

Bread had five British hits in all and 13 in the States, where the David Gates song 'Diary' went to Number 15 in the summer of 1972. 'Diary' featured on the 1973 album *The Best Of Bread*, one of their nine gold albums.

Handwritten lyrics by David Gates

Working lyrics annotated
by Neil Tennant

D J CULTURE

Imagine a war which everyone won
Permanent holiday in an endless sun
Peace without wisdom
One steals to achieve
Relentlessly one pretends to believe
Attitudes range from materialistic
To positive or frankly realistic
Which is terribly old-fashioned, isn't it?
Or isn't it?

(D J Culture)
Let's pretend
(D J Culture)
Wait and see
Living in a sattelite fantasy
Surving in a D J culture

Let's pretend we won a war
~~There are differences, others and the same~~
Like a football match, 10-nil the score
Anything's possible, we're on the same side
Or otherwise on trial for our lives
"And I, my lord, may I say nothing?"

I've been around the world for a number of reasons
I've seen it happen, the change of seasons
And I, My lord, may I say nothing?

Consider for a minute who you are
What you'd like to change, never mind the scars
Bury the past, empty the shelf
~~It's easy.~~ Decide to reinvent yourself
Like Liz before Betty, She after Sean
Suddenly you're missing then you're reborn
and say nothing

It's a matter of pride to ~~induldgae~~ your mood
No feast days or fast days or days of absitinenee intrude

DJ CULTURE

PET SHOP BOYS

COMPOSED BY **NEIL TENNANT/CHRIS LOWE**

AFTER MEETING IN A HI-FI
shop, former *Smash Hits* magazine
journalist Neil Tennant and
architecture student Chris Lowe
formed The Pet Shop Boys in 1981.
Through *Smash Hits* Tennant met
record producer Bobby 'O' Orlando
in 1983 which resulted in him
producing the duo. After a couple
of unsuccessful singles, including
'West End Girls', that song was re-
recorded and went to Number One
in eight countries including Britain
and the States. 'West End Girls'
won an Ivor Novello award for
International Hit Of The Year and
was voted Best Single at the Brits.

Tennant and Lowe went from
strength to strength, scoring 30 hit
singles in the UK including four
Number Ones. In 1991 they
charted four singles, including 'DJ
Culture' which was released to
promote their greatest hits
compilation album *Discography*.

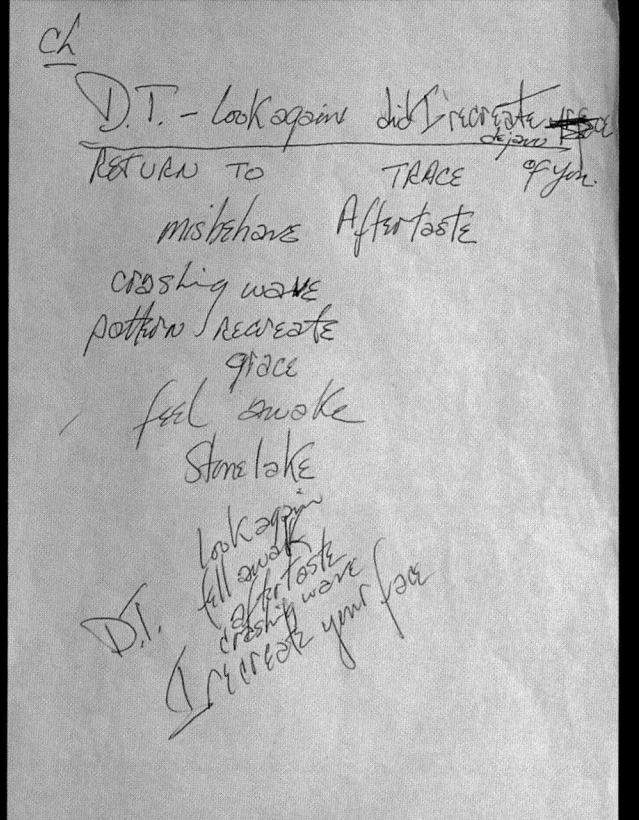

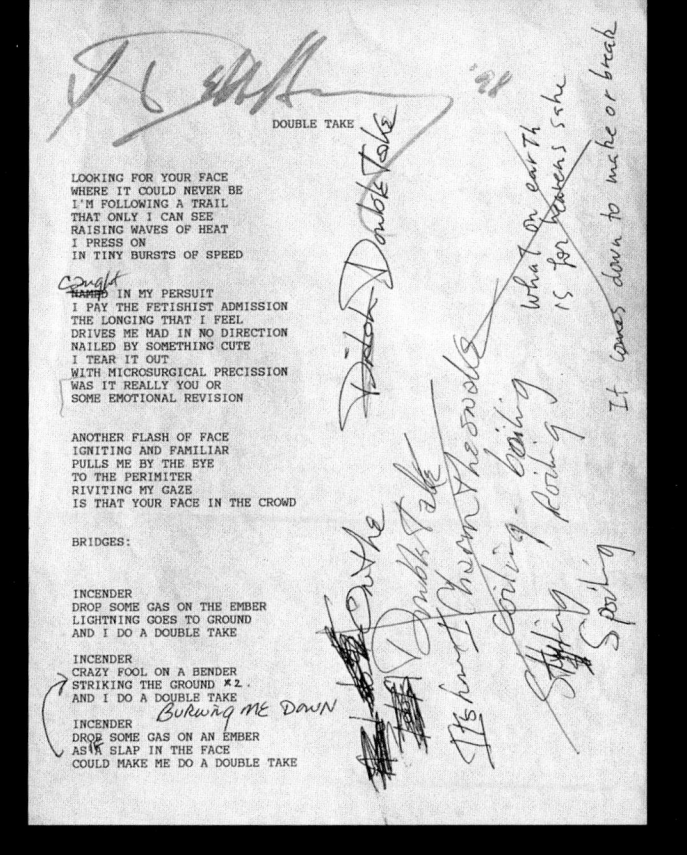

DOUBLE TAKE

BLONDIE

COMPOSED BY **DEBORAH HARRY/BLONDIE**

FRONTED BY DEBBIE HARRY, A former *Playboy* 'bunny' from Miami and singer with Sixties group Wind In The Willows, Blondie's debut single, 'X-Offender', was released in 1976. It was another two years before the group broke into the charts with a cover of Randy And The Rainbows' US hit 'Denise', which Blondie re-titled as 'Denis'. The single went to Number Two in the UK and their debut album hit Number Ten, but before long they'd notched up five UK and four US Number One singles.

Blondie split up in 1982 with Harry launching herself as an actress and solo star but they reformed in1998, releasing their first studio album for 16 years in 1999. Called *No Exit*, the album contained the Number One single 'Maria' plus a new track called 'Double Take' (pictured).

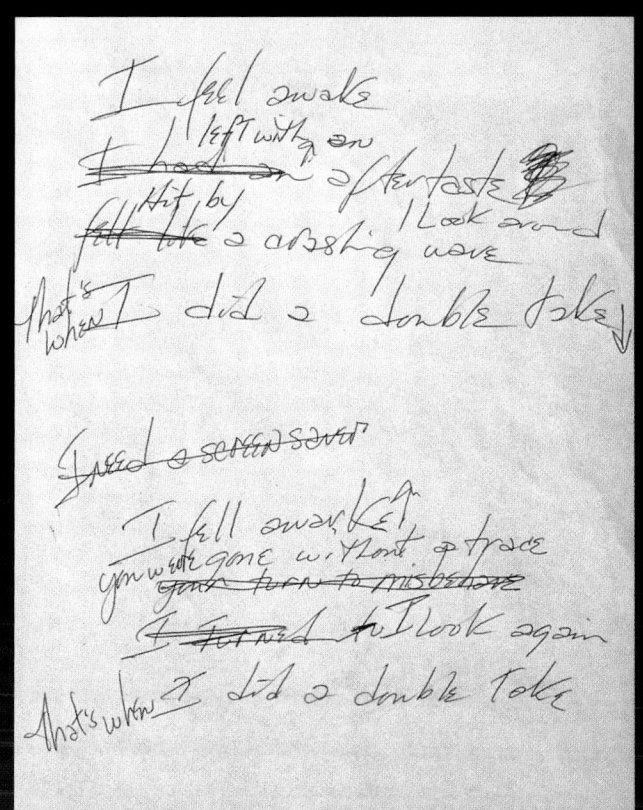

Working lyrics by Deborah Harry

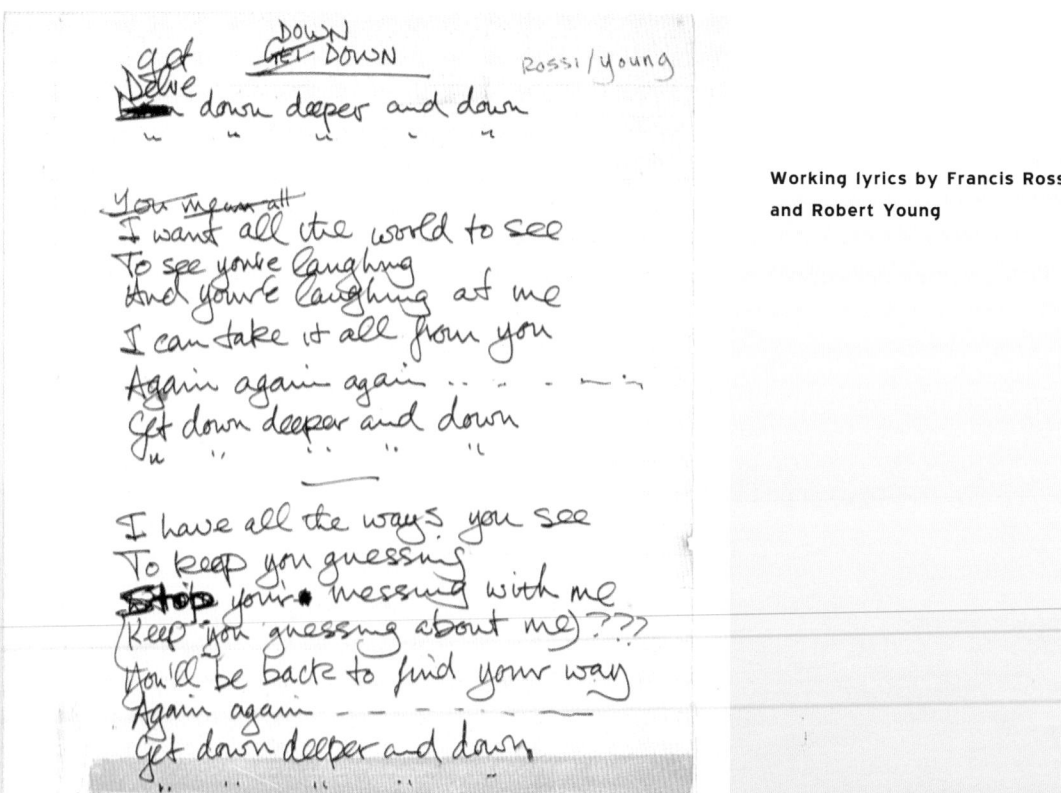

Working lyrics by Francis Rossi and Robert Young

DOWN DOWN

STATUS QUO

COMPOSED BY **FRANCIS ROSSI/ROBERT YOUNG**

STATUS QUO EVOLVED THROUGH THE SPECTRES AND Traffic Jam to have their debut hit with 'Pictures Of Matchstick Men' in 1968. By 1970 they'd shed psychedelia for a more 'heads down no nonsense' boogie approach with resounding success. An extraordinary chart – and concert – career over three decades has seen them spend 170 weeks in the UK Top 20, including 20 consecutive years without failing to chart. Of their eleven Top Ten singles, only 'Down Down' topped the charts, in 1974.

"I was sitting in a hotel room in Los Angeles trying to finish the song," explains Francis Rossi who, along with Rick Parfitt, has been the face and voice of Quo since the beginning. "I'd got most of the melody written back in England with Bob Young who I was working with at the time. We'd got most of the verse lyrics done, and looking back it was probably about my relationship at the time.

"We were stuck for a chorus, but felt that it had to have a 'de-de-de' kind of feel to it, like in T-Rex's song 'Deborah' – we needed something with that kind of push to it. We sat around for a couple of days, came up with nothing and ended up out of desperation resorting to 'down down' which meant nothing but suited the melody.

"We did *Top Of The Pops* and shortly afterwards went to France on tour. The BBC wanted us to come back and do the show again, but our management said we couldn't. The BBC retaliated by not playing it that week but we still went to Number One so they had to. And it was our only Number One in England, if only for a week."

With 52 British hit singles, Quo rank as the twelfth most successful chart act of all time. ▣

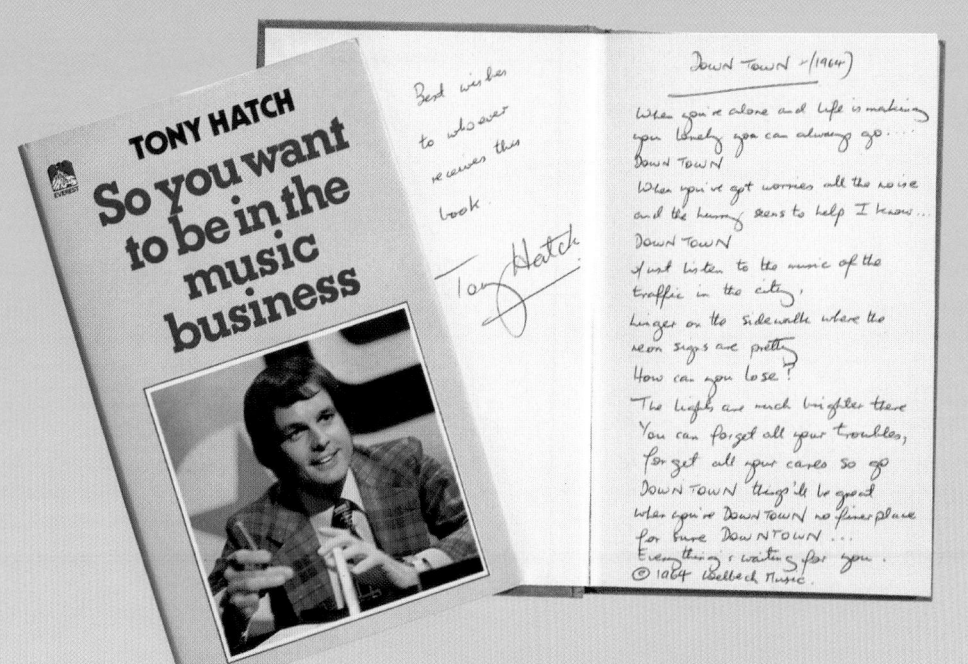

Handwritten lyrics
by Tony Hatch

DOWNTOWN

PETULA CLARK

COMPOSED BY **TONY HATCH**

EPSOM-BORN PETULA CLARK MADE HER STAGE DEBUT AT THE
age of seven in 1939, her recording career beginning ten years later. The first of more than 20 film roles came in 1944 and five years later her incredible 50-year musical career began. Clark's biggest hit, 'Downtown', written by Tony Hatch, hit Number One in the US (Number Two in the UK) in 1964, later remixed for another hit in 1988. As with a lot of classics, though, in reality it very nearly never happened – at least not for Petula Clark – as Hatch explains...

"I made my first short visit to New York in 1964," he recalls, "partly to immerse myself in the 'good vibrations' of one of the world's great entertainment centres, but also to visit some music publishers to try and pick up songs for my stable of Pye Records artists. As a record producer I had fair success covering US hits, but whilst this gave us some UK hits it didn't provide a continuing source of material.

"My first walk down Broadway to Times Square was the inspiration for the song which changed that situation and a couple of lives as well. I couldn't get the word 'Downtown' out of my head, and instinctively knew it was a great title for a song. A few days later, I was back in Studio One at Pye doodling on the Steinway whilst balance engineer Ray Prickett re-patched the desk for a mixdown. The melody fell into place in minutes – no words, but the title 'Downtown' knew exactly where it wanted to be. I decided to get it to Ben E King when it was finished, and thought what a great follow-up to 'On Broadway' it could be.

"Meanwhile there was a Petula Clark session to plan. Her record sales all over Europe were phenomenal, but my first year as her sole producer had yielded no UK chart entries. I also wrote the songs, so it was decided in late 1964 that Pet would make one further single with me for UK release although, whatever its fate, I would continue producing the continental singles and albums. I day-tripped to Paris armed with several of those New York publishers' songs and rehearsed with her at her apartment in the Bois de Boulogne. I took none of my own work, but

alas, she was not impressed with the American material and asked if I had anything else to offer, specifically something of my own. There I was in France, with the recording session in ten days' time and no lead song for the date. As an exercise in damage limitation, I reluctantly played Pet the sketch of 'Downtown'. She was on to it immediately even though it had no lyrics. Obviously she knew better than me what we were listening to. 'That will be a great song,' she said, 'and I want to record it.' There was no turning back (and no Ben E King record either) but Pet's enthusiasm also became my inspiration.

"As usual each Petula Clark recording session was a rush job with musicians and backing singers to book, conductor to hire, orchestrations to write and, of course, I still needed lyrics for the main song which had to be tailor-made for Pet. I decided to write them myself as it was my experience which had to be realised. I'm not saying I was under pressure but the second verse was finished in the studio toilet 15 minutes before the session commenced, with my secretary waiting outside with her typewriter! The song was recorded live in the studio and mixed down from eight-track on the same day. The atmosphere in the studio was electric. It seems that everybody except me knew that a classic was being created, I thought it was great but very British (not at all like Ben E) and that worried me. Ironically, that 'British' element was probably one of the record's greatest assets and I remember Joe Smith of Warner Bros Records securing 'Downtown' for the States long before we'd set a UK release date for its climb to Number Two in the *NME* charts.

"The rest is history. Three million singles worldwide, Number One in the States and a huge new market for Petula's wonderful talent. Versions in every singable language (others extraordinarily unsingable), plus dozens of cover versions and many cherished awards. More importantly, we'd found the chemistry that makes a successful producer/artiste relationship and consolidated it with twelve more hit singles, several albums and a valuable catalogue still greatly in demand today. I may have written and arranged 'Downtown' but Petula made it a hit."

DREAM ON DREAMER

THE BRAND NEW HEAVIES

COMPOSED BY **BRAND NEW HEAVIES**

THE CORE OF EALING-BASED OUTFIT THE BRAND NEW HEAVIES OVER THE last twelve years has been guitarist Simon Bartholomew, Jan Kincaid (drums/keyboards) and bassist Andrew Levy. The three, friends since their youth, initially teamed up with vocalist Linda Murial, and later with Jaye Ella Ruth. By 1991 they were working with soul singer N'Dea Davenport, with whom they had their first UK hit, 'Never Stop'.

During 1994, The Brand New Heavies chalked up four hit singles: 'Dream Come True', *Ultimate Trunk Funk* EP, 'Don't Let It Go To Your Head' and 'Stay This Way'. There were no hits during 1993, but they came roaring back in '94 with another four hits, headed by 'Dream On Dreamer' which went to Number 15 in the spring of that year. By 1997 Davenport had been replaced by Siedah Garrett.

Jacket designed by Brand New Heavies

ENJOY THE SILENCE

DEPECHE MODE

COMPOSED BY **MARTIN GORE**

'Keyboard' lyrics by Martin Gore

WRITTEN BY GROUP MEMBER

Martin Gore, Depeche Mode's 'Enjoy The Silence' was recorded at Puk Studios in Denmark, and became their 24th UK hit single, when it went to Number Six in 1990.

The sound of Andy Fletcher, Dave Gahan, Alan Wilder and Martin Gore became increasingly European, and the group went for a new leather-clad image. 'Enjoy The Silence' came from the album *Violator*, produced by Depeche Mode and Flood, promotion copies coming in a boxed presentation pack containing cassette, CD and vinyl copies of the album. *Violator* had also given them their previous hit single, 'Personal Jesus', and was to provide them with their next two hits, 'Policy Of Truth' and 'World In My Eyes'.

At the Ivor Novello awards in May 1999 Martin Gore was honoured with the Outstanding Song Catalogue award.

EVE OF THE WAR

JEFF WAYNE'S WAR OF THE WORLD

COMPOSED BY JEFF WAYNE

NEW YORKER JEFF WAYNE ATTENDED the Juilliard School of Music and was at one time a member of The Sandpipers. Moving to London in 1966 he continued to study music while working as an arranger and jingle writer. In the early Seventies he began working with David Essex as producer and musical director but solo success was to follow with the concept album of HG Wells' *War Of The Worlds*.

"In 1974 my father and I were chatting about my career and he pointed out that although I was doing quite well and was producing other people, I had no outlet at the time for my own compositions," Wayne recalls. "He urged me to find something that I believed in, something that would fire my 'composing juices'. With this in mind we both started to read different books and went through lots of styles and genres and composed a shortlist of three, of which *War Of The Worlds* was one. We felt it was both simple but visionary, and also the only one that suggested musical sounds and ideas to me as I read it.

"We found out the book was still very much under copyright, so over a nine month period we met up with the managers of HG Wells' estate and acquired all the remaining rights, including the right to create a musical interpretation, which became known as 'Jeff Wayne's Musical Version Of The War Of The Worlds'. It's a musical work that is continuous play and came out as a two-album set in the days of black vinyl. It has since gone onto cassette, CD and will be out on mini-disc and as a computer game shortly, even as a stage production.

"The album contains songs and themes as narrated by a journalist (played by Richard Burton) who has survived a Martian invasion from some six years earlier. He recounts the story and along the way he has flashbacks and comes across characters that are other artists that we were fortunate to attract, like Justin Hayward, David Essex, Phil Lynott, Chris Thompson and Julie Covington. The main theme is called 'Eve Of The War', and along with a song called 'Forever Autumn' [co-written with Paul Vigrass and Gary Osborne and sung by Justin Hayward] both have been big international hits." ▣

Working score by Jeff Wayne

The Eve Of The War from Jeff Wayne's Musical Version of 'The War Of The Worlds'

Handwritten score by Michael Kamen and lyrics by Bryan Adams

(EVERYTHING I DO) I DO IT FOR YOU

BRYAN ADAMS

COMPOSED BY **MICHAEL KAMEN/MUTT LANGE/BRYAN ADAMS**

ONTARIO-BORN BRYAN ADAMS' RECORDING career began in 1981 and by the following year he had built an excellent reputation playing live, touring with The Kinks and Foreigner. The hits started to come in the States in the same year, while 'Run To You' was the first to breach the British charts in 1985, reaching Number Eleven. In 1991 '(Everything I Do) I Do It For You', topped the singles charts in both the UK and US, notching up a record-breaking 16 weeks at Number One in the former.

The song was used in the film *Robin Hood: Prince Of Thieves* and was co-written by the film's orchestrator Michael Kamen. For him it was the chance to use an idea he'd been carrying for a while....

"I originally had the idea for what eventually became this song way back when I was in the New York Rock 'N' Roll Ensemble," says Kamen. "We were a very free-spirited band on stage, and I found myself improvising this little tune almost every night until it became too much for the others – they'd get fed up and tell me to stop. It had no words and I just know that it pleased me, but eventually I got talked out of playing it and sort of filed it away and went back to other things.

"I got an incredible chance later on to do a film score based on Robin Hood, who was one of my heroes of all time, right back from the original Richard Greene TV series in my childhood. In fact it was almost an obsession: I'd run around the Adirondack Woods in upstate New York during summer vacations, completely lost in this character, whittling arrows and looking for Maid Marian. So of course, when this opportunity came up, I (uncharacteristically) phoned my agent and said that I really wanted to do the movie. He had wanted to surprise me, but ended up telling me that he'd already been speaking to the right people, and that the producer, James Robinson, was flying to London at that very moment to try and convince me to do the music for the film. An even greater coincidence was getting asked to do another Robin Hood movie at the same, by another set of people.

"I chose to do the Kevin Costner version, and went to meet the director, Kevin Reynolds. Shortly after that I received the first footage of the film, and the first scene that I got was Robin Hood bathing naked under a waterfall, when Maid Marian comes across him in the glade. She looks at him in astonishment and embarrassment and with desire. I saw Mary Elizabeth Mastrantonio's incredible face and suddenly the song came burrowing from the back of my brain, straight up to the front. It was then that I realised what I'd written the song for. I was so excited that I did what I don't normally do, I became a child again, calling up friends and making them listen!"

Kamen's friends weren't the only ears tested out. "The production people in LA loved it too," he says, "and asked who should we get to sing it. The song was paraded in front of some great artists and quite a few of them wanted to do it, but usually in a stylistic way that wasn't appropriate to the film. Nothing had been decided by the time I got to LA to meet production and work on the score. We were on a tight deadline when David Kershenbaum and Jim Mazza, who were running the record company for the producers Morgan Creek, called me. They suggested Bryan Adams and although I didn't know him personally I agreed because I love his voice, his simple approach and the fact that he's a complete rock 'n' roller.

"At that point he hadn't issued a record in four years, I sent him a demo of the song with me playing on the harp and me singing a melody on top of it. Bryan called me and asked what the song was about and I told him it was a love song and to look at the scene in the movie where Robin asks Maid Marian if she'll do him a favour and go and take a message for the king – would she do it for the king? And she says no. But then she looks Robin meaningfully in the eyes and says, 'I'll do it for you.' Bryan got very excited and said he had 'got it', and about four days later FedEx showed up with a tape that was my original copy to Brian, returned with him singing over me humming. He had the words completed, including obviously, 'I'll Do it For You'. It gave the song meaning, it gave me the chills listening to it, and it was clear we had a hit, 25 years after I'd started carrying the tune around.

"The melody was used all the way through the film, every time Robin and Marian were together. And then at the end it turns into the song that we all know. The feeling that this tune had been re-purposed for the film and that it gave life to my childhood preoccupation with my hero was one of the most satisfying feelings ever – I still have to pinch myself even now. The record came out and it was an instant success as Mutt Lange had done a great production on it. He organised the middle eight and got a credit as a writer too, and Bryan and I wound up having one of those classic head-to-head battles about publishing which resulted in us being great friends to this day." ■

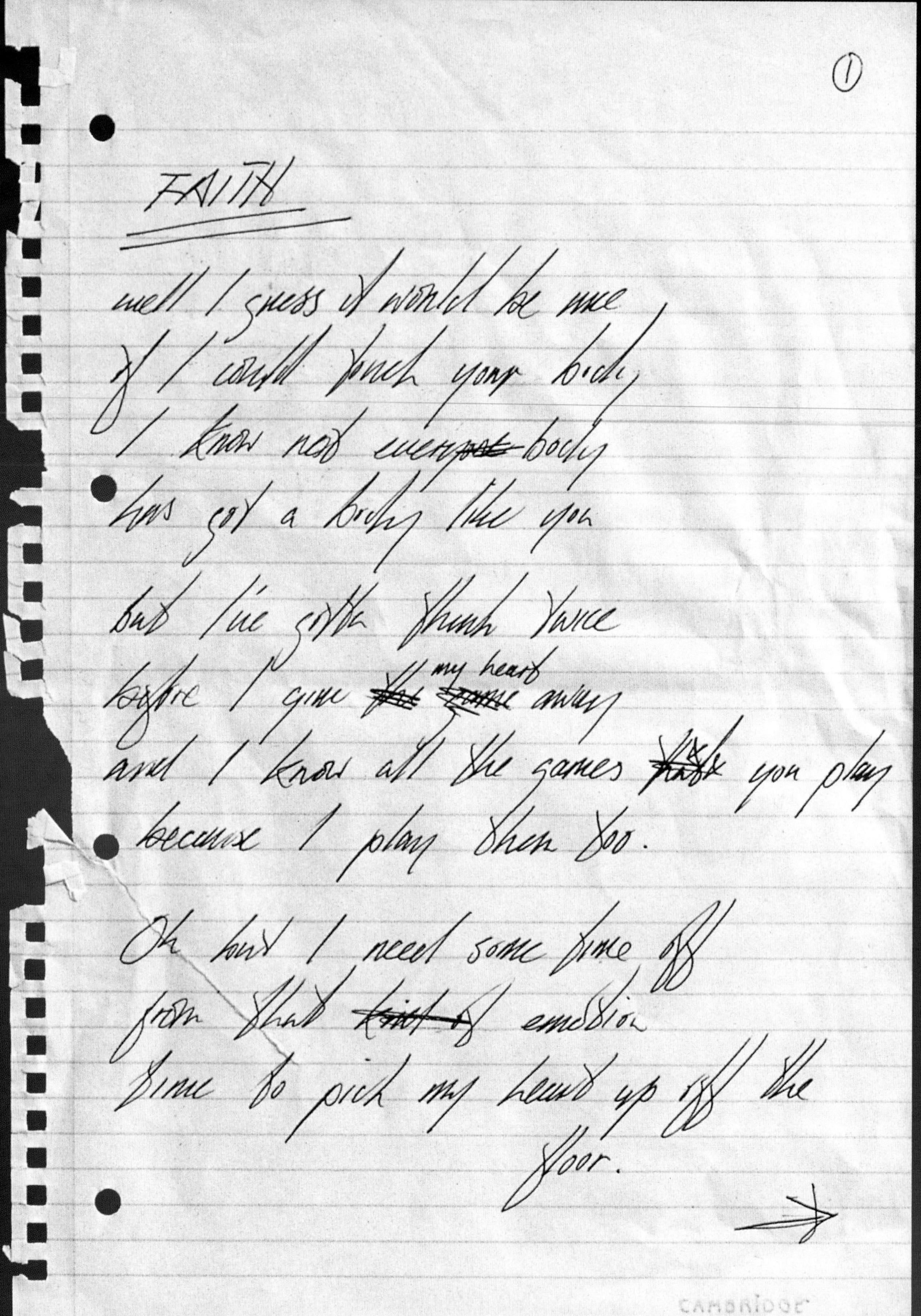

FAITH

well I guess it would be nice
if I could touch your body
I know not everybody
has got a body like you

but I've gotta think twice
before I give ~~it~~ ~~love~~ my heart away
and I know all the games ~~that~~ you play
because I play them too.

Oh but I need some time off
from that ~~kind of~~ emotion
time to pick my heart up off the
floor.

→

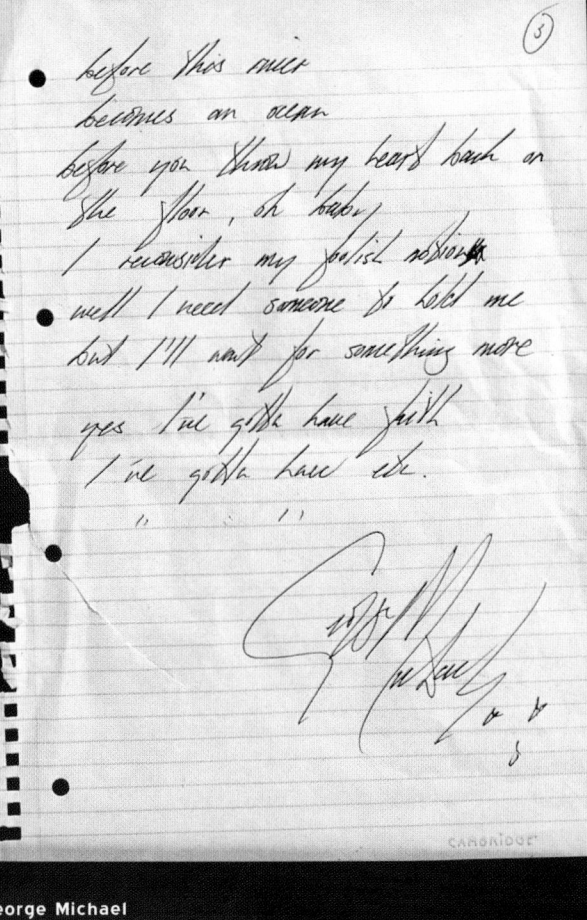

Handwritten lyrics by George Michael

FAITH

GEORGE MICHAEL

COMPOSED BY **GEORGE MICHAEL**

FROM TEEN SENSATION WITH WHAM! TO SOLO SUPERSTARDOM, GEORGE
Michael's career has been a success story from the beginning. Where others have tried and failed, he seemingly effortlessly made the step up from fun pop act to serious artist, beginning his solo career with 'Careless Whisper' in 1984 while Wham! were still at the height of their success. Other one-off singles followed – 'A Different Corner', 'I Knew You Were Waiting (For Me)' and 'I Want Your Sex' – until 1987 when his first solo album was released.

Faith topped the chart on both sides of the Atlantic, confirming Michael's international appeal, while the album's title track, written, arranged and produced by the singer, reached Number Two in the UK and Number One in the US.

In hindsight 'Faith' marked the mid-way point in George Michael's career, taking as its church organ-style intro the tune from the Wham! hit 'Freedom'. Three years and another image change later and the strong images associated with the song – the shades, the leather jacket, the guitar – were consciously destroyed in the video to 'Freedom '90'. ▨

falling into you

and in your eyes 👁 i see ribbons of color
i see us inside of each other
i feel my unconscious merge with yours
and i hear a voice say, "what's his is hers"

i'm falling into you . this dream could come true
and it feels so good falling into you

i was afraid to let you in here
now i have learned love can't be made in fear
the walls begin to tumble down
and i can't even see the ground

i'm falling into you . this dream could come true
and it feels so good falling into you

falling like a leaf
falling like a star ⭐
finding a belief
falling where you are

catch me, don't let me drop!
love me, don't ever stop!

so close your eyes and let me kiss you
and while you sleep i will miss you
i'm falling into you . . . . . .

words and music by billy steinberg, rick nowels and
marie claire d'ubaldo

Handwritten lyrics by Billy Steinberg

FALLING INTO YOU

COMPOSED BY **BILLY STEINBERG/RICK NOWELS/MARIE CLAIRE D'UBALDO**

FROM 1981 QUEBEC-BORN CELINE DION HAD BEEN A PROLIFIC French-Canadian recording artist, with some eleven albums to her credit. By 1988 her quest for international fame stepped up a gear when she won the Eurovision Song Contest – for Switzerland – and landed herself a Top Five hit in America. Success was slow coming in the UK, eventually arriving courtesy of Disney's *Beauty And The Beast* soundtrack, but it has since shown no sign of abating, with Dion headlining at Wembley Stadium for two nights in 1999.

In 1996 'Falling Into You', the title track of her multi-platinum album reached Number Ten in the UK and was written by songwriter Billy Steinberg with a couple of friends... "I was writing a lot at the time with Rick Nowels," Steinberg says, "when I was introduced to UK-based Argentinian singer/songwriter Marie Claire D'Ubaldo by Davitt Sigerson, a record executive working at PolyGram. He'd signed Marie Claire as an artist, so we all got together and wrote three songs including 'Falling Into You'. When I wrote the lyrics I had my future wife in mind at the time because we'd not long met. I actually went on to sing the song to her during the wedding ceremony and Rick and his wife accompanied me.

"I was very happy with this song and particularly like the line 'close your eyes and I will kiss you, while you sleep I will miss you, falling into you'. I find it a satisfying moment. When I work with Marie Claire and Rick, we all cross over somewhat but for the most part I write the lyrics first, then Rick writes the chords and Marie Claire writes the melodies, with a bit of input from Rick and myself.

"I submitted it to Celine Dion's people in Montreal, and they loved it. A guy from Sony in Canada called me and asked who I thought would would be a good producer for the project and although I hadn't done too much really, I went out on a limb and said that Rick and I would. They loved the demo (not knowing it was actually Marie Claire's finished version) and gave us the opportunity to produce it.

"I'm proud that Celine Dion chose it as the title of her album. It's happened a couple of times before, with 'Precious Time' by Pat Benatar, 'Like A Virgin' for Madonna and 'True Colours' for Cyndi Lauper, but Celine's album was such a phenomenal success, with over 25 million copies sold around the world. Truly amazing!"

FIELDS OF GOLD

STING

COMPOSED BY **STING**

FOLLOWING A HIGHLY SUCCESSFUL CAREER WITH THE POLICE, Sting released his first solo album in 1985, launching a new career for himself. Although he'd already had a hit single without the others when he released 'Spread A Little Happiness' in 1982, it wasn't until three years later that he began to record in earnest as a solo artist, releasing singles and albums of his own. His album *Nothing Like The Sun* topped the UK chart and went Top Ten in America, winning Best Album at the UK's Brit awards.

In parallel with his recording, he continued to pursue his acting career, which had begun with roles in *Quadrophenia* and *Dune*.

But it was Sting's 1993 album *Ten Summoner's Tales* that gave him two of his biggest hits, 'If I Ever Lose My Faith In You' and 'Fields Of Gold'. The songs reached Number 14 and Number 16 respectively in the UK chart. 'Fields Of Gold' gave its name to Sting's 1994 album, *Fields Of Gold: The Best Of Sting 1984-1994.*

Handwritten lyrics by Sting

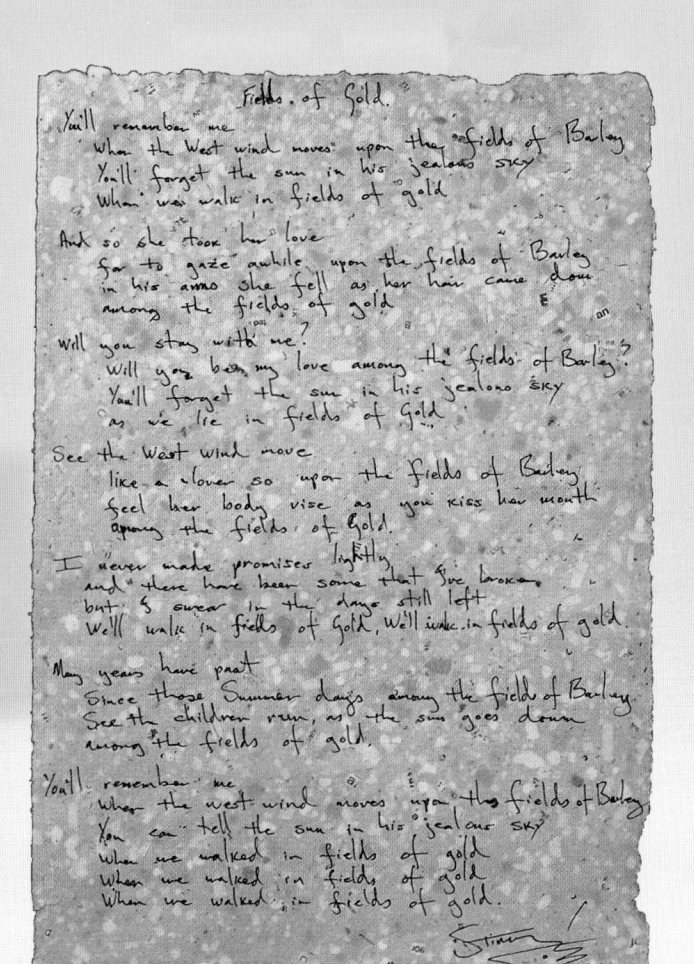

FIRESTARTER   THE PRODIGY

1. I'M THE TROUBLE STARTER   RUNNIN' INSIDE
   I'M THE FEAR ADDICTED, DANGER ILLUSTR
      CHORUS: I'M A FIRESTARTER, TWISTED
         YOU'RE THE FIRESTARTER, TWISTED
            I'M A FIRESTARTER, TWISTED

2. I'M THE BITCH YOU HATED, FILTH INFACT
      I'M THE PAIN YOU TASTED, FELL
      CHORUS.

3. I'M THE SELF-INFLICTED MIND DETON
      I'M THE ONE INFECTED, TWISTED

WORDS WRITTEN BY LIAM HOWLETT
                          KEEF FLINT

'Electric fire' lyrics written by Liam Howlett

FIRESTARTER

THE PRODIGY

COMPOSED BY **LIAM HOWLETT/KEITH FLINT**

KEITH FLINT AND LEEROY THORNHILL, HAVING first met at a rave in Essex, then saw Liam Howlett at an outdoor rave where he impressed Flint with the music he was playing. Further impressed by Howlett's tapes, Flint and Thornhill joined forces with Howlett to become The Prodigy, also recruiting MC Maxim Reality. Their first hit, 'Charly', arrived in 1991 and in March 1996 the band had its first Number One UK single with 'Firestarter'.

"'Firestarter' was the first song I tried to write for our last album," Howlett says. "It started off as an instrumental, I was just messing around with the use of guitars in dance music – I didn't believe that it had been done much with a cool flavour to it, on a real street level. I'd half finished the instrumental and Keith popped in. For the first time he said he'd like to have a go at some lyrics, so we sat down and talked about ideas.

"That gave me the inspiration to finish off for the next day and by then it had changed to a more structured piece, where I could see lyrics fitting. Keith and I set about writing them. It was mainly his input on the vocal side and I was just feeding back off him, the words are a total description of what's going on in his head. The music was recorded in three days at my home studio and then we did the main vocals at the Strongroom studio in London.

"The riff came from listening to lots of American rock – I was really into The Foo Fighters at the time. Their track 'Weeny Beeny' was an explosion of punk rock energy in the tune and I wanted to take some of that for 'Firestarter'. The riff isn't identical but you can see where the inspiration came from. The track isn't musical but it has some musical elements in it. I wanted the song to be a churning mass of sound but not too indistinguishable like Public Enemy used to be. When we'd finished it we knew we had something original but it still had some of the 'old' feel about it. Even though it was programmed, I think we managed to have an organic feel about it."

1996 proved to be the start of a major chart explosion by The Prodigy, hitting Number One again with 'Breathe' and scoring an incredible ten hits. ▤

"FOR WHOM THE BELL TOLLS"

VERSE: I STUMBLE IN THE NIGHT,
NEVER REALLY KNEW WHAT IT WOULD'VE
BEEN LIKE
BABY YOUR NO LONGER THERE TO
BREAK MY FALL,
THE HEARTACHE OVER YOU,
I GAVE IT EVERYTHING, BUT I COULDN'T
GET THROUGH
I NEVER SAW THE SIGNS
I'M THE LAST TO KNOW WHEN LOVE
IS BLIND.

RELEASE: ALL THE TEARS, AND THE TURBULENT
YEARS, WHEN I WOULD NOT WAIT
FOR NO ONE,
I DIDN'T STOP, TAKE A LOOK AT
MYSELF,
AND SEE ME LOSING YOU,

— HEART
CHORUS: WHEN THE LONELY BREAKS
ITS THE ONE THAT FORSAKES
ITS THE DREAM THAT WE STOLE
AND I'M MISSING YOU MORE
AND THE FIRE WILL ROAR,
THERE'S A HOLE IN MY SOUL.
FOR YOU ITS THE GOODBYE,
FOR ME ITS THE END,
FOR WHOM THE BELL TOLLS

Handwritten lyrics by Barry Gibb

FOR WHOM THE BELL TOLLS

THE BEE GEES

COMPOSED BY **M GIBB/R GIBB/B GIBB**

THE PHRASE 'FOR WHOM THE BELL tolls' comes from Elizabethan poet John Donne's 'Devotions': "Any man's death diminishes me/Because I am involved in Mankind/And therefore never send to know for whom the bell tolls/It tolls for thee." Donne, who became Dean of St Paul's in November 1621, has had his writings trawled for other pop song titles, including 'Catch A Falling Star' and 'No Man Is An Island'.

The purveyors of stunning three-part harmony and exceptionally high-ranging voices have chalked up five Number Ones in Britain, and seven in the States, where they ran out the most successful group of the Seventies. They've re-invented their style of music on more than one occasion, and have invariably had to prove themselves over and over again with each album. Gifted songwriters, the Brothers Gibb have written countless songs that have been commissioned for, or covered by, other artists, and have won a string of gold and platinum discs.

A different song called 'For Whom The Bell Tolls' was a small hit for Simon Dupree And The Big Sound in 1968, but The Bee Gees took theirs up to Number Four in the UK at the end of 1993, their 32nd hit single. 🗎

FOR YOU I WILL

COMPOSED BY **DIANE WARREN**   **MONICA**

FROM MEAT LOAF TO CELINE DION, ROD Stewart to Boyzone, the songs of Diane Warren have been recorded by the biggest names in music and in just about every genre possible. With her songs so far used in more than 50 hit films, Warren has picked up multiple Grammy and Oscar nominations. In 1997 she contributed 'For You I Will' to the Michael Jordan vehicle, *Space Jam*, performed on the soundtrack by R&B diva Monica.

"'For You I Will' is a title I had that I thought I could write a cool song around," Warren explains. "It's really about being there for the one or the ones you love, and going to any lengths or distance for somebody – 'I will cross the ocean for you, I'll go and bring you the moon.' A lot of the time I'll listen to the radio and hear people dedicating it to someone special in their lives. That really makes me feel good, to know that the message got through.

"I usually write everything in my little demo studio in my office, but I remember when I was working on this one, I had a meeting with Barbra Streisand about doing something for one of her movies. I was early for the meeting and I parked my car in front of her house and was writing the bridge in the car, which was quite funny really.

"It really worked out fine in the movie, and that's what I try to do, I try to write a song that will work as well outside the movie as it does within it. For instance, 'How Will I Live', which was in *Con Air* and recorded first by Trisha Yearwood and then LeAnn Rimes, is now the longest-running hit in US chart history.

"But I've also written songs that you just have to wait around to happen, and maybe the first version isn't going to be the one that hits. I still really want to write standards and copyrights that are going to last and which are going to transcend their time and place. That's what a great song will do, and it's not limited to one interpretation. Sometimes it can really blow you away, like my song 'I Don't Want To Miss A Thing' (also from a movie, *Armageddon*), which was a huge hit for Aerosmith and was also a Number One country hit for a guy named Mark Chesnutt. A great song will have a life of its own, and that's the kind of song I like to be involved with. It's my responsibility to do the best with the gift that I've been given." 🗎

Handwritten lyrics by Diane Warren

FROM A DISTANCE

BETTE MIDLER

COMPOSED BY **JULIE GOLD**

IN OCTOBER 1990 TWO VERSIONS OF 'From A Distance' entered the UK chart in the same week. The Cliff Richard version reached Number Eleven, winning the first heat. Bette Midler's version though, hot from the Number Two spot in the US, re-entered the UK chart the next year, peaking at Number Six.

"'From A Distance' is a song that I wrote in 1985," Julie Gold, the song's writer, says. "At the time I was a secretary at HBO and just about to turn 30. My brother was about to get married and I had just served as a juror on a very emotional and complex trial – you could say I was a bubbling cauldron of emotion.

"For my 30th birthday present, my parents sent me the piano I had grown up playing. I'd been without it for the eight years I had lived in New York. I'll never forget how it glistened in the sun on that cold winter's day when the movers took it off the truck and placed it in my apartment. They warned me not to play it for 24 hours because it was so cold from shipping. Here I was finally reunited with my best friend and confidante and I all I could do was polish it and hug it.

"All night long I woke up and looked down on it from my loft bed just to make sure it was really there. The next day when I finally played it, I wrote 'From A Distance'. I am sure I was granted that moment, and that song, by God."

Handwritten lyrics by Julie Gold

FROM RUSSIA WITH LOVE

MATT MONRO

COMPOSED BY **LIONEL BART**

A CLASSIC SONG FROM THE PEN OF THE LATE LIONEL Bart (born Lionel Begleiter) whose musical legacy includes such diverse pop material as Cliff Richard's 'Living Doll', Anthony Newley's 'Do You Mind?' and Tommy Steele's 'Rock With The Caveman', as well as co-writing the songs for Tommy Steele films *The Tommy Steele Story* and *Tommy The Toreador*. These included classics like 'Water Water', 'A Handful Of Songs' and 'Little White Bull'. Lionel also penned the scores for *Lock Up Your Daughters*, *Fings Ain't What They Used To Be* and the film that won six Oscars, *Oliver!*.

'From Russia With Love' was the title song for the 1963 James Bond film directed by Terence Young and produced by Harry Saltzman and Cubby Broccoli. It was the second film in which Sean Connery, then 33 years old, had portrayed Bond, his co-stars including Robert Shaw, Lotte Lenya, Bernard Lee, Eunice Grayson and Daniela Bianchi.

John Barry, the film's musical director, himself had a Top Ten hit in the UK when he recorded Bart's title song as an instrumental. But it was Matt Monro who took the more famous vocal version, produced by George Martin, to Number 20. British chart topper Craig Douglas also released a vocal version of the song.

Handwritten lyrics by Lionel Bart

GET HERE
Bred. Russell

You can reach me by Railway
You can reach me by Trailway
You can reach me on an airplane
You can Reach me with your mind
You can Reach me by caravan
cross the desert like an Arab man
I don't care how you get here
Just Get Here if you can

You can Reach me by sailboat
Climb a tree & swing Rope to Rope
take a sled & slide down slope
into these arms of mine
You can jump on a speedy colt
cross the border in a blaze of hope
I don't care how you get here just
GET HERE if you can

There are hills & mountains Between us
Always somethin' to get over
But if I had my way
Surely you would be closer
I need you closer

2. GET HERE

You can windsore into my life
TAKE ME UP ON A CARPET RIDE
YOU CAN MAKE IT IN A BIG BALLOON
BUT YOU BETTER MAKE IT SOON
YOU CAN REACH ME BY CARAVAN
CROSS THE DESERT LIKE AN ARAB MAN
I DON'T CARE HOW YOU GET HERE
JUST GET HERE IF YOU CAN

Handwritten lyrics by Brenda Russell

GET HERE

OLETA ADAMS

COMPOSED BY **BRENDA RUSSELL**

BRENDA RUSSELL FIRST CHARTED IN THE UK IN
1980 with a small double-sided hit, 'So Good So
Right/In The Thick Of It', her second hit here not
coming for another eight years: 'Piano In The Dark'.
That song was taken from her 1988 album *Get
Here*, the title track becoming a UK hit for Oleta
Adams in 1991 when it climbed to Number Four.

Russell, who wrote 'Get Here' and co-wrote 'Piano
In The Dark', had begun her career in the mid
Seventies, when along with her former husband,
Brian Russell, the pair recorded two albums for
Elton John's Rocket label.

Her solo career began in 1979, as she blossomed
into an all-round musician, songwriter, singer and
producer. For the album *Get Here* she worked with a
variety of production teams, including being reunited with former Rufus drummer Andre Fischer,
and legendary bass player Stanley Clarke. ▮

GOD GAVE ROCK 'N' ROLL TO YOU

LOVE YOUR FRIEND AND LOVE YOUR NEIGHBOUR
LOVE YOUR LIFE AND LOVE YOUR LABOUR
ITS NEVER TOO LATE TO CHANGE YOUR MIND
DON'T STEP ON SNAILS, DON'T CLIMB IN TREES
LOVE CLIFF RICHARD BUT PLEASE DON'T TEASE
ITS NEVER TOO LATE TO CHANGE YOUR MIND

GOD GAVE ROCK AND ROLL TO YOU,
GAVE ROCK AND ROLL TO YOU
PUT IT IN THE SOUL OF EVERYONE,
GOD GAVE ROCK AND ROLL TO YOU
GAVE ROCK AND ROLL TO YOU
SAVE ROCK AND ROLL FOR EVERYONE

IF YOU WANNA BE A SINGER OR PLAY GUITAR
MAN YOU GOTTA SWEAT OR YOU DONT GET FAR
AND ITS NEVER TOO LATE TO WORK NINE TO FIVE
AND IF YOU'RE YOUNG, THEN YOU'LL NEVER BE OLD
MUSIC CAN MAKE YOUR DREAMS UNFOLD
HOW GOOD IT FEELS TO BE ALIVE

GOD GAVE ROCK AND ROLL TO YOU
GAVE ROLL AND ROLL TO YOU ... ETC...

Russ Ballard.

Handwritten lyrics, including original 'Cliff
Richard' verse, by Russ Ballard

GOD GAVE ROCK AND ROLL TO YOU

KISS

COMPOSED BY **RUSS BALLARD**

FOLLOWING THE DEMISE OF THE ZOMBIES, THEIR KEYBOARD PLAYER ROD ARGENT
formed the group Argent with Russ Ballard, Bob Hewitt and Jim Rodford. Their Top 20 hit
'God Gave Rock And Roll To You' was later an upbeat stadium anthem for cartoon rock
band Kiss, but its roots were more personal for writer Ballard.

"I wrote 'God Gave Rock And Roll To You' with this feeling of well-being after coming out
of a year of total depression," he says. "Previously I'd just wanted to die, because every
day was grey, every day was black. There was always this cloud over me – what Winston
Churchill called 'The Black Fog'. I thought I was going mad but then I found somebody
who had compassion. Coming out of my depression was like moving into the light and
suddenly I was consumed by anger, aggression, resentment, envy – the whole gamut of
blocked emotions – and you can hear that in the words. Sometimes you write lyrics and
wonder where they come from, you just write them because they rhyme. But later you
look and you realise that that was exactly the way you were feeling at the time. I guess
that's expression. Writing this song was a cathartic experience to just get it out of myself,
so it's hard for me to say what the appeal for other people is because basically it was
written for me. The words 'God' and 'love' are probably over-used, but I suppose they
make us feel secure, and because humans are so fearful, they'll jump on to anything that
sounds like it's going to take away their responsibility.

"Kiss recorded the song in 1992 for the film *Bill And Ted's Bogus Journey*, but the record
company decided that the lyrics about Cliff Richard probably wouldn't be understood in
America so they changed a few lines. Effectively all they changed was four lines and they
needed three other writers to do it! I liked the Kiss version from the word go and again
was disappointed that it only got to Number Four because it was played a lot on MTV." ▮

Goodbye

No No, No No ×3

VI   Listen little child, there will come a day
when you will, able to say
Never mind the pain or the aggravation
you know there's a better way for you & me to be.

BRIDGE   Look for the rainbow in every storm
Fly like an angel heaven sent to me

CHORUS   Goodbye my friend (I know you're gone, you said your gone
but I can still feel you here)
It's not the end (gotta keep it strong before the
pain turns into fear)
So glad we made it, time will never change it no, no
you know it's time to say goodbye, no no no no no.

V2   Just a little girl, big imagination
never letting no one take it away.
went into the world, what a revelation
She found there's a better way for you & me to be.

BRIDGE 2   Look for the rainbow in every storm
Find out for certain loves gonna be there for you
ya'll always be someones baby

CHORUS.

M8   The times when he would play. about
The way we used to. scream & shout.
re never dreamt you'd go your own sweet way

Handwritten lyrics by Mel C

GOODBYE

THE SPICE GIRLS

COMPOSED BY **MATTHEW ROWBOTTOM/RICHARD STANNARD/THE SPICE GIRLS**

ORIGINALLY CALLED 'TOUCH', VICTORIA AD(D)AMS, GERI Halliwell, Melanie Chisholm, Melanie Brown and Emma Bunton – better known as Posh, Ginger, Sporty, Scary and Baby Spice – were groomed for stardom by Simon Fuller, the manager of Annie Lennox. Signing to Virgin Records, they released the first of their record breaking run of Number Ones in 1996, 'Wannabe'. Their eighth Number One, released as Geri left the group in 1998, was the ironically titled 'Goodbye'.

"'Goodbye' is a very special song for all of us," says Emma 'Baby Spice' Bunton, "and we think it's definitely one of our best. We were really happy when it became our third Christmas Number One in a row. It was a dream come true!

"One of our co-writers, Matt Rowe, put down a few ideas and played it to Mel C and me when we were in Dublin in May 1998. But we didn't actually get around to recording it properly until we reached Nashville, Tennessee, on our world tour last summer. We all worked on it together – bits of the words and melodies came from each of us.

"A lot of people tend to think the whole song is about Geri, but it's not, although Geri's departure obviously had a great influence. It's also about friends who decide to move onto the next thing, but, who you know will always be your friends, even though they go their way, and you go yours.

"Some of the lines that I had to sing were very moving, especially the words 'just a little girl, big imagination' – because that's Geri all over, isn't it? It was quite hard to sing, but I just had to pull myself together. I did think about Geri while I sang, but on some bits I had to stop thinking about her so I could concentrate properly!"

In 1997 the girls starred in their own film, *Spiceworld*, having said goodbye to their manager shortly before the film's release.

Govinda jaya jaya
Gopala jaya jaya
Radha-ramana hari
Govinda jaya jaya!

GOVINDA

KULA SHAKER

COMPOSED BY
WINTERHART/BEVAN/
MILLS/DARLINGTON

COMPRISING CRISPIAN MILLS,
Paul Winterhart, Alonzo Bevan and
Jay Darlington, Kula Shaker have
successfully paraded their love of all
things mystic – Indian and Arthurian
– in the charts in the late Nineties.
Mills, the son of actress Hayley and
director Roy Boulting, had previously
formed with Bevan The Objects Of
Desire and later The Kays with
varying line-ups, and from the last
group their debut album, *K*, took its
influence. 1996's 'Govinda', Kula
Shaker's third Top Ten hit, showed the
group's mysticism to the fore.

"'Govinda' was the first song we ever
played live, and it followed a trip I'd
made to India in the spring of 1993,"
Mills says. "When I got back I went to
the Glastonbury festival with friends
and we started rehearsing in a ten-
man army tent. We managed to talk
our way onto one of the stages there
and played the song as a sort of on-
the-spot improvisation but actually
quite similar to the way we play it
now. We then played it every single
gig for the next three years until we
got signed, and regarded it as our
'lucky song'.

"It's an Indian folk song about the
legends of Krishna, a little song that
the cowherd people sing, indigenous
to those people and we're very fond
of it. It was quite difficult to record
because it's better suited to live
performance and we learned a lot in
the process, but it's remained one of
our favourites." ▤

Handwritten lyrics by Crispian Mills

HEDONISM

SKUNK ANANSIE

COMPOSED BY SKIN/LEN ARRAN

SKUNK ANANSIE – SKIN, ACE,
Mark Richardson and Cass Lewis –
were formed in 1994 and began their
chart career the following year. Their
debut album, *Paranoid And Sunburnt*,
went gold yielding four hit singles
including the Top 20 'Weak'.
'Hedonism', their first single of 1997
went to Number 13.

"It's actually quite a painful song for
me to think about," Skin, formerly
Deborah Dyer says. "It was written in
tears at four am one morning
because I was upset over a very
personal situation. That was the
song, it was quite vindictive: 'I hope
you're feeling fucking happy now'
was the whole vibe of the song. The
original version of it had a really
more R&B feel to it, but we messed
around with it a lot and came up
with the final version, just a simple,
quiet, laconic song with the beautiful
guitar that grew to be a centrepiece
of the track.

"Lyrically it was just all about feeling
vindictive thoughts and hoping
someone would get a red hot poker
up their arse! It was my favourite
lyric on the whole album: 'just
because you feel good, doesn't mean
it's right.' That seemed to sum up so
many situations for so many people.
We do things and think, 'Are we
really happy about that when we
wake up in the morning?' Just
because it feels good doesn't mean
it's the right way to carry ourselves.

"I think that lyric just caught on to a
lot of people's thoughts at the time. I
think you can harness anger to push
you forward and propel you to do
things, that's the way I deal with it.
'Hedonism' was one of those more
tender moments when I was really
frustrated and angry and couldn't
sleep, I was in tears and just wrote
the song – which doesn't happen too
often these days, I must admit." ▤

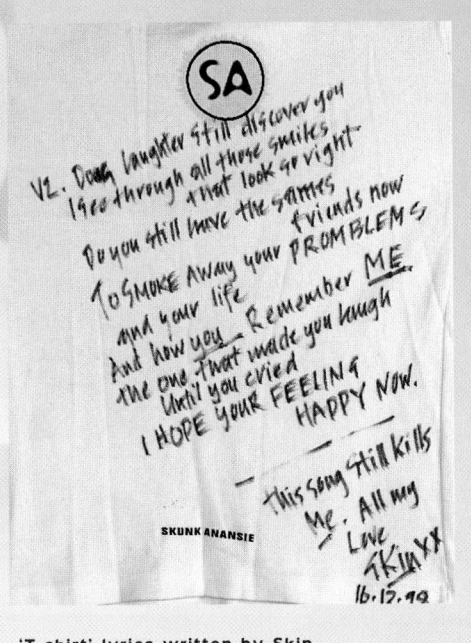

'T-shirt' lyrics written by Skin

'Umbrella' lyrics
handwritten by
Annie Lennox

HERE COMES THE RAIN AGAIN

EURYTHMICS

COMPOSED BY **DAVE STEWART/ANNIE LENNOX**

BY THE MID EIGHTIES THE EURYTHMICS HAD made the world's Top Tens their own with international hits like 'Sweet Dreams' and 'Love Is A Stranger'. 1984 was no exception as they charted with 'Sexcrime' and 'Here Comes The Rain Again', but the latter might never have happened without a certain climate, a certain city and a certain argument.

"The song started in the Mayflower Hotel in New York overlooking Central Park," Dave Stewart says. "It was a rainy day and I'd just got a tiny little synthesiser keyboard with me and was playing a little riff on it. Annie and I had had a minor argument about something because we were under such incredible pressure, like you do when you become successful. We were in hotel rooms all the time and it was a rainy, miserable day and I came up with this atmospheric little line on the keyboard, like a sequence. Annie liked it and wanted to play it herself, and then we were both fighting over the keyboard. She came up with the line 'here comes the rain again', which caught the atmosphere and the rain outside.

"It only took a couple of lines or an idea and we'd have the whole song almost done 15 minutes later. It was one of those songs that we finished very quickly. When we recorded it, we were busy building our studio, The Church in Crouch End, and converting this old building, but it hadn't quite been finished. So when it came to recording the orchestra, some of the string players were playing in the toilet and some were down the corridor, we were having to do them in different sections because the room wasn't ready. However the finished track turned out to be quite atmospheric despite all that going on.

"Like most of our songs, it's got a very strange juxtaposed lyric mixed with the music, like black and white, sweet and sour, which we always had. The verse is very gloomy – 'falling on my head like a tragedy' – and then the chorus goes to a major chord with 'talk to me like lovers do' and is very hopeful, then goes back to the tragic verses again. Nearly every Eurythmics song has got that contrast going on somewhere. As a songwriting duo we definitely had that spark, where one of us would say one thing and the other would say something else, and before you knew it, it was like 'bang', done. It used to shock people around us, they'd leave the room to make a cup of tea, and they'd come back in and we'd finished."

'Here Comes The Rain Again' reached Number Four in the US and Number Eight in the UK. ▤

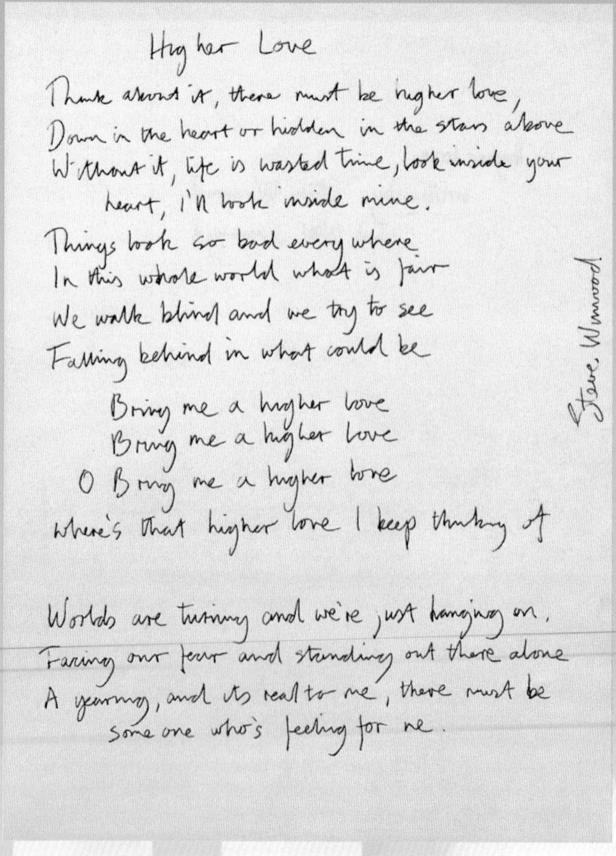

Handwritten lyrics (left page)

Higher Love

Think about it, there must be higher love,
Down in the heart or hidden in the stars above
Without it, life is wasted time, look inside your
heart, I'll look inside mine.
Things look so bad every where
In this whole world what is fair
We walk blind and we try to see
Falling behind in what could be

Bring me a higher love
Bring me a higher love
O Bring me a higher love
Where's that higher love I keep thinking of

Worlds are turning and we're just hanging on,
Facing our fear and standing out there alone
A yearning, and its real to me, there must be
some one who's feeling for me.

Steve Winwood

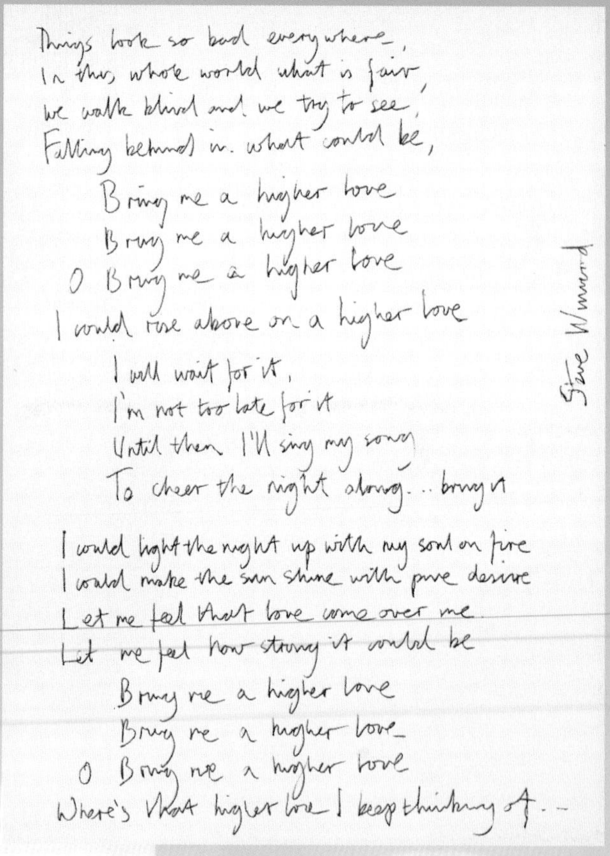

Handwritten lyrics (right page)

Things look so bad every where,
In this whole world what is fair,
We walk blind and we try to see,
Falling behind in what could be,

Bring me a higher love
Bring me a higher love
O Bring me a higher love
I could rise above on a higher love

I will wait for it,
I'm not too late for it
Until then I'll sing my song
To cheer the night along... bring it

I could light the night up with my soul on fire
I could make the sun shine with pure desire
Let me feel that love come over me.
Let me feel how strong it could be
Bring me a higher love
Bring me a higher love
O Bring me a higher love
Where's that higher love I keep thinking of. —

Steve Winwood

Handwritten lyrics by Steve Winwood

HIGHER LOVE

STEVE WINWOOD

COMPOSED BY **STEVE WINWOOD/WILL JENNINGS**

STEVE WINWOOD WAS JUST 17 WHEN he first topped the British chart with 'Keep On Running', in 1965, as vocalist and keyboards player with The Spencer Davis Group. He and the group had already had three hits. After eight UK and four US hit singles, Winwood left to form Traffic, having four US and four UK hits with the group before moving on to supergroup Blind Faith, and subsequently returning to Traffic. Between 1970 and the group's demise in 1974 they notched up four gold albums. Winwood's solo career as an artist got under way in 1977, his first big album coming in 1981 when *Arc Of A Diver* went into the Top Three and sold enough to warrant a platinum disc. His 1986 album, *Back In The High Life*, went triple platinum and yielded three hit singles, including 'Higher Love', written by Winwood and Will Jennings.

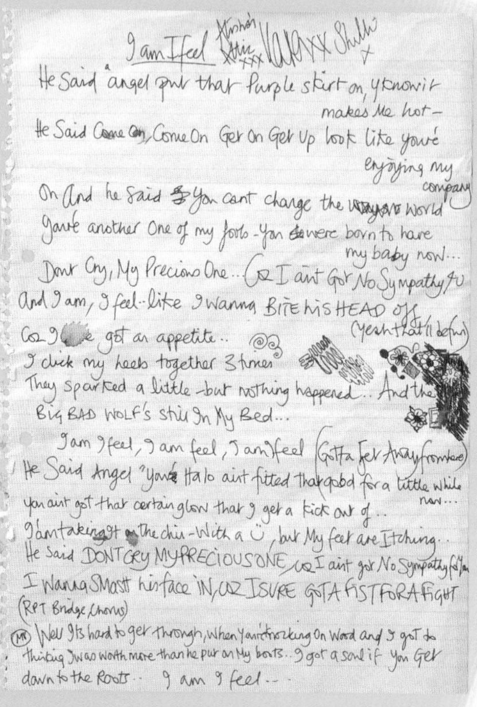

Handwritten working lyrics (I Am I Feel)

I am I feel

He said 'angel put that Purple skirt on, y'know it
makes me hot —
He said Come On, Come On Get On Get Up look like you're
enjoying my company
Oh And he said You can't change the world
You're another One of my fools - You were born to have
my baby now...
Don't Cry, My Precious One - Co I ain't Got No Sympathy for u
And I am, I feel like I wanna BITE his HEAD off
Co I got an appetite.. (Yeah that'll do)
I click my heels together 3 times
They sparked a little - but nothing happened... And the
BIG BAD WOLF's still In My Bed.
I am I feel, I am I feel, I am I feel (Gotta Get Away from him)
He said Angel your Halo ain't fitted that good for a little while
now...
You ain't got that certain glow that I get a kick out of...
I am taking it on the chin - With a ☺, but My feet are Itching..
He said DON'T CRY MY PRECIOUS ONE - Co I ain't got No Sympathy for u
I Wanna SMASH his face IN, Co I SURE GOT A FIST FOR A FIGHT
(RPT Bridge, chorus)
(M) Well It's hard to get through, When you're working On Wood and I got to
thinking I was worth more than the pub on My beats.. I got a soul if you get
down to the Roots... I am I feel ...

I AM I FEEL

ALISHA'S ATTIC

COMPOSED BY **KAREN POOLE/MICHELLE POOLE/TERENCE MARTIN**

NAMED AFTER AN IMAGINARY friend of sisters Shellie and Karen, Alisha's Attic came into being after the girls sent a home demo tape to Eurythmics star Dave Stewart. Impressed, Stewart secured the band a contract with Mercury Records and went on to produce their November 1996 album, *Alisha Rules The World*. Offering a different all-girl perspective to that other female phenomenon, The Spice Girls, Alisha's Attic have charted consistently since their debut single in 1996. That single was 'I Am I Feel', the original working lyrics of which are pictured here.

Working lyrics by Alisha's Attic

I'D LIKE TO TEACH THE WORLD TO SING

THE ANGLO-AUSTRALIAN OUTFIT
The New Seekers started their chart run with a version of Melanie's 'What Have They Done To My Song Ma' which they followed with a Number Two, 'Never Ending Song Of Love'. But it was their third single, written by Roger Cook and Roger Greenaway, that became their calling card.

"'I'd Like To Teach The World To Sing' actually started as a melody with no words whatsoever when Roger Cook and I were on holiday in Portugal round about 1969," Greenaway recalls. "We used to go with our families and stay pretty close to each other, and on every other day we'd sit on the beach and put ideas for songs down on tape, including about eight bars of what eventually became this song.

"At the same time we had been doing Coca Cola commercials for McCann Ericsson on a contract basis since 1965, and we'd done many commercials, maybe a dozen with different people for the product. Two guys used to come over from New York, one being Billy Davis who co-wrote some of Jackie Wilson's hits with Berry Gordy, and a guy called Bill Backer who was the account executive. We'd play them all the bits and pieces we had, and this occasion we played Billy this little tune which he liked, and so we finished it off for him. At that time it was called 'True Love And Apple Pie', and was eventually recorded under that title by a girl named Susan Shirley. Bill Backer came back to us a few days later and said, 'I love the melody but I hate the lyric.' So we sat down that same day and re-wrote it as 'I'd Like To Teach The World To Sing'.

"It was then recorded by The New Seekers as a two-minute commercial and went on to radio in America. However, we got very little reaction from it, and after about two or three months it was taken off and other commercials went on air. About a year later, a guy named Harvey Gabor was in the McCann Ericsson offices in New York, and said to Bill Backer, 'I've got this idea for doing a 30-second TV commercial with kids of all different nationalities, different colours and different creeds all standing on a hill, with a Coca Cola bottle and singing an anthem. Is there anything suitable in the Coca Cola song catalogue that we could use?' So Backer said, 'Look I'm busy, there's the library, everything that you need is in there.' Gabor started listening and came out after about three days saying, 'I've got it, it's called "I'd Like To Teach The World To Sing".'

"Gabor then came to London to record the commercial with all the kids, but the weather was so awful that he transferred the shoot to one of the hills in Rome. They then trawled all the local embassies for the children of the diplomats, so all those kids you see are dressed up in their own national costumes. However, because of an accident causing damage to a helicopter whilst filming, the shoot went over budget by a quarter of a million dollars and Gabor was sacked on his return to New York. Anyway, about two months later the commercial went on air in the States, and apparently within two weeks Coca Cola had received over 10,000 letters from people asking where they could buy the music from the ad.

"By chance, The New Seekers happened to be working at a hotel in New York, so we rushed them into the studio, recorded the song and got it released in a few days. Of course it zoomed up the charts there, and it came out about a month later in the UK just before Christmas and did over a million singles in ten days here. That's how it happened, it wasn't planned, it all came about more by default. And to this day virtually no one has heard the original version of the song, when it was called 'True Love And Apple Pie' and had a middle eight, which was never used on the later version."

The New Seekers' version reached Number One in the UK and Seven in the US in 1971. 🖹

THE NEW SEEKERS

COMPOSED BY **ROGER COOK/ROGER GREENAWAY/ BILLY BACKER/BILLY DAVIS/PETER BOYLE**

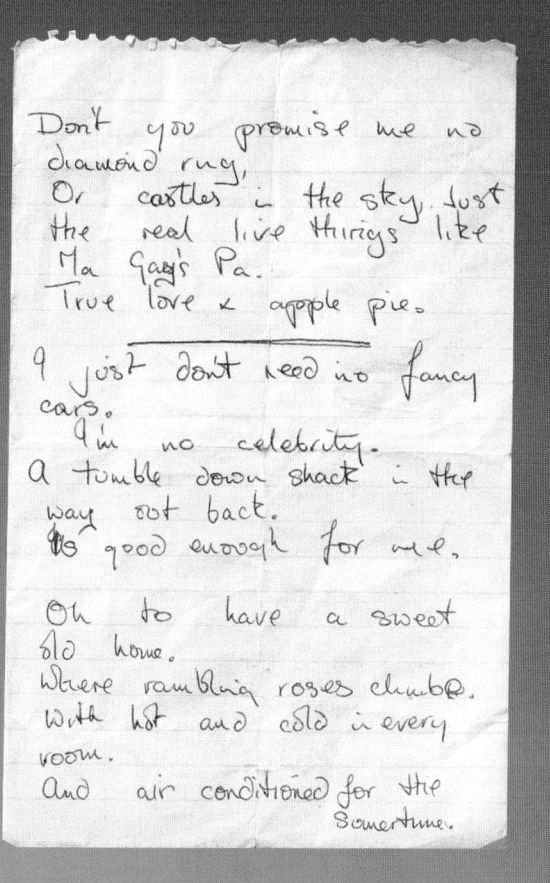

Working lyrics by Roger Greenaway

I DON'T WANNA FIGHT

TINA TUNER

COMPOSED BY **LULU/STEVE DUBERRY/BILLY LAWRIE**

AFTER FOUR HIT SINGLES IN THE UK AND 21 in the US as Ike & Tina Turner, the duo split in 1975. Divorcing Ike in 1976 Tina launched upon a tremendous solo career, charting first in the UK with 'Let's Stay Together'. In 1993 she reached Number Seven in the UK with 'I Don't Wanna Fight', a track co-written by Lulu, herself the singer of 23 British hits.

"My brother Billy persuaded me to write," Lulu says. "I was nervous so he agreed to help. He was managing writer Steve Duberry so we got him to do the melody. For my first attempt I found it a safe place to express myself. Little did Steve, Billy and I have any idea that it would go on to have the success it did. We haven't stopped writing since!"

Both Lulu and Tina seem to enjoy duets – Lulu with Bobby Womack and Take That, Tina with Rod Stewart, Eric Clapton, Bryan Adams and Barry White – so a duet between the two must be on the cards!

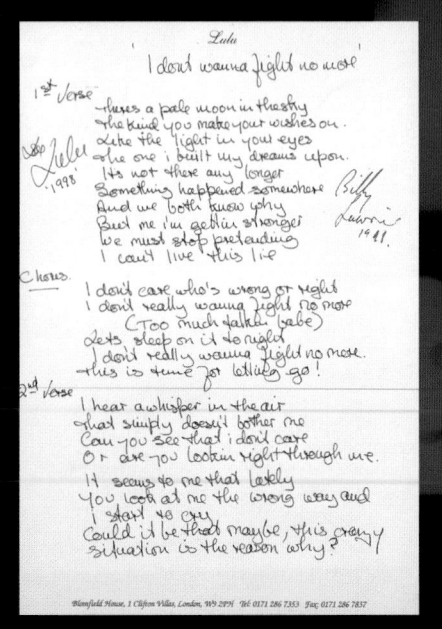

Handwritten lyrics by Lulu

(I JUST) DIED IN YOUR ARMS

CUTTING CREW

COMPOSED BY **NICK VAN EEDE**

'(I JUST) DIED IN YOUR ARMS' WAS CUTTING CREW'S FIRST HIT single and although it only reached Number Four in the UK charts in 1986 it topped the charts in the US.

"'(I Just) Died In Your Arms' started out as just a title originally," the band's frontman, Nick Van Eede admits, "and I still love the way it works on lots of levels. Titles are really important. A lot of people say that the title meant so much to them regardless of what the song was about. The song was born when I spent some time lodging at my friend Pete's in Epsom. I had no money, I'd sold my last Telecaster to get through the last two months and I moved into Pete's house with his 15 guitars, keyboards and drum machine. Sometimes the best thing for a writer is to get a new toy because it's the most exciting thing to have new sounds, like real posh strings or a dirty bass. You are either going to write something fantastic in the first six hours or you've lost the moment – and that's what happened with 'Died In Your Arms'.

"I moved in, strapped on Pete's Gibson SG or something, cued up the drum machine, keyboards and at the risk of sounding cliched, the whole thing – words, intro, keyboards, the cello line, the harmonies, everything – was done in about two hours. I've read it told by others, but it just seems to happen that way. I think I changed a couple of lyric lines later on, but this title just kept coming out, and I remember all I had on paper were the lyrics more or less as they eventually went on the record.

"The biggest hurdle was trying to retain all the ideas and basic sounds I had on my little demo, and get them transferred to the final master. That took a lot longer than expected with quite a lot of hassle. Cutting Crew got signed to Siren, a subsidiary of Virgin, within three months of the band being in existence in November 1985, and we were in New York a month later recording the songs. However the tracks didn't work out as well as we would have liked, so we ended up back in London still working on them, but again things weren't happening. I called our A&R man at midnight from Air Studios in Oxford Street and said, 'For God sake, it's gone wrong again. I know there's only one producer that can do this for me, and his name is Terry Brown.'

"Terry was a mate of mine from Canada who had done all the early Rush albums and had produced my old band, The Drivers, in Toronto. However my request caused a tantrum between our manager and the A&R man, but Terry came over (I'd already asked him before telling the record company!) and from that day on it just went smooth as anything.

"Peter Vitesse, the keyboard player we used, also did a lot for the song. He took my little demo and said, 'I think I know what you're getting at here.' He got this big posh keyboard sound and kept it faithful to the original, which I loved about him. The boys in the band played great, Kevin McMichael played a great guitar solo and arranged the guitars."

The finished product became the band's first single. "Nobody gave a toss who Cutting Crew were," Van Eede admits, "so we only got one review – which was lovely – in *The Guardian*. It became a big hit in the UK, and it then became a Number One in 23 countries including the States. I've even heard Richard Branson say that it was the song that launched Virgin Records in the USA – although he always forgets our name and calls us Crowded House!"

Verse

BMIN – GMAJ7 – A6 – F#min?

DIED IN ARMS (8MIN)

Handwritten lyric fragments scrawled across the chart:

- Chorus
- I just died in your arms tonight
- of a kiss I said did
- It must have been something you said
- some kind of
- been
- I should've walked away
- x2
- I need to
- should've
- Sweetly
- I keep (on) looking for
- can't
- Broken hearts lie all around me
- away / way
- and I don't wanna get all caught up / to get out of this !!!
- 2-30 Phone Gary !!!
- Verse

	Los Angeles	Miami	Minneapolis	Nashville	New Orleans	New York City	Oklahoma City	Omaha	Philadelphia	Phoenix	Pittsburgh	St. Louis	Salt Lake City	San Antonio	San Diego	San Francisco	Seattle	Washington
	1946	595	906	214	425	760	761	821	665	1587	526	484	1589	875	1891	2139	2182	552
	2329	946	936	687	998	184	1180	1025	90	1899	210	737	1864	1407	2296	2457	2334	57
	2611	1258	1284	942	1367	187	1509	1262	281	2300	496	1058	2105	1764	2588	2704	2486	414
	1745	1197	334	409	837	740	693	416	678	1440	412	258	1249	1041	1723	1886	1720	590
	1900	948	396	230	701	589	756	614	507	1569	256	308	1440	1025	1805	2036	1964	411
	2053	1080	622	448	922	425	954	733	363	1742	105	467	1569	1246	2031	2161	2023	310
	1984	990	627	337	806	483	866	689	405	1671	144	410	1529	1140	1965	2120	2017	322
	1246	1110	853	822	437	1383	181	585	1296	879	1061	546	1010	247	1182	1476	1670	1163
	849	1716	693	1023	1067	1638	500	485	1569	588	1302	781	381	793	840	956	1019	1464
	1979	1146	528	466	936	508	916	651	453	1681	201	440	1489	1215	1966	2079	132	385
	1397	964	1046	663	305	1417	395	793	1324	1015	1124	667	1204	191	1308	1636	1874	1189
	1815	1021	503	249	708	684	689	517	542	1489	325	229	1365	986	1783	1944	1866	499
	1363	1239	394	486	690	1113	312	152	1039	1043	769	229	981	697	1337	1498	1489	927
	236	2175	1300	1587	1500	2248	986	2099	2183	255	1910		368	1069	248	414	869	2077
		2342	1536	1797	1671	2475	1187	1330	2401	370	2106	1592	590	1210	109	337	954	2288
	2342		1501	806	674	1090	1223	1393	1013	1972	1013	1068	2088	1143	2264	2585	2925	919
	1536	1501		695	1040	1028	694	282	580	1270	726	448	991	1097	1532	1589	1399	909
	1797	806	695		471	766	615	612	675	1448	462	271	1403	822	1751	1969	1918	542
	1671	674	1040	471		1188	567	844	1094	1201	918	604	1428	495	1599	1911	2087	969
	2475	1090	1028	766	1188		1345	155	94	2143	340	892	1989	1587	2446	2586	2421	229
	1187	1223	694	615	567	1345		418	1268	833	1010	462	865	407	1136	1383	1520	1158
	1330	1393	282	612	841	1155	418		1094	1037	821	342	869	824	1313	1433	1368	1000
	2401	1013	980	675	1094	94	1268	1094		2082		813	1932	1502	2376	2521	383	136
	370	1972	1270	1448	1301	2143	833	1037	2082		1814	1262	587	847		651	1109	1956
	2136	1013	726	1462	918	340	1010	821	267	1814		553	1659	1277		2253	2124	184
	1592	1068	448	271	604	892	462	342	813	1262	553		1156	786	1577	1735	1709	696
	590	2088	991	1403	1428	1989	865	839	1932	507	1659	1156		1086	626	599	689	1839
	1210	1143	1097	822	495	1587	407	824	1502	843	1277		1086		1129	1482	1775	1361
	109	2267	1532	1969	1999	2446	1136	1313	2376	304	2106	1557	626	1129		447	1053	2253
	337	2585	1589	1969	1911	2586	1383	1433	2521	651	2255	1735	599	1482	447		678	2419
	954	2725	1399	1918	2087	2421	1520	368	2583	1109	2124	1709	689	1775	1053	678		2307
	2288	919	909	542	969	229	1158	1000	136	1956	184	696	1368	1364	2253	2419	2307	

"I KNEW YOU WERE WAITING"
(FOR ME)

LIKE A WARRIOR THAT FIGHTS & WINS THE BATTLE
I KNOW THE TASTE OF VICTORY
THO I WENT THRU SOME NIGHTS CONSUMED BY THE SHADOWS
AND I WAS CRIPPLED EMOTIONALLY

★ ★ ★

SOMEHOW I MADE IT THRU THE HEARTACHE
YES I DID ... I ESCAPED
I FOUND MY WAY OUT OF THE DARKNESS
KEPT MY FAITH ... KEPT MY FAITH

★ ★ ★

WHEN THE RIVER WAS DEEP I DIDN'T FALTER
WHEN THE MOUNTAIN WAS HIGH I STILL BELIEVED
WHEN THE VALLEY WAS LOW IT DIDN'T STOP ME
I KNEW YOU WERE WAITING ...
I KNEW YOU WERE WAITING FOR ME

★ ★ ★

WITH AN ENDLESS DESIRE I KEPT ON SEARCHIN'
SURE IN TIME OUR EYES WOULD MEET
NOW LIKE THE BRIDGE IS ON FIRE THE HURT IS OVER
ONE TOUCH AND YOU SET ME FREE

★ ★ ★

I DON'T REGRET A SINGLE MOMENT
NO I DON'T ... LOOKING BACK.
WHEN I THINK OF ALL THOSE DISAPPOINTMENTS
I JUST LAUGH ... I JUST LAUGH

★ ★ ★

WHEN THE RIVER WAS DEEP ......

★ ★ ★

AND SO WE WERE DRAWN TOGETHER THRU DESTINY
I KNOW THIS LOVE WE SHARE IS MEANT TO BE
I KNEW YOU WERE WAITING ... I KNEW YOU WERE WAITING ...4 ME

★ ★ ★

Dennis Morgan

I KNEW YOU WERE WAITING (FOR ME)

ARETHA FRANKLIN & GEORGE MICHAEL

COMPOSED BY **SIMON CLIMIE/DENNIS MORGAN**

LIKE MARVIN GAYE, ARETHA FRANKLIN IS a serial duettist, charting with George Benson in 1981, The Eurythmics in 1985, Elton John in 1989 and Whitney Houston the same year. But her biggest success as one half of a duo came in 1987 when she teamed up with George Michael to have a Number One on both sides of the Atlantic co-written by Climie Fisher's Simon Climie and Dennis Morgan.

"My whole approach was to come over to England trying to find people to collaborate with," Morgan says, "much like I was doing in the USA with Steve Davis and Kye Fleming. At the time I was into the soul period as much as country music. There was this wonderful circle, and I knew that if I could find the right partners we'd snap right into place and have a huge hit, bigger than anything.

"In September 1984, after several trips over here, I met Simon Climie after an Everly Brothers concert at the Royal Albert Hall. We didn't write at that time, but later in January 1985, when I was on my way to Midem in Cannes, we wrote three songs in London. They were titled 'Pray For Peace', 'An Angel Cries' and a song called 'I Knew You Were Waiting (For Me)'. The day before 'I Knew You Were Waiting' happened, we were at Salisbury Cathedral and I remember sending up a prayer, like you do. I knew that I would seriously have to connect with something to make this journey down to Cannes even work, because I reckoned the people there just weren't going to be interested in my past even though it was very interesting. So the next day, this title was just hanging in front of me when Simon and I sat down. He's a great songwriter, I really like working with him, he's very fast, he sings great, he's really talented, and we wrote this thing in about an hour, with probably two hours of tweaks and little minor re-writes.

"However, I remember about three quarters of the way through this song, I felt so strongly about it, I just really knew it was something special. When the flow is happening, it's very wrong to stop and question it, you should just go ahead and let it run its course. In other words this is what is called inspiration. I remember at one point we stopped for about 30 seconds to say, 'Is this title right? Is this right, is that middle eight right?' I remember getting a bit forceful, saying, 'It's right, let's just finish it, then we have a song.' So we worked on the demo a bit before I went down to Cannes, and then Simon finished it while I was away. By the time I got back to America, it was on hold for Aretha and George, literally, it was that fast. Tom Sturgess who was Simon's publisher at the time, had pitched it to Clive Davis at Arista, who had the idea of putting Aretha and George together. We didn't write it as a duet, but it lent itself, and once we heard they were interested, we said, 'Of course, we knew it would work that way!'

"When it came out, I saw the video over here for the first time and I got that old feeling back, that buzz, that tingle, that chill, and that enthusiasm, almost equal to that first time I saw The Beatles on *Ed Sullivan*. My contribution to it was mainly the lyrics, and Simon and others may interpret differently, but to me what it was always about was overcoming the forces of adversity, like a warrior that fights and wins the battle. Also, because I have the Christian faith in my life, I look for things that are spiritually tuned in. I don't know if that makes sense but the song is very uplifting. It's much more than a positive thinking song, I hate that term. It's a real got down into the spirit, come to grips with whatever's holding you back and standing up and fighting against it song. And it's a love song too.

"As a result, I started my publishing company, Little Shop Of Morgan Songs, with a share in a Number One hit all round the world. The song also won an Ivor Novello award that year, which was a great thrill for me as an American, especially as Paul McCartney happened to be present at the ceremony. I can tell you that little bronze statuette has pride of place in my office in Nashville – thank you very much, Salisbury Cathedral!" ▨

Handwritten lyrics by Dennis Morgan

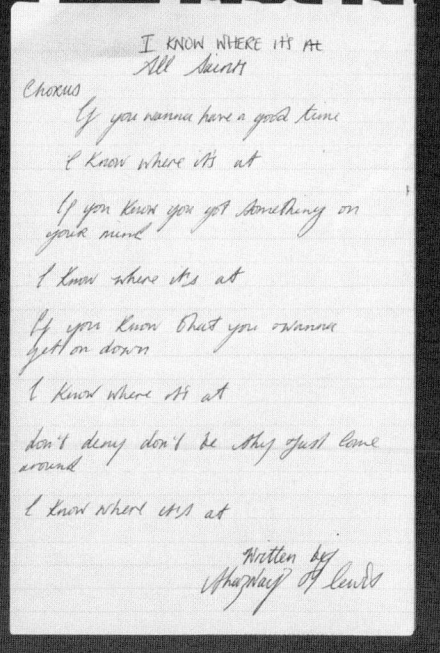

I KNOW WHERE IT'S AT

ALL SAINTS

COMPOSED BY **SHAZNAY LEWIS**

ALL SAINTS WERE FORMED IN 1993 AND named after a road in London. Comprising London-born Shaznay Lewis and Melanie Blatt, plus Canadian-born sisters Nicole and Natalie Appleton, they had their debut hit (Number Four) in 1997 with 'I Know Where It's At'.

"This was the first song that All Saints recorded together," writer Shaznay explains. "I wrote it in 1995 when it was just me and Mel in the band, we demo'd it but never went back to master it and then we got signed to London Records. They picked it as the first single so it was the first song that Mel, Nicky, Nat and I recorded together and made a video to.

"It wasn't written for anyone in particular, it's just a happy song. As far as songwriting influences, I like Alanis Morissette a lot, she's a very clever writer. I also really like Lauryn Hill and Stevie Wonder's writing."

A run of chart toppers followed, including 'Never Ever', 'Under The Bridge/Lady Marmalade' and 'Bootie Call'. Despite their short career, by the end of 1998 All Saints were already the 50th most successful act of the decade and were the top act of that year with 'Never Ever'. ▨

I'M NOT IN LOVE

10cc

COMPOSED BY **GRAHAM GOULDMAN/ERIC STEWART**

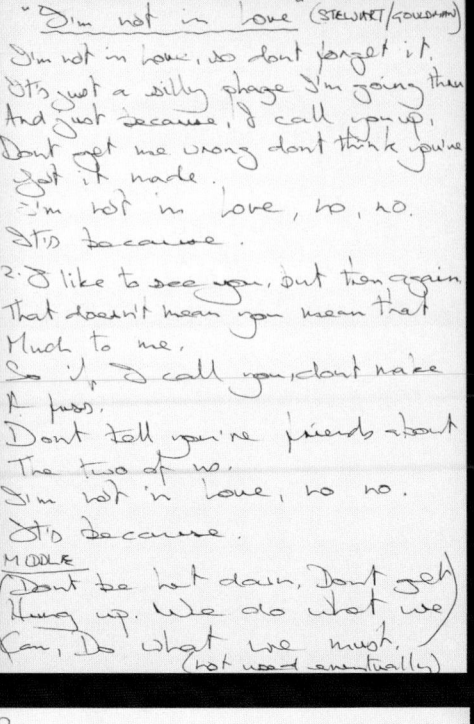

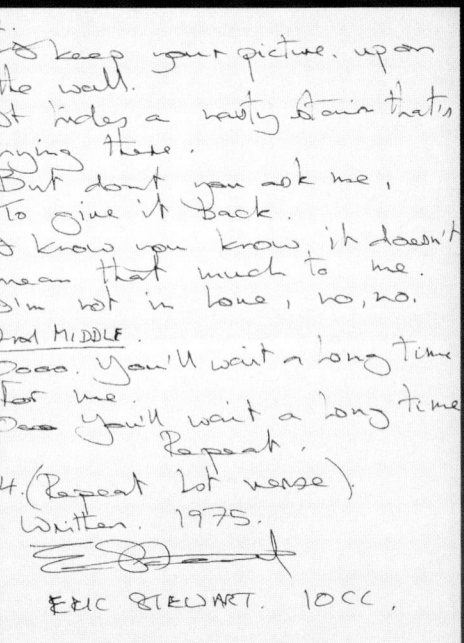

Handwritten lyrics by Eric Stewart

BORN OUT OF HOTLEGS WHO HAD A HIT

with 'Neanderthal Man', 10cc were Graham Gouldman, Kevin Godley, Lol Creme and Eric Stewart, four talented Manchester musicians. Hits like 'Donna', 'Rubber Bullets' and 'Life Is A Minestrone' proved them able to mix pure commercial pop without being a comedy act, but it was their least quirky single, 'I'm Not In Love', which was to prove the most enduring, reaching Number One in the UK and Two in the US in 1975. As Eric Stewart reveals, it was the first song of its type from the two writers.

"Graham Gouldman and I had never written a ballad before," he admits. "I'd had what we thought was a very 10cc-ish idea for a love song which didn't actually say I love you. Instead, it would say, 'I'm not in love with you,' then give all the reasons for being totally in love. It was written very quickly, though originally we envisaged it as a lightweight, shuffly Latin American number, almost like 'Girl From Ipanema'. However, when we tried recording it that way, we all hated it. The original demo also had a different middle eight, which on the released version we turned into an instrumental after the second verse.

"We put the song aside to work on the rest of the *Original Soundtrack* album, but every time we walked into the studio, either the secretary or one of the assistant engineers would be singing 'I'm Not In Love'. We said to each other, 'There must be a way we can do this song, because the idea is great,' and it was Kevin Godley who came up with the key idea, which was to record it uniquely, using just voices for the whole song – choir sounds, string sounds, everything. Lol Creme devised the notion of making a loop of each individual note of the song, and we spent three weeks making loops of a chromatic scale. We recorded the first note on a 16-track machine, then Kev, Lol and Graham just sang 'aaah' in the studio for days, while I, as the group's engineer, kept recording and multi-tracking them until I got this block of 'aaahs' and we had a chromatic scale, 13 notes, on the 16-track.

"Then, on one of the free tracks, to give us the timing, we put down a Moog synthesiser bass drum note, which just went 'bom bub-bom, bom bub-bom'. Guided by that, we then all manned the control desk and fed the

chords in, with all of us moving faders so that the chorus changed throughout the song as the lyrics were going to change – there were no lyrics on this at that point! It took three weeks, and a lot of sweat, to do that. When we'd finished the backing tack, we thought it might need something a bit more human on it, so Graham played a very simple acoustic guitar, and I laid down a Fender Rhodes acoustic piano, somewhat cack-handedly because I'm not really a pianist. Sat among those vocals, it took on an incredible feeling. We sat for hours just listening to the backing track, we were so impressed with it ourselves. We didn't hear it as a hit but it was a wonderful experience just listening to this wall of sound.

"The lead vocal was me singing solo, and it too was put down very simply, with no double-tracking. Then Kev and Lol kept coming with more way-out ideas: 'We've got to do something else in here as well – let's have somebody talking on it.' The studio secretary, Cathy Redfern, had a lovely telephone voice, so they had her saying the words, 'Big boys don't cry, be quiet, big boys don't cry.' When that was added, we knew we had something quite special.

"When the album was released, we started getting phone calls. Richard Williams at Island (not our label) rang me and said, 'Eric, you've got a song on your album called 'I'm Not In Love' – why isn't it a single? Every girl in this office has got your album on, and is playing that song. I'm from another record company, and I shouldn't be telling you this, but that's a hit – release it!'

"We'd avoided going with it initially because it was a love ballad, which wasn't what we thought 10cc was all about; we wanted to do quirky, strange songs. But, due to massive pressure from everybody, we released it. We were at the Reading Festival the weekend the single was released, and woke up on the Sunday morning to hear Dave Lee Travis play it on his Radio One show over every transistor on the site. The feeling to wake up to that was incredible. Everybody sat up and looked at each other: 'Jesus, that's it – exactly that feeling we got in the studio! This is going to be very big'. And it was!"

'Shirt' lyrics handwritten by Richard Fairbrass

I'M TOO SEXY

RIGHT SAID FRED

COMPOSED BY **RICHARD & CHRISTOPHER FAIRBRASS/ROBERT MANZOLI**

BROTHERS RICHARD AND FRED FAIRBRASS (THE LATTER having had trials for both Chelsea and Fulham football clubs) came together with Rob Manzoli to form Right Said Fred, taking their name from the 1962 Bernard Cribbens hit. Between 1991 and 1994 they had eight hits, including the Number One, 'Deeply Dippy', and their trademark song, 'I'm Too Sexy'.

"That was originally another song called 'Heaven' with a completely different bass line," Richard Fairbrass says. "One sunny afternoon we were working with a guy called Brian Pugsley, just messing around when we started singing, 'I'm too sexy' along with this line. We thought this was extremely funny and very silly, but we took it away and thought about it. When we added the 'I'm a model' bit the song immediately made sense. Fred wrote the rest of the lyrics, I came up with the title and Rob wrote another part of the melody. It took us about nine months to record it because we had no money, we had to keep on going back and doing it in bits and pieces.

"We went into the studio with Tommy Dee at that stage and he added the little drum rolls, that's how it came into fruition. Really the idea sprang up because Fred had been out with a lot of models – 'I'm a model, you know what I mean?' is a line he actually heard! The 'I'm too sexy for your whatever' lines don't really mean anything, they could relate to the chair, the house, the garden – we had 30 or 40 alternatives along with the ones we settled for in the song. It could have been 'I'm too sexy for Stallone, too sexy for Doris Day' – we could have gone on forever but names give the song a date as opposed to inanimate objects, so we settled for the funniest and least obvious comparisons.

"We were surprised at the success of the song, punters pick up on things that you don't notice and sometimes the strongest ideas are the ones you don't see, especially because we'd spent nine months on it. The final mix sounded great but we didn't think it had a cat in hell's chance of being so successful. We used The B-52's 'Love Shack' as a template, not for production but for the spirit of the song; it's a very 'in your face' song and we played it in the studio to remind ourselves of what we wanted. 'Love Shack' is also a nonsense song but very effective. The only trouble with fun songs is that they're not regarded very highly with those in the know, like the awards people. If you do comedy acting or music, people literally don't take you very seriously. It was a clever but tongue in cheek song.

"We needed an instrumental but not a solo in it, and because Rob's a big Jimi Hendrix fan what we ended up with was a bit of 'Third Stone From The Sun', which we didn't realise until this bloke came up to us at a gig up north and told us. The Hendrix Foundation were incredibly cool about us using it and just wanted a credit on the CD and album just so young people knew where it came from.

"When it came out, everything went bananas, which in retrospect wasn't really how we'd have wanted it. It was a bit like enjoying a pleasant walk one minute and then being dragged round the park by a mad dog. No control and no idea of where you're going to end up. It took us all over the place and we ended up promoting it in territories two years after it was all over. America especially wasn't interested in anything else because they wouldn't stop playing it. 'Sexy' should have been the fourth single ideally. It's been the goose that laid the golden egg. It was Number One in about 26 countries and the most performed song, as was 'Deeply Dippy'. The album did huge business and we sold quite a few other singles but everyone remembers us for 'I'm Too Sexy'." ▯

INVISIBLE TOUCH

GENESIS

COMPOSED BY ANTHONY BANKS/PHIL COLLINS/MICHAEL RUTHERFORD

THE GENESIS OF GENESIS OCCURRED IN 1967 AT Charterhouse School, 358 years after it first opened its doors. School group Garden Wall featured Peter Gabriel and Tony Banks while Mike Rutherford and Anthony Phillips played in rival ensemble The Anon. Gabriel, Phillips, Rutherford, Banks and different drummers were re-christened Genesis by former Charterhouse pupil Jonathan King, who became their mentor. In 1970 Flaming Youth's Phil Collins joined on drums, later to replace Gabriel as vocalist as part of the Banks/Rutherford/Collins trio that achieved phenomenal success, never more so than with 'Invisible Touch' in 1986.

"It was initially written for our album of the same name," Collins explains, "and was the first time that we had no other material from other sources. The three of us just sat around in the studio, someone would start a riff, somebody else would start chord sequences and take it from there. I set up a drum pattern because it makes ideas easier to sing to and found myself repeating the main hook line, 'She seems to have an invisible touch, oh, oh, oh.' From then on we started to work out the bones of the song. A lot of the lines were spontaneous whilst we were forming it and of course then you sit down and re-write the wild lines and make everything fit.

"When it came to recording we sat down and apportioned who had what. I got that song because I'd been singing the hook on it. Basically it's about a girl, someone who has that indefinable thing, she's able to get right under your skin and do what she wants with you. We've all had that feeling before. You know, when you keep bouncing back to someone who's not good for you but you can't stop yourself.

"It was our first Number One in America, both the album and the single. I thought it would be our big hit in England but it wasn't. The video was great fun – I think it still stands up now. We were all influenced by the early Police videos and we tried the same approach. Just ourselves capturing the moment without any high tech stuff. We filmed it in a huge grain store with a little stage in the middle. The crew gave us hand-held cameras and we just mucked about. I think it was one of our best, a non-concept video but great fun. The reason I liked the song then, and still do, is because it reminded me of a Sheila E song that I really liked. That was fine by me – any excuse to try and steer Genesis into a hipper area!"

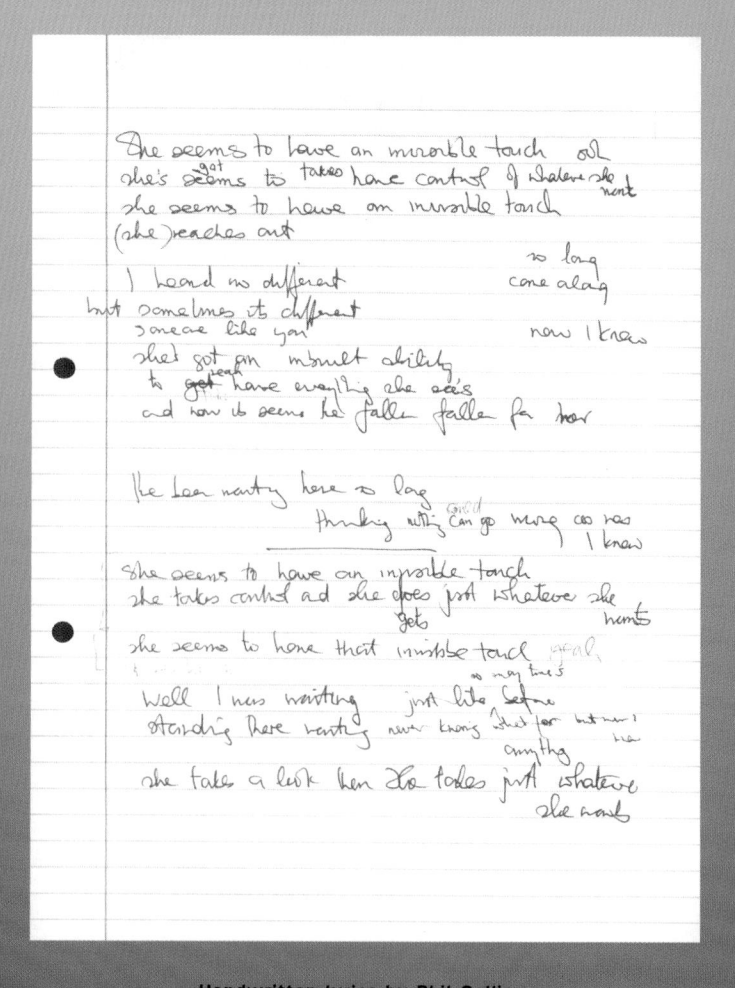

Handwritten lyrics by Phil Collins

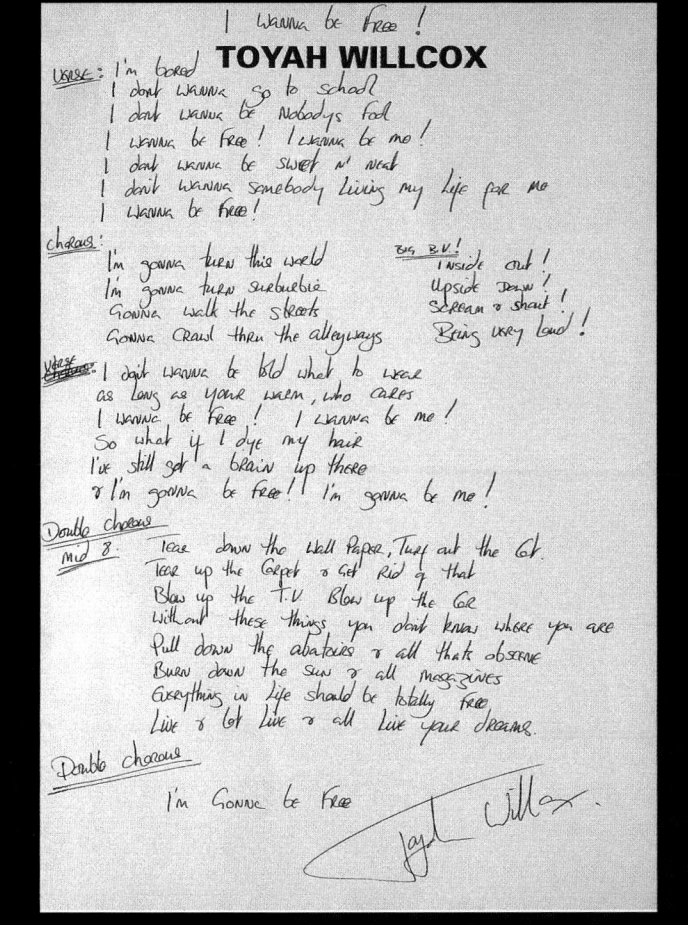

Sheet music signed by The Rolling Stones

Handwritten lyrics by Toyah

IT'S ONLY ROCK 'N' ROLL (BUT I LIKE IT)

THE ROLLING STONES

COMPOSED BY **MICK JAGGER/KEITH RICHARDS**

'IT'S ONLY ROCK 'N' ROLL' IS OFTEN VIEWED AS A
hybrid of self-deprecating parody and 'heads down, no-nonsense good old rock 'n' roll', but writer Mick Jagger admits, "I wrote it quickly one day…it's a bit..rock 'n' roll revival in parts…but that was done quite subconsciously. It was originally done with just me and Ronnie Wood [then still with The Faces]." Dismissing the rumours that David Bowie was on the original session Mick later confessed, "David just happened to come by the studio when we were doing the vocal."

Both the song, and its parent album, were recorded by the Stones in Munich in the summer of 1974, and it was the last of the group's albums to feature guitarist Mick Taylor. As well as the band members, the single 'It's Only Rock 'N' Roll' also featured Billy Preston, Kenney Jones and Willie Weeks.

The album and single also marked the debut of Jagger and Richards' pseudonym as producers, 'The Glimmer Twins'.

I WANT TO BE FREE

TOYAH

COMPOSED BY **TOYAH WILLCOX**

TOYAH'S FIRST RELEASE CONTAINED TRACKS WHICH WERE
featured in an episode of the TV show *Shoestring*, starring Trevor Eve, but her first chart entry came in 1981 with the EP 'Four From Toyah'. Three more hits followed that year – 'I Want To Be Free', 'Thunder In The Mountains' and 'Four More From Toyah' – contributing to her 39 chart weeks in the UK in 1981 and her position as Fourth Best Female Singer in the *NME's* poll. More hits followed in the early Eighties but towards the end of that decade she turned her attention more towards acting. Married to King Crimson's Robert Fripp, they live in Cecil Beaton's former residence.

JUST A NOTION ①

1: JUST A NOTION
THAT'S ALL
JUST A FUNNY FEELING
DEEP INSIDE
THAT YOU'RE OUT THERE WAITING
YOU'RE NOT SURE I'M ALONE
AND YOU WONDER
IF I'M OCCUPIED
SO YOU'RE HESITATING
JUST A NOTION
THAT YOU'LL BE WALKING
UP TO ME IN A WHILE
AND YOU'LL SMILE
AND SAY HELLO
AND WE'LL BE
DANCING THROUGH THE NIGHT
KNOWING EVERYTHING FROM
THERE ON MUST BE RIGHT
JUST A NOTION
BUT SOMEHOW I KNOW I'M NOT WRONG
~~~~~~~~~~~~~
~~~~~~~~~~~~~
THERE'S SOMETHING HAPPENING
THAT I JUST CAN'T EXPLAIN
IF I TRY IT'S ALL IN VAIN
BECAUSE IT'S

2: JUST A NOTION ②
THAT'S ALL
JUST A FEELING THAT YOU'RE
WATCHING ME
EVERY MOVE I'M MAKING
AM I READING YOU'RE MIND
CAUSE IT'S ALMOST LIKE YOU'RE
TOUCHING ME
THERE IS NO MISTAKING
JUST A NOTION
THAT YOU'LL BE WALKING ....
.... I KNOW
I'M NOT WRONG
IF IT'S OUR DESTINY
THERE'S NOTHING WE CAN DO
AND TONIGHT IS VERY SPECIAL
IT'S THE NIGHT
FOR ME AND YOU

Working lyrics by Benny Andersson

JUST A NOTION

ABBA

COMPOSED BY BENNY ANDERSSON/BJORN ULVAEUS

SWEDISH SONGWRITERS BENNY ANDERSSON AND BJORN ULVAEUS
began their writing partnership after meeting in Vastervik, Sweden, in
1966. Six years later, Andersson, Ulvaeus and their respective partners,
Anni-frid Lyngstad and Agnetha Faltskog formed Abba, Andersson and
Ulvaeus embarking on a new era in their writing career which would make
them two of the world's most successful songwriters. As Bjorn recalls,
"We'd get together at something like 10am, either at my home or his, and
we'd sit there hour after hour, and something would usually come
up…but often it didn't…nothing good anyway…so we just continued to
slog on until we had something. Then we'd go away somewhere, just to
be able to write night and day – to my summerhouse on an island outside
Stockholm, for instance."

The two of them would invariably write three or four songs, for which
Bjorn would later provide dummy lyrics, before trying out the keys with
the girls. They would then go into the studio with some of Sweden's best
musicians, and work the songs up into commercial propositions.

To date, 'Just A Notion' has yet to be released.

KAYLEIGH

MARILLION

COMPOSED BY **DEREK DICK/MARK KELLY/STEVEN ROTHERY/PETER TREWAVAS/IAN MOSLEY**

WHEN 'KAYLEIGH' BECAME AN INTERNATIONAL HIT IN 1985 IT marked the upturn in fortunes for Marillion. The story behind the song, however, like the inspiration behind many classics, is one of sadness – particularly for lead singer Fish (aka Derek Dick).

"The lyrical idea for it originally came in 1984 when we were in Wales working at Rockfield Studios on the *Fugazi* album," he recalls. "I was breaking up then with a long-term girlfriend who was called Kay, and just when we were about to cut the last thread we came back together again, but we never sorted out the mess that had caused it in the first place.

"We later started to write the *Misplaced Childhood* album, but by this time my relationship with Kay was dead. I came back from Rockfield to our place in Belsize Park where we were staying – a dreadful depressing place, with a kitchen and one room – which is mentioned in the song. We'd had the big argument just before and I said, 'This is it.' I came back and everything that had belonged to her had gone. The phones and electricity were cut off, there was just my stuff lying in darkness in the room, which all came out in the song. Kay just disappeared and I didn't know where she was at all.

"However, I remember listening to a Clifford T Ward song at that time – I think it was 'Home Thoughts From Abroad' – which goes on about the plumber or something, 'have you fixed that leaky sink?' and then goes 'by the way, how's your broken heart?'. I just thought that was so cool, and I think that was the first sort of subconscious inspiration which led to 'Kayleigh'.

"What I did was mount a sort of pastiche about various different relationships within the lyrics. Everybody thought that the song was about one person, but it wasn't, it was about a number of different people, probably four I'd say. It was about things that had happened in my student days doing forestry in Galashields, and about later joining the band. It also conveys images of me sitting back in the hotel room, and thinking about what could have been if I'd followed a particular direction instead of the one I pursued.

"When it came down to the title of this song, I decided to call it 'Kayleigh', sort of intentionally obscure because Kay had the middle name Lee. I really didn't want to get into revealing her identity and causing problems for her, so I made this composite name up. However, the band really didn't want the song to be called 'Kayleigh' and they all objected, saying, 'We all know it's Kay.' I said, 'Well look, I'm not changing it to "Rosemary" or anything like that.'"

The song began to take shape at a Chessington studio which belonged to John Giblin, a bass player who worked with Simple Minds.

"Steve Rothery came up with this riff, which as soon as I heard it I knew would fit the basis of the rough words I'd written beforehand. It was one of those perfect marriages of music and lyrics. The problem was that although I knew the format, I hadn't finished all the lyrics. We left it while we went on a Christmas tour but I kept writing lots of possible verses, agonising over getting the right words and the right

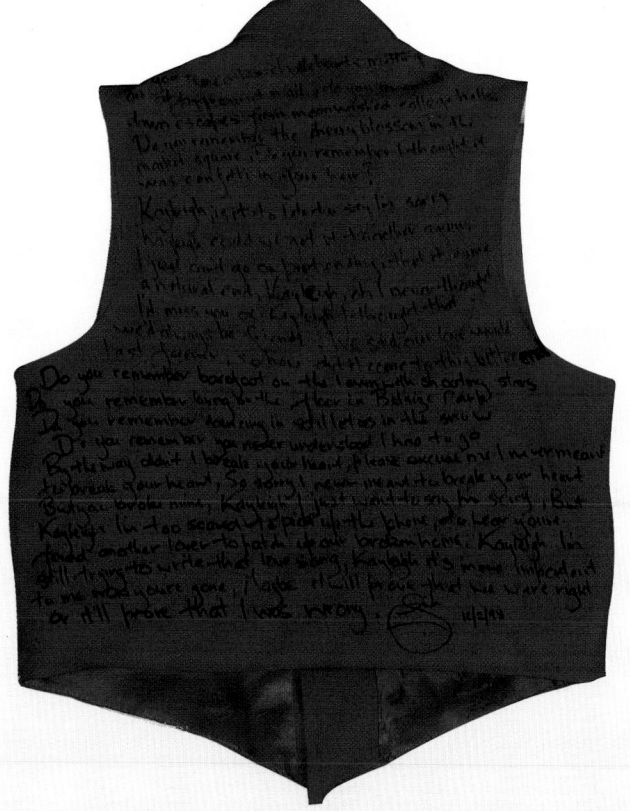

'Waistcoat' lyrics handwritten by Fish

images, right up until we went into record at Hansa Studios in Berlin in April of the following year. Virtually the whole song was there, except for one verse that was missing. Our producer, Chris Kimsey, kept saying, 'When are you going to sing "Kayleigh"?' and I would say, 'Oh, I'll do it tomorrow.' One night he just said, 'The band and I are going to dinner, we'll be back in two and a half hours and I want that fucking song done now!'

"So I sat in the studio and basically in two hours – well actually in about ten minutes after they walked out the door – I had it. I got it down and it was beautiful. It's a lyric I'm very, very proud of because the imagery is cinematic but at the same time it's kept tight and controlled."

The would-be classic was nearly kept from the public after all.

"When EMI first heard it, they didn't like *Misplaced Childhood* and they didn't think 'Kayleigh' was a single, until we eventually persuaded them otherwise. To give them credit, when it did come out they threw everything behind it and when it went into the Top Ten it was phenomenal, it was three and a half minutes that changed our lives. It was also quite strange because everybody at the time wanted to know who 'Kayleigh' was. The tabloids were actually offering me money to reveal her identity, and I just said, 'No way.' I never saw her afterwards until we played Hammersmith Odeon, and she was there, because she actually thought that the song was an attempt to try and get us back together again, which it wasn't. However, I'm also very proud that 'Kayleigh' is now used as a real name by girls, and appears in those books listing kids' names, which mention that it was 'originally a single by Marillion'."

Despite EMI's fears, the album went to Number One in the UK and the single, 'Kayleigh', to Number Two, being held off the top spot by The Crowd's charity record, 'You'll Never Walk Alone'. 'Kayleigh', Marillion's sixth UK single also gave them their first US chart success. ▤

KIDS IN AMERICA

Verse I Looking out a dirty old window
Down below the cars in the city go
                                    rushing by

I sit here alone — and I wonder why?

Friday night and everythings moving
I can feel the heat — but its soothing
Heading down — I search for the beat
                    in this dirty Town

Down town   the young ones are going
Downt town   the young ones are growing

(Chorus) Were the Kids in America —
         Were the Kids in America
         Everybody lives for the music — go round

Verse II   Bright lights — the music gets faster
            Look boy dont check on your watch
            Not another glance
            I'm not leaving now honey
                            not a chance

            Hot shot — give me no problems
            Much later baby you'll be saying now
                            never mind

Handwritten lyrics by Marty Wilde

KIDS IN AMERICA

KIM WILDE

COMPOSED BY **MARTY WILDE/RICKY WILDE**

FROM 1958 TO 1962 SINGER MARTY WILDE CHARTED 14 singles to become one of the most successful British rock 'n' roll balladeers. Unlike many solo performers whose careers foundered with the advent of the beat boom, Wilde has continued to perform, appearing in films and carving a separate career as a songwriter, writing hits for Status Quo, Lulu, The Casuals and his daughter, Kim Wilde. Her version of 'You Keep Me Hanging On' reached Number One in the States, but it was 'Kids In America', written by Marty and Kim's brother Ricky, that started it all.

"The lyrics were really just an observation that I made about the attitude of American teenagers at the time, who frightened me to death," Marty Wilde says. "I just thought that some of the harshness and coldness which some of the youngsters of that time displayed was good subject matter. There were lines in it like, 'kind hearts don't grab any glory, kind hearts won't make a new story', which is saying the same sort of thing as people say about newspapers, ie nice stories don't sell papers. The attitude that I wanted to get over in the song was also the beginning of the girl power thing, at least for Kim, where she was telling the guy, 'Don't look at your watch, don't tell me what to do – I'm telling you.' The song was really just a comment about how I imagined a small section of American teenagers, where they might walk into a toy shop and walk out with a machine gun or something.

"I was thrilled for Kim because it launched her career, and it was also very satisfying for both myself and Ricky because it did so well. I thought it was a record of its time, but I'm still particularly proud of the synth sounds on it, particularly the opening stabby bars with the old Moog which were great. That bass end still hits you in the guts.

"It became a big hit round the world, which took us rather by surprise. I remember that when Mickie Most at Rak Records first heard the record, he said he thought it would be a very big hit. When I came home from the meeting, I said to my son Ricky that if it came out as a single I thought it could make the Top 50, not knowing that it would have the sales impact that it did. I remember one evening when Kim was talking on the phone to Mickie after it had been released, the company used to give us the sales figures. He told her it had sold something like 250,000 in just one day, which was quite a shock for a record that I thought might just make the Top 50!"

'Kids In America' reached Number Two in the UK in 1981 and 25 in the US a year later. ▤

LADY IN RED

CHRIS DE BURGH

COMPOSED BY **CHRIS DE BURGH**

CHRIS DE BURGH BEGAN WRITING SONGS WHILE ATTENDING Trinity College, Dublin, later signing a record deal with A&M. Despite a couple of fine albums and a turntable hit with 'A Spaceman Came Travelling', it wasn't until 'Don't Pay The Ferryman' that his chart career in the UK and US caught up with his success in other countries. 'Lady In Red' was to become his biggest hit, reaching Number One in the UK in 1986 and Number Three in the States a year later.

"This song, like most of mine, wasn't specifically written with anybody in mind," de Burgh insists. "With me they tend to arrive like trains in the night, no idea where it comes from but it has to be developed like a seed that's been planted. Generally the lyrics and music come together. A melody and a few words appear, and I try hard to get a melodic song structure to put the words in. The music gives an indication of what it's all about but the lyrics are the hard part.

"The song started off as an idea called 'The Way You Look Tonight' and when people ask how long it took, I say, 'Five months and 20 minutes' because the initial ideas are there almost immediately, but it can take five months to get the thing right.

"It became 'Lady In Red', quite frankly, because the words fitted. 'Lady In Green' doesn't sound right, red just fitted properly. However, the imagery behind it is about how relationships have to be worked on to keep things together. The couple in the song have rowed, split up at the party, he's looking over at her thinking, 'Mmm, who's that?' then she turns round and he sees it's his lady. He hadn't noticed her properly before. It's a romantic idea that women like to hear and men find awkward to talk about.

'Red dress' lyrics by Chris de Burgh

"I had pretty much most of the song written when I went out one night to a disco after an awards party and my wife Diane was looking great in a red outfit. Everything sort of slotted into place from there. It was produced by Paul Hardiman and myself but recording was difficult. After a week of trying we wiped the tape clean and began again. What you hear is the final result.

"It's been a huge song, especially in America. It went to Number One in about 25 countries, and legend has it that it was even Princess Diana's favourite song. I don't get bored of hearing it. I'm still listening and trying to analyse what made it so successful." ▤

FORMED IN 1971, BRIAN May, Roger Taylor, Freddie Mercury and John Deacon signed to EMI Records later that year. In 1973 they released their eponymous first album and their debut single 'Keep Yourself Alive', although it was to be the exciting 'Seven Seas Of Rhye' the following year which would give them their first hit single.

The musical virtuosity of May, Taylor and Deacon, coupled with the voice, flamboyance and showmanship of Mercury, led to them becoming one of the world's most successful groups, The Beatles being the only group to have more Top Ten singles in Britain.

The ability of each member of the group to write high quality songs gave them a run of hit singles around the world, up to and after Mercury's death in 1991, and a long list of gold and platinum discs. In 1995, May, Taylor and Deacon released a new album, *Made In Heaven*, which topped the UK chart and yielded five hit singles, including 'Let Me Live', written out here by the song's main composer, Roger Taylor. The single, on which Mercury, May and Taylor share lead vocals, reached Number Nine in the UK in the summer of 1996.

"Let Me Live"

why don't you take another little piece of my heart
" " " " it & break it & tear it all apart
V1   all I do is give, & all you do is take,
all that I'm askin' — is an even break
so let me live — let me live — let me love — we'll make a brand new start
(Br) if you need anybody, you can always depend on me
if you ever get lonely, you know where I will be.

why don't you take another little piece of my life,
V2 why don't you take it, & stake it, & tear it with a knife
cos all you do is live, & all I do is die,
why can't we just be friends — stop-livin' a lie!
so let me live — let me live
let me love — no need to say goodbye.

+ If you need anybody — you can always depend on me
If you ever get lonely, you know where I will be

Why don't you take another little piece of my soul
" " " you shake it & shape it, till you're really in control
all you do is take
+ all I do is give
all that I'm asking — is a chance to live.

Let me live
" " "
" " love   take another little piece of my heart now baby.
" " love

G   C C   G   E E
E   A A   E   C C
C ——— — — —— F F   C ,,,,,,,,,   G G

Working lyrics by Roger Taylor

76 INSPIRATIONS

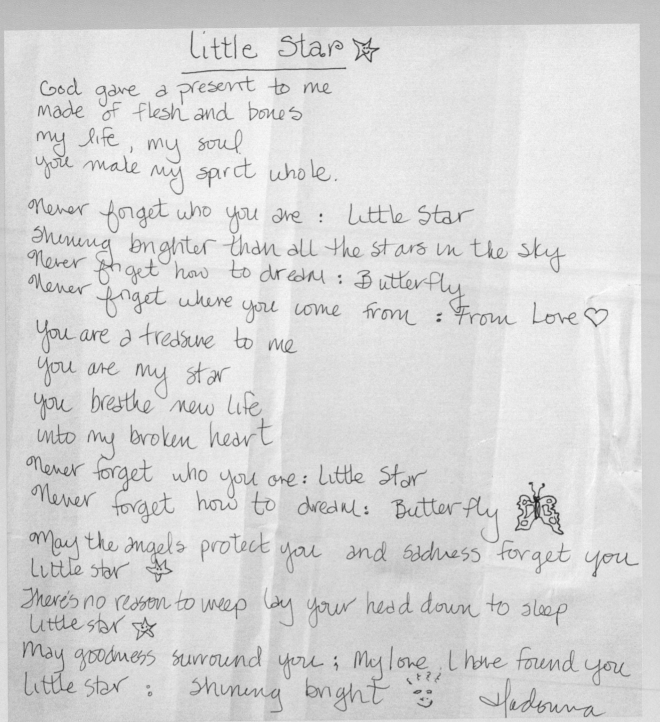

Little Star ⭐

God gave a present to me
made of flesh and bones
my life, my soul
you make my spirit whole.

Never forget who you are : Little Star
Shining brighter than all the stars in the sky
Never forget how to dream : Butterfly
Never forget where you come from : From Love ♡

You are a tresure to me
You are my star
You breathe new life
into my broken heart

Never forget who you are: Little Star
Never forget how to dream: Butterfly

May the angels protect you and sadness forget you
Little star ⭐

There's no reason to weep lay your head down to sleep
Little star ⭐

May goodness surround you ; My love, I have found you
Little star : shining bright   Madonna

LITTLE STAR

MADONNA

COMPOSED BY MADONNA/RICK NOWELS

FOR THE THIRD MOST SUCCESSFUL ARTIST OF ALL TIME IN THE British chart, 'Little Star', coupled with 'The Power Of Goodbye', was Madonna's 49th hit single in Britain, and her 43rd Top Tenner.

The song was taken from the 1998 Grammy award-winning album *Ray Of Light*, the title track of which had been written in 1970 by two British musicians, Clive Muldoon and Dave Atkins, the latter having previously been the lead singer with Sixties recording group Dave Curtiss And The Tremors. Originally called 'Sepharyn', from the opening ling 'Zephyr in the sky…', Muldoon's niece, Christine Leach, had been listening to Madonna's producer William Orbit working on a backing track, when she began singing the song over the top of it. Orbit was impressed; so was Madonna, and re-titling it from another line in the song, it became 'Ray Of Light'. It was a great result for Atkins after all his years in the business, although his co-writer Muldoon had passed on.

Madonna chose to donate and write out the lyrics to 'Little Star' for *Inspirations* because the song is about her daughter, Lourdes, and the proceeds from the book will be going to charities that work often with disadvantaged children. The song was written by her and Rick Nowels. ▯

<u>Love is all around</u>   By Reg Presley

I feel it in my fingers, I feel it in my toes
Well love is all around me, and so the feeling grows
It's written on the wind, it's everywhere I go
So if you really love me, come on and let it show

You know I love you I always will
My minds made up by the way that I feel
There's no beginning they'll be no end
Cos on my love you can depend

I see your face before me, as I lay on my bed
I kinda get to thinking, of all the things you said
You gave your promise to me, and I gave mine to you
I need someone beside me, in everything I do.

You know I love you I always will
My minds made up by the way that I feel,
There's no beginning they'll be no end
Cos on my love you can depend.

It's written on the wind, it's everywhere I go
So if you really love me, come on and let it show.
Come on and let it show
Come on and let it show

Love from

Love is all around!
Best wishes,
Duncan Kennedy

LOVE IS ALL AROUND

WET WET WET

COMPOSED BY **REG PRESLEY**

MOST SONGS' ORIGINAL VERSIONS ARE never bettered whereas others somehow outgrow their earlier constraints. Despite The Troggs taking it to Number Five (Seven in the US), for most people the definitive version of 'Love Is All Around' was made by Wet Wet Wet in 1994. Released as the theme to the film *Four Weddings And A Funeral*, it spent 15 weeks atop the UK charts and certainly paid back the efforts of its writer, Troggs frontman Reg Presley.

"The Troggs had been doing a pretty hard tour, and I'd just come home after being away for several weeks," Presley says. "It was good to be back at home, and it put me in a very settled and loving mood. This particular day was a Sunday, and I'd just had my first proper Sunday lunch in weeks, and went to lie down afterwards on the sofa. As I did so, I realised the TV was on, and went to turn it down. The programme on at the time featured The Joy Strings, the Salvation Army band, and they were shaking their tambourines and singing along together. As I moved over to the telly to turn it down, the idea came to me for 'Love Is All Around', literally in a flash. Maybe if it had been another programme or another band, I would have never had the inspiration, I don't know.

"Anyway, I didn't get my lie-down on the sofa, as for the next 20 minutes I was writing. Some of the songs I'd written before had happened very quickly, and this was the same. I don't know how it happens, I don't know why it happens, it just seems as though they come out of the ether at the right time. Anyway I got it down, and called our guitarist, Chris Britton, over to go through the chords and cement it down. We both agreed that it had potential, and then went into the studio and recorded it several weeks later, and it turned out to be a very nice

hit for us in 1967, getting us back into the Top Ten.

"There have been several covers, and in fact REM actually did it before Wet Wet Wet. When we worked with them on the *Athens To Andover* album, we went over to record in their home town of Athens, Georgia, which is about the same size as Andover. We were amazed to hear that in their early days they played a lot of our numbers on stage. I couldn't believe it. They were in awe of us, we were in awe of them, and I think we just walked around each other for about five minutes going, 'Cor!' They actually did a pretty good version, although I wish Michael Stipe had sung it rather then Mike Mills, to be honest.

"However, this was just before we heard about Wet Wet Wet's version, which for me was absolutely superb. When I first heard it I thought, 'It's got to go somewhere, you just can't ignore it.' Funnily enough, not many people realise that it was a Number One in England before *Four Weddings And A Funeral* came out. It had been out in the States but not over here, and to some extent the single helped to build up the film. It stayed at Number One for 15 weeks, the second-longest span at Number One and just one week short of Bryan Adams' record.

"Writing a song like that which has become so successful really enhances everything else on the down side of the rock business, it sort of levels it all out. The song has been played at weddings, at funerals – I think they've played it more or less everywhere now! The nice thing was later on getting a hat trick of Ivor Novello awards for it, as Best Selling Song in the UK, PRS Most Performed Work and International Hit Of The Year. That was an incredible day for me – as a songwriter, not a singer – and made me very proud." 📄

'Guitar' lyrics handwritten by Reg Presley, signed by Hugh Grant, Duncan Kenworthy and Richard Curtis

LOVE POTION NUMBER NINE

THE SEARCHERS

COMPOSED BY **JERRY LEIBER/MIKE STOLLER**

JERRY LEIBER AND MIKE STOLLER, THE WRITERS OF 'LOVE Potion Number Nine', first came together in 1948, as Mike recalls: "I got a call from Jerry, who I'd never met, who said he'd got my name from a friend of his, and had heard I could write notes – music on paper – and I agreed to meet him, although I wasn't enthusiastic about it." A mutual love of the blues fused the partnership, and they became one of the major songwriting teams of the Fifties and early Sixties, penning dozens of classic pop songs including 'Kansas City', 'Hound Dog', 'Jailhouse Rock', 'Yakety Yak', 'Searchin', 'Charlie Brown', 'Poison Ivy' and 'Stand By Me'.

'Love Potion Number Nine' was a US hit in 1959 for The Clovers, The Searchers charting with it in the States and the UK in 1965, and The Coasters giving it a third outing in the American listings in 1967. In 1982 The Tygers Of Pan Tang had a UK hit with it.

Many other artists have recorded this classic, including The Ventures, The Surfaris, Elkie Brooks, Wayne Fontana and Sam The Sham.

Handwritten lyrics by Jerry Leiber

MACARTHUR PARK

RICHARD HARRIS

COMPOSED BY **JIMMY WEBB**

BORN IN IRELAND IN 1933, ACTOR RICHARD HARRIS MADE HIS
name in such classics as *The Guns Of Navarone* and *A Man Called Horse*.
In 1968, following his role in the musical *Camelot*, he recorded Jimmy
Webb's classic 'MacArthur Park'.

"The idea behind 'MacArthur Park' was always that it should be a piece
of classical proportions," Webb says. "Bones Howe's original request had
been for a 'classical-sounding piece'. Really, the song that everybody
knows was only the beginning of that idea – and quite enough, I might
add, as I don't believe we really needed 30 minutes of 'MacArthur Park'.

"The lyrical meaning is not that difficult to understand: the song is about
a lost love, a love that's not coming back. Quite why some people find
such a mystery about it, I don't understand, but I've come under some
criticism from time to time, with people saying, 'Well, that song doesn't
mean anything.' Of course, the late Sixties, that era of hallucinogenics
and psychedelia, was rife with material that was completely
impenetrable but this is simply a song about a love affair gone wrong.
The specific images are from real life. MacArthur Park, on Wilshire
Boulevard in LA, is where I used to meet my girlfriend Susan, and we'd
lunch there in the park. The couple in the song are also picnicking under
the trees, and the rain ruins their cake, which the song takes as an
allegory for the disintegration of the affair itself. There's no psychedelic
imagery there, and some of the listeners just construed that because
people were writing that stuff at the time. It obviously meant something
to somebody, though, which is why the song still won't go away…

"Richard Harris's vocals for 'MacArthur Park' and the whole of his album
A Tramp Shining were recorded in London, something I was very glad to
do because I'd had an instant love affair with the city that has never gone
away. We recorded at Lansdowne Studio and all we needed was just to
have Richard go into the room, stand in front of the microphone and lay
the voice down, because everything else was done. I had put the
orchestra on in LA, and the whole arrangement was complete which was
actually kind of chancy because I could have written something that
would have completely interfered with what he intended to do. It didn't
take him a terribly long time, and I'd just like to set the record straight –
there weren't any real technological magic acts performed on that stuff
to get those tapes together. Richard sang well, he sang strongly, he got
through those tracks nicely, and there wasn't a lot of time involved.

"I think the first and foremost appeal of the record was its arrangement,
for which I got a Grammy award. It had that uptempo kind of rocking
thing in the middle that breaks down tempo-wise and goes into a very
wide, expansive, emotional finish. Probably the real hook in the record is
when you come out of the allegro – the fast section – and go into where
it just opens up like a film score. I find that kind of a thrilling moment. It
also had a very pretty love song right in the middle of it, called 'After All
The Loves Of My Life' which stands on its own. In fact, that's the only
part that Frank Sinatra recorded! He didn't really tackle the first part or
the fast section, but just went for the piece that he liked.

"The biggest cover by far was Donna Summer's which was made ten
years later. It was a surprise, because I had no idea that she was going
to do it. But I was delighted, because I rated her so highly, and the song
is so right for her. Whereas Richard and I had made Number Two,
Donna's version of 'MacArthur Park' was the first Number One record of
my career, and on the day it reached the top I cut the charts out of all the
trade papers and framed them!

"From that moment on I have never needed to go out and look for
someone to record one of my songs. Since then I have usually been
contacted by people saying, 'Do you have anything? If you don't, would
you consider writing something?' That's a lot different from being out on
the street with your songs under your arm just praying that someone
would only listen to you."

Handwritten lyrics by Steve Harley

MAKE ME SMILE (COME UP AND SEE ME)

STEVE HARLEY AND COCKNEY REBEL

COMPOSED BY **STEVE HARLEY**

AS FORMER JOURNALIST STEVE HARLEY AND HIS GROUP
Cockney Rebel hit the UK chart with 'Judy Teen' and 'Mr Soft', Harley was becoming a controversial interviewee. Just before the release of 'Make Me Smile', he said, "I set myself exceedingly high standards, I can't help it, I just do. However, I don't go out of my way to push it down people's throats." A love/hate relationship with the music press led to him being voted Klutz Of The Year, ahead of The Bay City Rollers and Gary Glitter, by readers of the *New Musical Express*, in February 1975.

Ironically, his new single 'Make Me Smile' blasted its way into the chart, and cruised comfortably to Number One, confounding his critics, and becoming one of the most durable hits of the Seventies. "You can't be a contented genius if you want to write things that are extra special and truly great," he said at the time. "I haven't even started yet. Truly great writers don't produce their finest work until they've been around a bit longer."

The song was reissued in 1992 when it reached Number 46, a second reissue three years later attaining Number 33. Steve is still playing and writing in the late Nineties, and presented the BBC Radio Two series, *Sounds Of The Seventies*. ▨

MELLOW YELLOW

DONOVAN

COMPOSED BY **DONOVAN LEITCH**

GLASGOW-BORN DONOVAN LEITCH MOVED TO
Hertfordshire as a boy and made his first public appearance at the age of 18 in 1964. He was spotted while playing at Clacton by songwriter Geoff Stephens, and following appearances on *Ready Steady Go* was signed to Pye Records. Of his ten UK and 14 US hits 'Mellow Yellow' has been the most frequently misinterpreted. Donovan puts the record straight:

"Whilst holidaying in Greece awaiting the release of my previous record, 'Sunshine Superman', I began to compose songs for the album to follow, including a cheeky little song for the title track called 'Mellow Yellow'. It's usually best not to describe what a song means, as for a song to be popular worldwide it can often mean different things to different people. However, in the case of 'Mellow Yellow' the interpretation of my lyric meant a lot it seemed, so I will give you some idea of where I was coming from, 'man'.

"Like 'Sunshine Superman', this song was once again termed by many as 'drug-orientated', and this time I was said to be singing about smoking bananas. What I actually meant by the title was that I was a laid-back kind of dude, and smoking the safe little green herb (called by many names) was in part responsible, and not the dried banana skins as was assumed.

"As with some of John Lennon's songs at the time, I 'pasted' images together from newspapers, billboards and magazines, just as pop artists had also done since Picasso and Braque. The 'electric banana' was a reference to the vibrators which had become available as 'marital aids' on the back pages of periodicals. Andy Warhol would use the image of a banana on the cover of a Velvet Underground album a year later in 1967. The rest of the lyric is culled from books of 'saffron-robed monks' and 'saffron-cake' from Cornwall. And there was an obvious reference to my teen-girl fans at the time, who were mostly 14 and just 'mad about music'.

"The session arranger was the young John Paul Jones, later of Led Zeppelin. I wanted a New Orleans jazz feel. Having been to the city and heard some of the old jazz cats play, I wanted a march with a mellow mood. Many of the best horn players in London were in the studio that day (Advision, I think), and the jazzers were in a mood of celebration as they had very little chance in the Sixties to make the sort of music they appreciated.

"I sang live in the studio and we recorded a few takes.

Handwritten lyrics by Donovan

However, something was wrong. The producer, Mickie Most, came over and asked me what it was: the arrangement? No, the parts were perfect. A strained atmosphere developed between me and Jones. I couldn't put my finger on it. Then a lesser-known horn player spoke up as I tried to explain the problem with the sound. The jazzer said, 'I know what Don means. He means we should put the 'ats on!' The hats are the horn mutes shaped like bowler hats. The musos all went down into the studio, put their 'ats on and played. A soft and 'mellow' sound wafted out through the speakers – this was it.

"John Paul smiled and I laughed as the track was recorded – the sound before the 'ats had been like a stripper's song in a night club. It wasn't mellow, but now it was. Mickie Most beamed out at me: he knew he had a hit, he knew before the session, he always did. Paul McCartney also came into the session, as he often did, although contrary to what most books say, he did not sing the whisper vocal, 'quite rightly'. I sang this piece, and Paul joined in on the 'party' parts.

"'Mellow Yellow' followed 'Sunshine Superman' into the single charts all over the world in 1966, and by the following year, I was one of the hottest concert tickets in the States – I was having a real ball."

The song reached Number Two in the US and Eight in the UK.

i step off the train
i'm walking down your street again
and past your door
but you don't live there anymore
it's years since you've been there
                now 've
have you disappeared somewhere ?
like outer space
or some better place
and i miss you   like the deserts miss the rain
what's become of you, what's become of you ?

would you be dead ?
you always were two steps ahead of everyone
we'd walk behind while you would run
i look up at your house
i can almost hear you shout down to me
i'm here where i always used to be —
and i miss you   like the deserts miss the rain

so i asked around
and finally i tracked you down

back on the train
i ask why did i come again
can i confess
i've been hanging round your old address
and the years have proved
to offer nothing since you moved
you're long gone, but i can't move on

you left me here
wasted, wasted years
you wouldn't believe
how little i've achieved

Tracey Thorn

Ben Watt

MISSING

EVERYTHING BUT THE GIRL

COMPOSED BY **TRACEY THORN/BEN WATT**

HERTFORDSHIRE-BORN TRACEY THORN, AND LONDON-BORN BEN WATT MET AT HULL
University in the early Eighties, releasing solo albums and albums with The Marine Girls before
forming Everything But The Girl. Their hits began in 1984, but they didn't dent the Top Ten, or
even the Top 20, until their version of 'I Don't Want To Talk About It' gave them a Top Three, and
their seventh, hit.

As Ben Watt recovered from a serious illness, the hits continued, with 'Missing' reaching
Number 69 in 1994.

That wasn't to be the end of the story of that particular song though, as a version remixed by
DJ Todd Terry became a smash around the world, including the US, where it made the Top Ten,
staying on the chart for three months. ▢

MOVE IT

CLIFF RICHARD

COMPOSED BY IAN SAMWELL

EVERY GREAT STORY HAS TO HAVE A BEGINNING, AND for Cliff Richard, the UK's most successful act – 120 hit singles, 63 Top Tens, 89 Top 20s – the beginning was a song written by his then bass player, Ian Samwell.

"'Move It' was the first song I ever wrote, the first hit Cliff Richard ever had, and the first honest-to-goodness original and genuine rock 'n' roll record ever to come out of Great Britain," Samwell says. "Amazing! Especially if you consider that none of us had the slightest idea what we were doing. Some things are just meant to be, and 'Move It', I think, was just one of those things.

"George Ganjou, a theatrical agent whom I discovered by reading the ads in *Variety*, was eventually persuaded to see Cliff Richard And The Drifters perform at the Gaumont, Shepherd's Bush. As a result, we made a demo at a tiny mono recording studio above HMV in Oxford Street, London. We recorded two songs, 'Breathless' and 'Lawdy Miss Clawdy' and Mr Ganjou sent our demo to Norrie Paramor who then invited Cliff, drummer Terry Smart, and myself to his office at EMI. He said that he liked what he heard and would give us a decision when he came back from holiday in three weeks' time. It was the longest three weeks of my life!

"When Norrie returned, news was good. He had arranged an initial date for us at Abbey Road Studios, and had found a song, 'Schoolboy Crush' (already an American hit for Bobby Helms). Now all we needed was a B-side. I'm not sure how the news reached me, but I came to understand that Norrie had asked if we had any of our own material. We didn't, but having dabbled a little bit with poetry and written a couple of short stories, I decided to take a shot at it.

"The story about my writing 'Move It' on the top of a double decker bus on the way to Cliff's house in Cheshunt is actually true. I went upstairs and was relieved to find that I was the only passenger on the top deck. If there had been anyone else there, I would have been too embarrassed to get my guitar out, and the song never would have been written. I scribbled down the lyrics as they came to me, there were no re-writes. The first part of the lyric was inspired by an article in *Melody Maker* by jazz critic Steve Race. It began, 'So rock 'n' roll is dead is it? Well, my obituary consists of two words, good riddance.' I suppose that around that time the initial burst of rock 'n' roll had started to slow down a little bit, but anyone under the age of 25 could have told you it wasn't going to die any time soon.

"I wrote out the lyric in such a way as to enable Cliff to read it directly off the lyric sheet as in 'C'mon pretty baby, let's a-move it an' a-groove it', because it is quite difficult for a singer on the spur of the moment to avoid the pitfalls of correct, and consequently stiff, pronunciation. As you may have noticed, there is only one verse to 'Move It'. It is sung twice with a solo in between. I had started a second verse, but I couldn't think of a way to finish it in time. When you get to the end of the introduction the last two notes form the basis of the rhythm guitar pattern that drives the whole thing along."

"Jack Good, the TV producer, heard 'Move It' after EMI had released it as the B-side of 'Schoolboy Crush'," Cliff Richard adds. "Thank heavens he was the kind of producer who would bother to turn a record over. He didn't like the official A-side, and didn't want me to sing it on *Oh Boy!*. For that I was, and am, very grateful, because EMI agreed, on the basis of Jack's opinion, to switch the sides. They were clever enough to see the potential for me, as a new artist, if I were to be seen singing my records on this new, high-profile rock 'n' roll show, and therefore they were prepared to change all the press, all the publicity, from 'Schoolboy Crush' to 'Move It'. From then on, it became 'Move It, Cliff Richard's exciting debut single'."

The new A-side reached Number Two in the UK in 1958. Almost 40 years later Ian Samwell sent Cliff the long awaited second verse to 'Move It' which the singer incorporates into his stage act today. ▤

1954 'Move It' songsheet signed by Sir Cliff Richard

MY HEART WILL GO ON

CELINE DION

COMPOSED BY **JAMES HORNER/WILL JENNINGS**

***TITANIC*, THE FILM RELEASED IN 1997 STARRING LEONARDO DI**
Caprio and Kate Winslet, became the highest grossing film in history,
taking more than one billion dollars and justifying the $200million that
it took to make. As well as a commercial success, *Titanic* equalled
Ben Hur's record for winning the most Oscars – including an Academy
Award for its theme song, performed by Celine Dion.

"I'd been working on some other films with *Titanic*'s composer, James
Horner, and he called me and told me about this project which turned
out to be *Titanic*," lyricist Will Jennings says. "Up to that point, all I'd
heard were negative reports on the project from the papers and from
Hollywood, but I loved the image of the Rose character, and when
James played me this tune and told me the story of the script I was
hooked. In fact when he played me the tune, I'd already got a lot of
the lyrics right there, maybe a quarter of the song was in my head by
the time I left his place.

"It evoked memories of a lady potter that I'd met a couple of years
before in Ojai, California named Beatrice Wood. Her career had begun
before the first World War and she'd once been the lover of Marcel
Duchamps in Paris and wound up in Ojai back in the Forties, working
at her wheel every day. I had seen the premiere of a movie, which
was based on her life of romance and adventure in Greenwich Village
at the beginning of WWI, and Beatrice Wood came to it. She was very
much alive and alert and we had a chat after the film, she actually
shook hands with each person who had come. When she touched my
hand I got such a feeling of life coming out of her that it was
incredible. She stayed on my mind so much when James told me the
story, I immediately went to her mentally for the inspiration for 'My
Heart Will Go On'.

"Celine Dion liked the song and recorded the demo, which James
presented to director James Cameron, and he loved it. I didn't meet
Cameron in person until the night of the Golden Globe awards. He
asked me, 'Did James tell you what I said?' In his opinion, the song
had completed the film and the title and the lyric had continued it
beyond the 'heart' of the story. I said thank you, but I did have some
help on it because I had met this 100-year-old woman a couple of
years before who had helped to inspire me. Cameron just looked
amazed and admitted that the character of Rose had also been
inspired by an older woman – the same Beatrice Wood. In the film,
when you see Rose at the window in her potters studio, what you're
actually seeing is Beatrice in California. And just a few days before the
Oscars she died, aged 104."

'My Heart Will Go On' topped the charts in the UK and US in 1998. 🗐

My Heart Will Go On

Every night in my dreams
I see you, I feel you
That is how I know you go on

Far across the distance
And spaces between us
You have come to show you go on

Near, far, wherever you are
I believe that the heart does go on
Once more you open the door
And you're here in my heart
And my heart will go on and on

Love can touch us one time
And last for a lifetime
And never let go till we're gone

Love was when I loved you
One true time I hold to
In my life we'll always go on

Near, far, wherever you are
I believe that the heart does go on
Once more you open the door
And you're here in my heart
And my heart will go on and ON

You're here, there's nothing I fear
And I know that my heart will go on
We'll stay forever this way
You are safe in my heart
And my heart will go on and on

Celine Dion

Lyric: Will Jennings
Music: James Horner

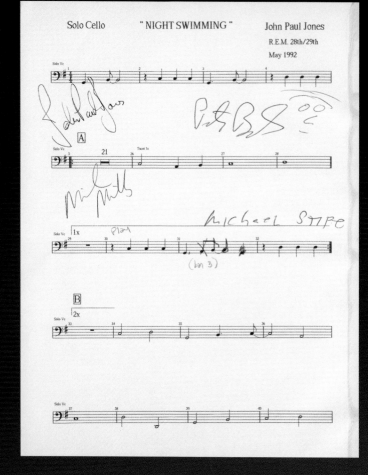

NIGHTSWIMMING

REM

COMPOSED BY **MICHAEL STIPE/PETER BUCK/MIKE MILLS/BILL BERRY**

MICHAEL STIPE, PETER BUCK, MIKE MILLS AND BILL BERRY, collectively known as REM, came together at the University of Georgia, Athens, USA, first performing in 1980. They toured with The Police and signed to the small Hib-Tone label before moving to IRS in 1982. Another tour with The Police and the release of their debut album, *Murmur*, in 1983 meant REM had arrived. Ten years later – following a string of international successes – they achieved their 14th UK hit single with 'Nightswimming'.

"'Nightswimming' is one of the few songs that Michael ever wrote where he had the lyrics before we had the music," says REM guitarist Peter Buck. "He wrote them during the *Out Of Time* record, and we just couldn't fit anything to it. It was at the very end of the sessions, when we were mixing the last couple of songs, Mike came up with the piano thing for it and we all kind of sat around the piano and arranged it. I guess there was some discussion about getting it on the record, we had just about finished and it seemed like a long time so we said, 'Okay, that's definitely on the next album,' which was *Automatic For The People*.

"Lyrically, the song is about when the band was first starting out down in Athens, Georgia, which is a hot muggy place, and there were only about 100 people on the whole scene who would go out and see the kind of bands that we were in – there was ourselves, a band called Pylon, Love Tractor and The Method Actors, while The B-52s had just moved away from town.

"So at the end of the shows during summertime it would be about 100 degrees and everyone would be soaked through, and there were a couple of swimming places that were illegal to go to at night, but there would be a convoy of about eight or ten cars, everyone would hop out and take their clothes off and dive in and swim – it was a great place if you hadn't connected already to meet people of the opposite sex, or the same sex, after the shows. They were really young, innocent days when we were in our late teens or early 20s, and I have real strong memories of diving into this place called Ball Pump, it's a really nasty, muddy pond but after you've been dancing in 98% humidity it sure felt awful good.

"So that's what inspired the song, and the strings on *Automatic For The People* were arranged by John Paul Jones. Working with that guy was pretty amazing, we had a great time making the record and ended up recording in Criteria Studios in Miami, using the grand piano that was used on 'Layla', so it's got a few interesting historical connections. John Paul wrote out a bunch of notated scores, and we got a few signed for ourselves which we all wanted to have, and Michael also wrote the lyrics out for the string players to follow, hence the donation to the auction."

The late Nineties have seen the group's members involved in varying activities, with Stipe producing the Seventies film *Velvet Goldmine*, and Berry leaving the band. ▤

1959

PATTI SMITH

COMPOSED BY **PATTI SMITH/TONY SHANAHAN**

IN 1969 CHICAGO-BORN PATTI SMITH WAS LIVING IN PARIS before moving to London and finally to New York. During the early 1970s she wrote for *Rock* and *Cream* magazines, worked as a guitarist and published her poetry. Her recording career, influenced by Dylan and The Rolling Stones, began in the mid Seventies, although she continues to issue her poetry as well as singles and albums.

"I was a twelve-year-old schoolgirl in 1959 and it was a very dramatic time in America," Smith recalls. "The cars had wings and were big and beautiful, there was optimism everywhere rising out of a complacent post-war conformity and a desire to be free and express oneself. I was seeing the rising of beatniks, and I remember hearing songs like 'Stagger Lee' and 'Kansas City'. People were going on the road, there was jazz music and books by Jack Kerouac.

"At the same time a whole world away in Tibet, the roof of the world, people were spinning prayers for nature, brotherhood, love and the Earth. It was such a contrast, they just tended to themselves. America had new and total freedom at the same time as theirs was taken from them by the invading Chinese. Their temples were burned and their

spiritual leader, the Dalai Lama had to disappear. As a twelve-year-old girl who was into Tibetan culture I was completely mystified as to how this was allowed to happen.

"My parents had told me about World War II, my father had fought in it and I thought that our parents had done it all, that the world would now be free and clean. To see people completely ignoring Tibet shocked and confused me. I still find it mystifying and heartbreaking, but I never realised that I would have the privilege to write a song about this and do some small thing to raise consciousness of the situation. I've since shaken the Dalai Lama's hand and in writing the song I hope to keep reminding people that every day, as we taste our freedom, there is still a little land on the roof of the world that is in captivity.

"'1959' is my little song about such a huge issue, written with Tony Shanahan and myself. I hope it makes you think, and makes you pray for the Tibetan people who spend most of their life praying for us."

Patti Smith retired in 1980, came back in 1988 and again re-emerged in 1996 with a new album.

NO ONE IS TO BLAME

HOWARD JONES

COMPOSED BY **HOWARD JONES**

'NO ONE IS TO BLAME' FIRST SAW THE light of day on Howard Jones' 1985 album *Dream Into Action*, alongside 'Life In One Day', 'Look Mama' and 'Elegy'. Produced by Rupert Hine, it was Jones' second album and it climbed to Number Two behind Phil Collins, while the single 'No One Is To Blame' was, ironically, produced by Phil, with Hugh Padgham. The track went to Number 16 in the UK and to Number 34 in the States in 1986.

Howard was born in Southampton, but moved with his parents to Canada, where he lived until returning to Britain to become based in Manchester. His run of success as a singer and songwriter began in 1983 when he scored with 'New Song', his early live performances featuring mime artist Jed Hoile.

In 1986 Howard Jones contributed his royalties from the song 'Little Bit Of Snow' to the anti-heroin project *Live-In World*, proving, as does the gift of lyrics by so many artists to the Hits Under The Hammer charity that, thankfully, altruism does have a place in the cut and thrust of the music business.

NUTBUSH CITY LIMITS

IKE & TINA TURNER

COMPOSED BY **TINA TURNER**

'NUTBUSH CITY LIMITS' WAS WRITTEN BY TINA TURNER (formerly Annie Mae Bullock) about the town in which she'd once lived. Produced by her husband Ike, at Bolic Sound, Inglewood, California in May 1973, it returned the duo to the charts after a seven-year absence. It brought them their third gold disc over a 13-year period, and resulted in them becoming the first American act to receive the Golden European Record award.

The track's lead guitarist was T Rex front man Marc Bolan, who'd met Ike and Tina in Los Angeles earlier in 1973, and with whom they said they'd like to record. Marc played on several songs for the duo, including 'Sexy Ida' and 'Baby, Get It On'. In 1982, the British group Geordie released a frenetic, driving, heavy metal version of 'Nutbush', but it failed to chart.

Lyrics signed by Tina Turner

"NUTBUSH CITY LIMITS"

WRITER: TINA TURNER

CHURCH HOUSE, GIN HOUSE
SCHOOL HOUSE, OUT HOUSE
HIGHWAY NUMBER 19
THE PEOPLE KEEP THE CITY CLEAN
THEY CALL IT NUTBUSH
OH NUTBUSH
THEY CALL IT NUTBUSH CITY LIMITS
NUTBUSH CITY LIMITS

25 WAS THE SPEED LIMIT
MOTORCYCLE NOT ALLOWED IN IT
YOU GO TO STORE ON FRIDAY
GO TO CHURCH ON SUNDAY
THEY CALL IT NUTBUSH
OL' NUTBUSH
YEAH, NUTBUSH
THEY CALL IT NUTBUSH CITY LIMITS

YOU GO TO FIELD ON WEEK DAYS
AND HAVE PICNIC ON LABOR DAY
YOU GO TO TOWN ON SATURDAYS
GO CHURCH EVERY SUNDAY
THEY CALL IT NUTBUSH
OL' NUTBUSH
THEY CALL IT NUTBUSH CITY LIMITS

NO WHISKEY FOR SALE
YOU GET DRUNK
NO BAIL
SALT PORK AND MOLASSES
IS ALL YOU GET IN JAIL
THEY CALL IT NUTBUSH
OH, NUTBUSH
THEY CALL IT NUTBUSH CITY LIMITS
NUTBUSH CITY LIMITS

LITTLE OL' TOWN
IN TENNESSEE
QUIET LITTLE OL' COMMUNITY
ONE HORSE TOWN
YOU GOTTA WATCH WHAT YOU'RE PUTTEN DOWN
OL' NUTBUSH, NUTBUSH CITY LIMITS

OCEAN DRIVE

THE LIGHTHOUSE FAMILY

COMPOSED BY
PAUL TUCKER

SONGWRITER PAUL TUCKER was studying in Newcastle when he persuaded fellow student Tunde Baiyewu to sing on the demo of a song he'd written, 'Ocean Drive'. This led to them signing for Polydor Records, re-recording 'Ocean Drive', and releasing it as a single as The Lighthouse Family. "We were soul, which is the family part, and I think a lighthouse is a friendly thing!" Tucker says, explaining the name.

In the spring of 1997 they had a small hit with 'Lifted', following it with 'Ocean Drive' which came to a halt in the lower reaches of the Top 40. The following year both songs were re-mixed with better results: 'Lifted' making it to Number Four and 'Ocean Drive' to Number Eleven. 'Ocean Drive' was used on a TV commercial for a breakfast cereal, and off the back of that featured on the album *Turn On Tune In*, a compilation of the very best of soul and jazz from the coolest TV commercials.

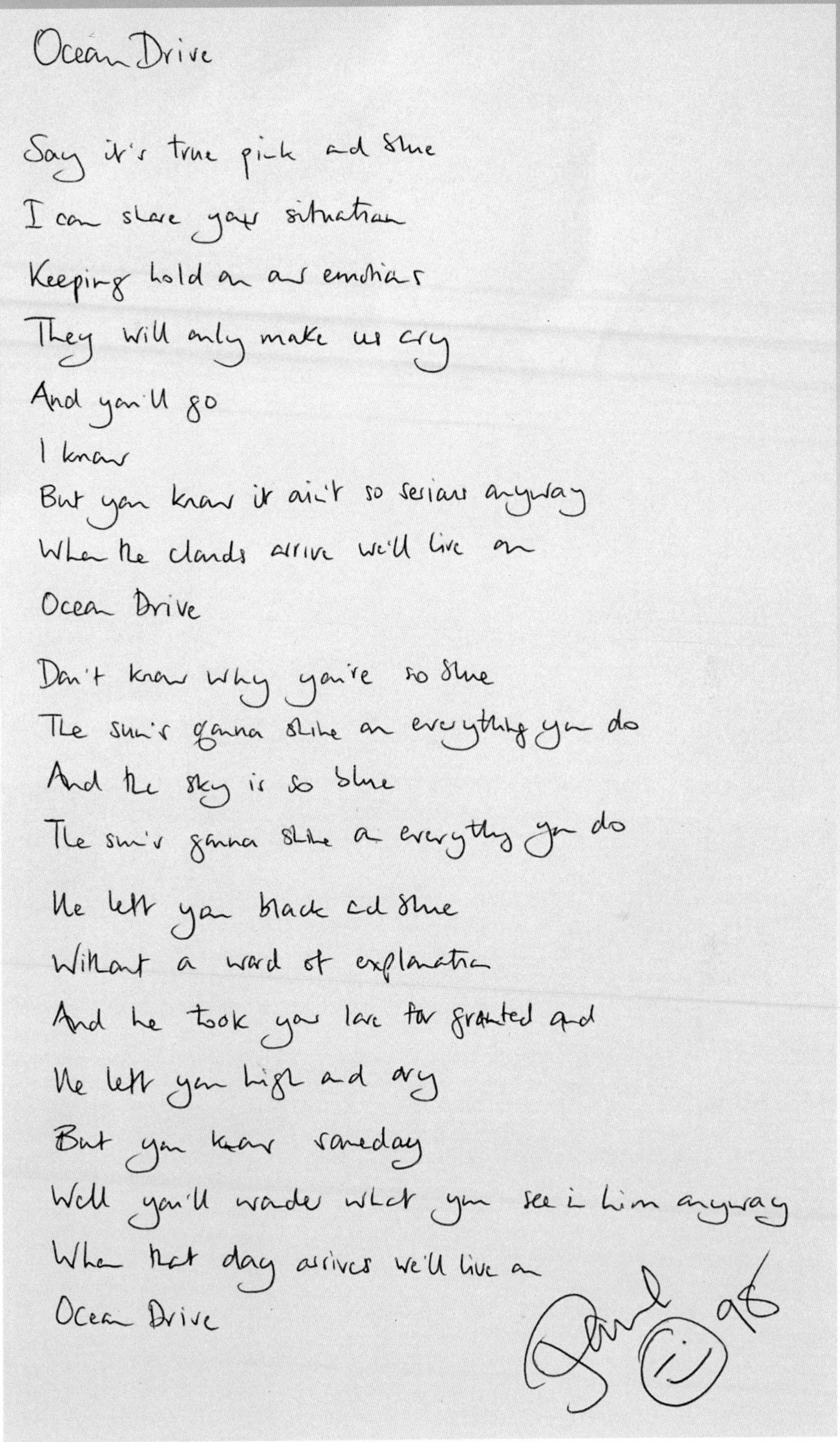

Ocean Drive

Say it's true pink and blue
I can share your situation
Keeping hold on our emotions
They will only make us cry
And you'll go
I know
But you know it ain't so serious anyway
When the clouds arrive we'll live on
Ocean Drive

Don't know why you're so blue
The sun's gonna shine on everything you do
And the sky is so blue
The sun's gonna shine on everything you do

He left you black and blue
Without a word of explanation
And he took your love for granted and
He left you high and dry
But you know someday
Well you'll wonder what you see in him anyway
When that day arrives we'll live on
Ocean Drive

Handwritten lyrics by Paul Tucker

Handwritten lyrics by Billy Steinberg

ONE AND ONE

A sky isn't always blue
A sun doesn't always shine
It's alright to fall apart sometimes

I am not always you
And you are not always mine
It's alright to fall apart sometimes

After all is said and done
One and one still is one
When we cry, when we laugh
I am half, you are half

A heart isn't always true
And I am not always fine
We all have an angry heart sometimes

After all is said and done
One and one still is one
When we cry, when we laugh
I am half, you are half
Look how far we have come
One and one still is ...

One moon, One star
I love the One we are
One thread, One line
That runs through our lives

Words and Music by Billy Steinberg, Rick Nowels and
Marie Claire D'Ubaldo

ONE AND ONE

ROBERT MILES FEATURING MARIA NAYLER

COMPOSED BY BILLY STEINBERG/RICK NOWELS/MARIE CLAIRE D'UBALDO

SWISS-BORN ROBERT MILES FIRST ENTERED THE CHARTS WITH 'Children', a Number Two hit inspired by the Yugoslavian conflict. In 1996 he was voted Best Newcomer at the Brit awards by which time he'd sold 13 million singles, many of them for 'One And One', a track written by the same team who wrote Celine Dion's 'Falling Into You'.

"The credit for this song should really go to Rick Nowels," says the song's co-writer, Billy Steinberg. "We'd been working together with Marie Claire d'Ubaldo and our first writing session was just about to end because she had to get back to London. We started messing around, working in that very short time as the session was winding down, and all we came up with was the line: 'After all is said and done, one and one still is one.' We put it down onto our Walkman, but really both myself and Marie Claire dismissed it, as we were all tired having done three songs already that day.

"When we got back together quite a long time later, Rick dragged out that cassette again and said he felt that there was a great chorus there. He'd been guarding it ever since our last meeting! When I think back now, the chances of us getting it right were very slim doing it that way because, for me, it's very hard to take a little chorus from so far in the past and then write verses and a bridge to it. I prefer to work all at once. Also, to get the right melody was very hard because the chorus was in a major. It would have sounded too 'saccharine' if we'd continued in that vein so we wrote the verse in a minor key, that gave it the uplift into the chorus.

"The middle eight came about the easiest and that to me is the most satisfying part of the song. I suggested we did it twice, like The Beatles tended to do with their strongest middle eights because I liked it so much. It was influenced by some of the Bernstein/Sondheim songs from *West Side Story* that Rick and I had been listening to. I think it just sort of seeped in there!

"We submitted it to Clive Davis at Arista – he's the best in the business, a great advocate of songwriters in general – and he plugged the song into the Robert Miles project, urging him to do it. It took several times to get right, as Clive had a vision and the first few attempts weren't what he wanted to hear. No expense or effort is spared to record something properly when he believes in it and finally his tenacity won over.

"I'm looking forward to hearing a cover of this, particularly because it has the capacity to be done in a different way from the Euro sound that Robert Miles had. The one regret I have for this and also 'Falling Into You' is that they've been more successful in England and Europe than the USA. I'd have liked to have heard it more on the radio in the States."

'One And One' reached Number Three in the UK in 1996. ▤

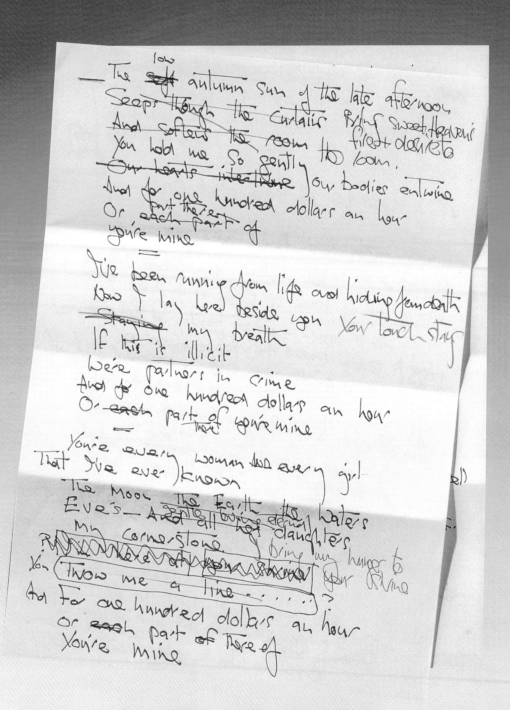

$100 AN HOUR

RICHARD O'BRIEN

COMPOSED BY **RICHARD O'BRIEN**

RECENTLY A TV PRESENTER IN THE UK, RICHARD O'BRIEN IS best known for writing the ultimate piece of audience participation theatre, *The Rocky Horror Picture Show*. Still showing in London's West End after 20 years, the movie of the show made household names of Tim Curry and Susan Sarandon and brought transvestism out of the closet. As '$100 An Hour' proves, O'Brien has lost none of his songwriting ability – or his sense of humour.

"I was doing a movie in Australia and I was on stand-by, which meant that I had lots of time on my hands," he says. "I'd done an album before I left but when my record company sent me a copy of the CD I was only happy with six out of the twelve tracks. So seeing

as I had all this spare time I decided to set myself a target and write a song a day.

"I did write and record them and this song was on there. The inspiration behind it was watching the autumn sun get lower in the sky, like a fireball. And then the words just came to me: 'The low autumn sun of late afternoon, brings sweet heaven's fire and desire to the room, you hold me so gently our hearts intertwine and for $100 an hour or part thereof you're mine...'

"It's about a man running from life, not necessarily about the sex act, more about being held and how tragic it is that he has to pay for it." ▤

COMPOSED BY **LEO SAYER/DAVID COURTNEY**

BETWEEN 1973 AND 1983 LEO SAYER HAD TOP
Ten records all over the world, two Number Ones, his own BBC TV series and even won a Grammy. Cited by Take That's Gary Barlow as "my reason for getting into showbusiness", Leo's celebrity has spanned generations, as proved by the range of audiences at his 1999 concerts. 'One Man Band' was a hit in 1974 but it had been around for a while...

"That song originally came to me when I was run over by a taxi cab in Ladbroke Grove around 1968," he says. "I was crossing the road in a dream heading to a pub called Finch's, and ended up about ten foot in the air when this taxi driver didn't see me. It was a late Saturday morning and hardly anyone else was around, no witnesses or anything, and I thought it was just my luck, another knock when I was trying to make my way in life. I was working as a commercial artist but every chance I could get I was sneaking away to make music. It was the days of all the folkies like Donovan, Bert Jansch and Davy Graham all playing on the street and I used to go and jam with them on harmonica when they were busking outside the pub.

Working lyrics by Leo Sayer

"I wasn't badly hurt, so I sat down on the kerb and started writing this song: 'Everybody knows down Ladbroke Grove, you've got to leap across the street, you could lose your life under a taxi cab, you've got to have eyes in your feet.' It wasn't until a few years later that I looked at my jottings and thought, 'Hang on, that's a song.' Then about 1971 or 1972 I eventually showed Dave Courtney the lyric and he said, 'Oh, that's interesting, what about this idea,' and he started playing one of his bits of music. Usually we'd both write things at different times and put the two things together, and we often ended up with something magical.

"I suppose 'One Man Band' first got known by being sung by Roger Daltrey. We had a bunch of songs ready for my first album, *Silverbird*, but we actually had more than we needed so I was stockpiling for my second album. We were down at Roger's home studio recording 'The Show Must Go On' and half a dozen other tracks when Roger came in and said, 'I really like your songs, I want to do a solo album, can you give me any tracks?' Dave and I looked at each other and thought, 'Well, we could give him "One Man Band" and "Giving It All Away" and some others.' We didn't actually think that those songs were going to fit with our project, so we decided to give him some from our next bunch.

"The original recording for my record was made in Los Angeles, but I actually didn't make the session because I was doing a gig somewhere else. Dave and my manager Adam Faith got the session together and I believe there were quite a few illustrious names on it like Ry Cooder and members of Tower Of Power, who were in the band at Warner Brothers studio in Burbank, and who were also working with Randy Newman at the time. However, Adam didn't think the track had the right feel, so he brought it back over to England to work on, but I think some of those original players might still be on it. Roger Daltrey also made his own version with Russ Ballard.

"It's become a bit of a classic to me because it sums up all the things that were going on through my life at the time. I thought I was the only person that had the answers to what was necessary to me and actually felt like a one man band, hence: 'Nobody knows nor understands, is there anybody out there gonna lend a hand (meaning the busking) to my one man band.'"

The song reached Number Six in the UK in 1974.

One Man Band.

(1) everybody knows down Ladbroke grove
you have to leap across the street
you can lose your life under a taxi cab
you gotta have eyes in your feet.

find a nice soft corner and you sit down
take out your guitar and play
then the ~~bastards~~ police come say move along
and so you move along all day...

(2) for three days now I haven't eaten at all
my my I must be getting thin
soon my cap will be large enough
to fit a head a crown in

[So hey there mister dont you look so sad dont look so ill at ease
I can play you any song you choose
to cheer up the life you lead.

Cho [Oh I'm a One Man Band
No body cares nor understands
and Is there anyone there wanna lend a hand
to my One Man Band.

M. [And OOh Oh Oh look at the rain falling
OOh look at the rain falling.....

(3) No One comes down here in the afternoon
the whole city falls asleep
Its enough to make all the buildings flee from the street
Rep - Solky the Nickelk;
No things rushing here but a post office
at the poor starving fool
who the bad way to London town and broke all the heart...

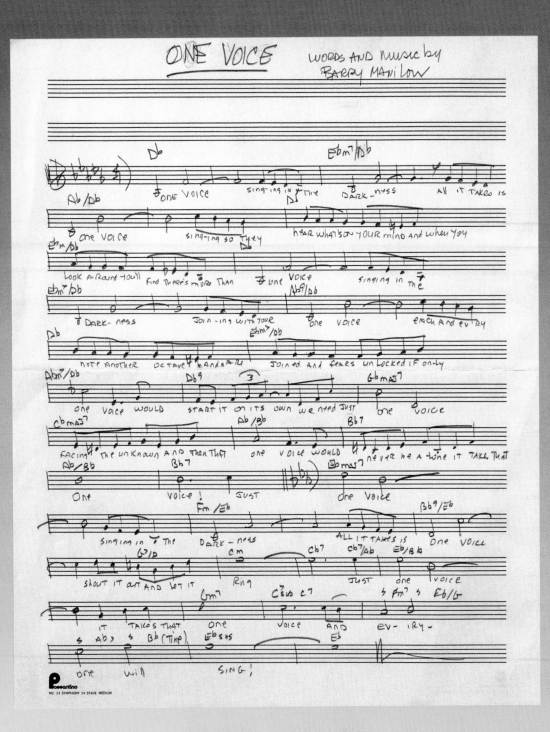

ONE VOICE

BARRY MANILOW

COMPOSED BY **BARRY MANILOW**

'ONE VOICE' HAS ALMOST BECOME BARRY MANILOW'S
signature tune. He invariably ends his show with it, often featuring a
local choir, and on television and variety shows it inevitably heralds
his departure from the stage. Produced by Barry and Ron Dante, the
original 1979 recording from the album of the same name featured
Manilow overtracking his voice 40 times.

He remembers dreaming the song, much as Paul McCartney had done
with 'Yesterday': "One morning I woke with an entire song running

through my head," he recalls. "It was completely written. I stumbled
to the piano, pressed the record button on my cassette player,
croaked my voice onto it, and then went back to bed. When I played
the cassette back later on it was all there and complete. I don't know
how this happened."

A live version of the song written in a dream also appeared on the
1982 album *Barry Live In Britain*, the same live version also appearing
on the 1993 album *Hidden Treasures*.

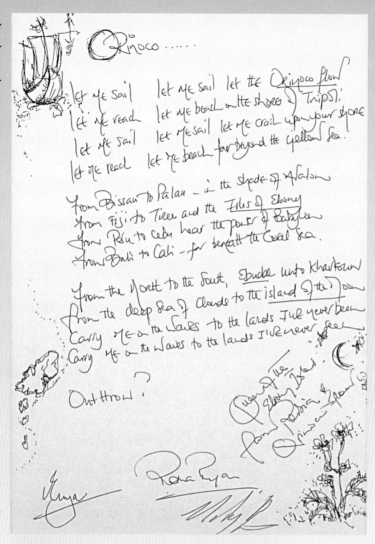

Handwritten lyrics by Enya

ORINOCO FLOW

ENYA

COMPOSED BY **ENYA/ROMA RYAN/NICK RYAN**

BORN EITHNE NI BHROANAIN IN 1961 IN GWEEDORE, DONEGAL, INTO A
musical family, Enya's father, Lee O'Bhroanain, led an Irish showband using the
anglicised name of Brennon. In 1976, his sons and daughter and an uncle formed
the group Clannad (Gaelic for 'family'), which Enya joined three years later. Under
the wing of manager Nicky Ryan, she left after a couple of years to pursue her
own musical path. Clannad went on to have a string of hits, following their 1982
Top Ten hit 'Theme From *Harry's Game*'.

Enya's first solo album, *Enya*, was released in 1987, and included music for a TV
series that later became *The Celts*. *Watermark* in 1988 became a gold album,
and yielded the Number One single 'Orinoco Flow'. As with her other songs, Enya
was responsible for the music, while Nicky Ryan's wife, Roma, wrote the lyrics.
The success of 'Orinoco Flow' led to Enya being nominated for Best International
Female Artist and Best Newcomer in the 1989 Brit awards. During the Nineties hit
singles and albums continued to flow, giving her ten hit singles in ten years, with
the sales of albums running into millions. ▨

OUR HOUSE

MADNESS

COMPOSED BY **CARL SMYTH/CHRIS FOREMAN**

THE ROOTS OF MADNESS BEGAN IN 1976
when three of their members – Chris Foreman,
Mike Barson and Lee Thompson – from Gospel
Oak School, Camden formed The North London
Invaders. Carl Smyth, known on stage as Chas
Smash, joined the following year with Graham
'Suggs' McPherson, Mark Bedford and Dan
Woodgate completing the line-up in 1978. The
hit singles began in 1979, the group charting 26
times in the UK. In 1983 'Our House' became the
group's most successful US single, reaching
Number Seven.

"We were in a rehearsal situation and I had this
idea for each band member to write something
about their different personal circumstances,"
co-writer Carl Smyth says. "Most of us had
separated or absentee parents, which meant that
we were sort of loners. That's the secret of the
band I think, which brought us all together.

"I thought it would be interesting to have a stab
at writing about family situations. Next thing I
remember is flying back from America and the
lyric started coming to me, which I began writing
on a napkin. I had no tune or anything, until one
day I walked into rehearsals and the band was
already playing what was to become the song.
Chris (Chrissy Boy) Foreman, my co-writer had
got the band all playing this tune, and I came in
and the verse which I'd written on the plane
seemed to fit really well. So that's how it was
born. Needless to say no one else in the band
bothered to write their own personal family story.

"The song did really well in the charts and was
nominated for an Ivor Novello award. Chris and I
were invited along to the dinner but we were
rehearsing for a tour and thought that there
wasn't much point in going as we didn't expect
to get anything. The band tended to avoid all
those glitzy gala events, preferring to keep a bit
more down to earth. However, the next day our
manager came down to the studio with two Ivors
statuettes for Best Pop Song Of 1992, so we
missed out on our moment of glory receiving
them. We were always surprised, and still are, at
the longevity and success of our songs, but it felt
great knowing we were being honoured by our
peers in the industry." ▨

PARKLIFE

BLUR

COMPOSED BY **DAMON ALBARN/GRAHAM COXON/ALEX JAMES/DAVID ROWNTREE**

Caption: Paul Carrack's handwritten lyrics on an x-ray of his own shoulder

Handwritten lyrics text:
Over My Shoulder
Lookin' back over my shoulder
I can see that look in your eye
I never dreamed it could be over
I never wanted to say goodbye.

Everybody told me you were leaving
Funny I should be the last to know
Baby please tell me that I'm dreaming
I just never want to let you go

I don't mind everybody laughin'
but it's enough to make a grown man cry
I can feel you slippin' through my fingers
I don't even know the reason why

Everyday it's a losing battle
Just to smile and hold my head up high
Could it be we belong together
baby won't you give me one more try

Paul Carrack

OVER MY SHOULDER

MIKE AND THE MECHANICS

COMPOSED BY **MIKE RUTHERFORD/PAUL CARRACK**

'OVER MY SHOULDER' REACHED NUMBER TWELVE IN BRITAIN IN THE SPRING of 1995, spending nine weeks on the chart, and giving Mike And The Mechanics their seventh UK hit. It was taken from their fourth album, *Beggar On A Beach Of Gold*, a Top Ten hit in Britain, featuring covers of songs by The Miracles and Stevie Wonder, with the title track having been written by BA Robertson.

Mike And The Mechanics were formed in 1985 by Genesis bass player Mike Rutherford, and comprised ex-Ace front man Paul Carrack (vocals/keyboards), former Sad Café singer Paul Young, top session drummer Peter Van Hooke, and ex-Toyah keyboards player Adrian Lee. Their first hit, 'Silent Running', came in 1986, but their finest hour in the singles chart came two years later, when 'The Living Years', written by Rutherford and Robertson went to Number One in Britain and America, giving them their second gold album. ▣

Formed in 1988 by Damon Albarn, Alex James, Dave Rowntree and Graham Coxon, Blur initially went out as 'Seymour', taking their name from JD Salinger's 1963 novel. The name 'Blur' came when they signed a record deal and they made their first appearance on *Top Of The Pops* in 1991 with 'There's No Other Way', which reached Number Eight in the UK.

Blur's 1994 album *Parklife* became the torch bearer for the 'BritPop' movement in the UK, a fact that annoyed the group but didn't harm sales, with two million copies sold. 'Parklife' the single, featuring *Quadrophenia* star Phil Daniels on vocals and in the video, was the epitome of the album's anglocentricity, as the band's designer, Rob O'Connor, explained to *Record Collector*: "Damon lifted the story of everyday British culture and set it in the locale he was living in, Notting Hill. He read *London Fields* which for him embodied that 'everyman' way of life, cruising around pubs and betting shops, playing darts, drinking beer, being a Jack the lad…"

'Parklife' reached Number Ten in the UK in 1994. ▣

Handwritten lyrics by Damon Albarn

Parklife

© 1993

Confidence is a preference for the habitual voyeur of what is known as ▓▓ and morning soup can be avoided by taking a route through what is known as / John's got brewers droop he gets intimidated by the dirty pigeons they love a bit of it ➤ You should cut down on your PORKLIFE MATE get some excercise

all the people so many people and they all go hand in hand through

MEANTIME

I got up when I want except on wednesday when I get rudely 👁👁 by the dustmen / I put my trousers on have a cup of tea and think about leaving the house / I feed the pigeons I sometimes feed the sparrows too it gives me AN ENORMOUSENSE (FRANK MUIR) OF WELL BEING

and then I'm happy for the rest of the day safe in the knowledge that there will always be a bit of my heart devoted to it

(long deliberation by Phil Daniels on how to say this)

damon XX

Oct 1998

PATIENCE OF ANGELS

EDDI READER

COMPOSED BY **BOO HEWERDINE**

FOLLOWING THE DEMISE OF FAIRGROUND
Attraction in 1989, Glasgow-born Eddi Reader embarked on a solo career. 'Patience Of Angels', written by singer/songwriter Boo Hewerdine, was her biggest hit.

"When I first heard the song it affected me because it explained the struggle of a woman on her own with kids," Eddi Reader says. "The emotion that it evoked was empathy because at the time there was an awful lot of attacks on single mothers, both socially and

politically. I felt it was a strong and supportive song and I wanted to communicate it to as many people as possible. I sang it for the first time at an Irish Centre and asked the audience what they thought. They loved it, and I haven't actually done a concert without performing it since then."

"I wrote 'Patience Of Angels' in 1990 for what was to be The Bible's doomed third album," Hewerdine explains. "My flat was just the right height for people on the top deck of buses to stare into my room ('From the top of a bus she thought she saw him wave...'). My baby daughter's cry had developed a keening quality that could make the hairs on the back of my neck bristle ('And the baby won't stop crying...'). What must it be like to be a lonely single mother?

"As soon as I had finished 'Patience' I knew I had done it. First I played it to my girlfriend, it made her cry (this was a good sign), then I played it to Neill the guitarist – he thought it was great (he played it to his girlfriend and it made her cry too). Unfortunately, the rest of

the band, the manager, the A&R man and anyone who didn't go out with me or Neill just thought it was 'all right'. The Bible never recorded it and within a year had split.

"When I came to record my first solo album I made a really good demo of the song – surely now they would see. The managers and A&R men did their stuff but it was shelved yet again. Eventually I stopped playing it at gigs because it reminded me of all the naff things that had happened over the previous couple of years.

"In 1993, Eddi Reader, Clive Gregson and I did a UK tour together. While we were rehearsing, Eddi brought up 'Patience Of Angels'. 'I don't do that one anymore,' I grunted. But by the third gig of the tour she had persuaded me and I remembered how much I liked it. Later that year Eddi went to California to record an album and she asked me about doing some of my songs. 'Patience' came out as a single, it was played loads on the radio and it was a hit. Only a little one, but still enough for me to think of all the people who had been iffy about the song in the past and go 'ha'."

PERFECT

COMPOSED BY **MARK NEVIN**

FAIRGROUND ATTRACTION

AFTER MARK NEVIN AND EDDI READER
began to collaborate as writers in 1985 they formed Fairground Attraction, bringing in Simon Edwards and Roy Dodds. In 1988 their single, 'Perfect', shot to Number One.

"The lyric had first occurred to me about ten years before in a dark and dank Cricklewood

bedsit," writer Mark Nevin explains. "I laid awake in the middle of the night while my 'imperfect' girlfriend of the time slept unaware of my treacherous musings. I wanted out and I wanted 'it' to be perfect. The song didn't really get written until a couple of years later when, in Akron, Ohio with yet another imperfect partner I declared that 'too many people take second best' and that I 'wouldn't take anything less', yes it had to be, 'Perfect'. I left my rejected girlfriend crying at the airport and took a flight back to London.

"Back home Eddi Reader and I used to play around in pubs. We did lots of miserable songs and were in desperate need of some light relief in the set. There was a kind of unwritten agreement between us that we disagreed with whatever the other one said at all times, and since I thought that 'Perfect' would be a good song to do in our set I played it to Eddi and said that I didn't think we should do it. She

promptly disagreed, and so we did it at the next gig.

"It was the first time that all four members of Fairground Attraction had played together. We hadn't rehearsed the song, we just busked it as the second encore. Eddi didn't know all the words so she just repeated the last verse over and over. It didn't matter. The response was phenomenal and the audience sang along with the chorus as though they'd always known it.

"Nine months later it was Number One. Our lives changed so quickly, everything was a panic. A year after that it was over – we'd sold 1.5 million albums, won all sorts of awards, travelled the world and couldn't speak to each other any more. That was over ten years ago. Eddi and I are friends again now, and musically I'm working on the successor to 'Perfect'. It's called 'Let's work together for an equal and mutually supportive relationship'..."

PIANO IN THE DARK

BRENDA RUSSELL

COMPOSED BY **BRENDA RUSSELL/JEFF HULL/SCOTT CUTLER**

'PIANO IN THE DARK' FROM BRENDA RUSSELL'S 1988 ALBUM
Get Here, gave her a Top 30 hit, the single peaking at Number 23 and staying on the chart for three months. She wrote the song with Jeff Hull and Scott Cutler, Hull playing synths and programming the drums for the recording, with Russell Ferrante and James Harrah playing guitar and Joe Esposito featuring as male vocalist.

As a writer, Brenda Russell has had songs covered by such artists as Earth Wind & Fire, Anne Murray, Chaka Khan and Rufus, Luther Vandross, Roberta Flack and Patrice Rushent.

The single 'Piano In The Dark' was recorded by Russell with Andre Fischer and Peter Ekberg at Atlantic Studios, Stockholm, Sweden and various studios in Los Angeles and Hollywood for Herb Alpert's A&M label.

Finished and working lyrics by Brenda Russell

PILGRIM

ERIC CLAPTON

COMPOSED BY **ERIC CLAPTON**

DURING 1963, CLAPTON, FORMER KINGSTON COLLEGE OF ART STUDENT
and budding guitarist, joined his first group, the locally based Roosters. He then
had a brief spell with Casey Jones And The Engineers, before joining The
Yardbirds late in 1963. Leaning more towards blues than pop, he enlisted in
John Mayall's Bluesbreakers in 1965, soon leaving to form Cream with Ginger
Baker and Jack Bruce. Following the demise of Cream after a glittering three-
year career, Eric became part of the short-lived supergroup Blind Faith, before
forming the equally short-lived Derek And The Dominos.

As well as guesting both live and on record with many rock luminaries, he
began to expand and grow as a solo artist, clocking up almost 30 solo hit
singles in Britain alone. Despite a run of personal problems, he has topped both
the US and UK charts, collected a pile of gold and platinum discs, won a whole
clutch of Grammys, countless other awards and in 1995 was awarded the OBE.
In 1998 he released *Pilgrim*, his first album for four years, contributing his
handwritten lyrics of the title track to Hits Under The Hammer. ▤

Handwritten lyrics by Eric Clapton

Pilgrim

How do I choose, and where do I draw the line
between truth and necessary pain
How do I know and where do I get my belief
that things will be all right again
What words do I use, to try and explain
to those who've witnessed all my tears.
What does it mean to know all these things
when love's been wasted all these years (rpt.)

(chorus)
standing in the shadows
with my heart right in my hand
removed from all the people
who could never understand
that I was a pilgrim for your love

Its like living in a nightmare
like looking in the blackest hole
like standing on the edge of nothing
completely out of control
where have I been all these years
and how come I couldn't see
like a blind man
walking round in darkness
I was a pilgrim for your love (rpt.)

(chorus)
standing in the shadows (etc.)

Please.

So you never knew love,
until you crossed
the line of grace
and you never felt wanted
until you'd someone
slap your face
and you never felt alive
until you'd almost wasted away.

you had to win
you couldn't just pass
the smartest ass
at the top of the class
your flying colours
your family tree
and all your lessons in history..

Please...Please...Please
get up off your knees
Please — Please — Please.
leave it out .....

PLEASE

U2

COMPOSED BY **BONO/THE EDGE/ADAM CLAYTON/LARRY MULLEN JR**

ORIGINALLY CALLED FEEDBACK, U2 dallied with Hype before settling for the name which would make them stars in 1978. The next year saw the Dublin band top the Irish charts, but it wouldn't be until 1980 that *Boy* saw U2 make their first impact in the UK and the US. During the next 18 years they chalked up almost 30 UK hits, storming the charts on both sides of the Atlantic and winning an array of Brits, Grammys and other awards.

After the group's radical reinvention of themselves with the *Achtung Baby* album, they've continued to make thought provoking music, occasionally about non 'pop' subjects. 'Please', from the album *Pop*, reached Number Seven in the UK in 1997 and was one such song, as Bono explains: "That song was written around the breakdown of the peace process in Northern Ireland," he says. "Melodically, it came out of jamming with Howie B who is a producer, writer and DJ, and who has an extraordinary take on what U2 are all about. Larry, our drummer, wasn't around so Howie would spin records and beats and grooves and I started singing over one beat. During a ten-minute period, I was singing the tune of what became 'Please'. It happened in one roll and had a few lyrical clues but at the time was just 'Bongalese', as we call it round here!

"We dug around a bit and with a bit of archaeology we found where the song was going. The peace process was breaking down in our country at the time, so the references to the dates 'September streets capsizing, shards of glass

Handwritten lyrics by Bono

splinters like rain' – that referred to the Docklands bombing. Although that was February, we were just referring to the different points when the ceasefire was breaking down. The song is a conversation with a Provos sympathiser and their lover. You get a tiny minority of these people in Ireland who like to dress up in the cause of 'revolution', the sort of people who do political signs at college and support the Provos and the armed struggle. Personally, they make me ill but you bump into them sometimes and this is the story of one. It's a lover's row with such a person. Edge had a lyrical idea along the lines of 'I never knew this, I never knew that' and I turned it round on him to 'you never knew this, you never knew that'. He also had a beautiful line, 'the heaven you keep, you stow'.

"In context it's an intensely personal song. About watching someone you've known over the years grow in a distorted way. Reaction-wise, Elvis Costello said it was his favourite tune of last year and I regard that as a huge compliment.

"We performed the song during the PopMart tour with the Irish flag moving behind us, and even though some people didn't pick up the context, I think they sensed the bile behind it. We played it at the MTV awards – which is the land of pure pop – and we weren't sure what to expect. But it was a nice song to drop in, and it went well. We have also donated it to be used on the Omagh charity album, Across The Bridge Of Hope, and we are more than pleased to contribute to Hits Under The Hammer."

and you never knew
how low you'd stoop
to make that call
and you never knew
what was on the ground
till they made you crawl
and you never knew
that the heaven you keep
you stole...

your catholic blues
your convent shoes
your stick on tattoos
now they're making the news
your holy war
your northern star
your sermon on the mount
from the boot of your car.
Please... Please... Please...
get up off your knees
Please... Please... Please...
leave me out of it...

'Jacket' lyrics handwritten by Martin Fry

POISON ARROW

ABC

COMPOSED BY **ABC**

ABC CAME INTO EXISTENCE IN SHEFFIELD AFTER MARTIN FRY interviewed local members of Vice Versa, Mark White and Stephen Singleton, for his fanzine. This resulted in Fry joining as singer and a name change to ABC. Success came early with their debut single, 'Tears Are Not Enough', breaching the Top 20 in 1981; a year later 'Poison Arrow' reached Number Six in the UK and 25 in the States.

"That song was a collaboration between the whole band," Fry says. "It's a tale of unrequited love and sold millions so there must be a lot of heartbroken people out there! It came out in 1982 and the title says it all. It's a bitter song, because when somebody dumps you, you hate them even though you want to love them. I think the appeal of the song is that a lot of people identified with that spirit, the emotion. That's the universal motive that makes songs popular. However, right up to recording there was nothing in the middle. We got bored of the sound of the sax solo in the middle eight and when we came to record it with Trevor Horn there was this big space in the middle of the record.

"Of course we had a deadline, so just five minutes before it was up, in desperation we got the receptionist at Sarm to do a little dialogue with me. On the record I say, 'I thought you loved me but it seems you didn't care,' and Karin Clayton said, 'I care – but I can never love you,' then we had a massive drum break – problem solved! It was also great working with Trevor. Actually *Lexicon Of Love* was the first album that he ever did, and was an integral part of that early Eighties scene of changing production standards.

"It was our first single and got to Number Six, which was a massive buzz for us especially because it was on our own label. People still sing the singalong bridge ('Who broke my heart – you did, you did') to me as I walk down the street even today. I've also got a great version in Cantonese by a guy in Hong Kong which is a great accolade. That and hearing it in the background on *Coronation Street*. I don't know if anyone else has covered it but I've heard it in a few working men's clubs up and down the country. Aargh, it's entered the world of cabaret!"

QUIT PLAYING GAMES (WITH MY HEART)

THE BACKSTREET BOYS

COMPOSED BY **MAX MARTIN/HERBIE CRICHLOW**

WHILE THE LIKES OF BOYZONE AND FIVE DOMINATE THE UK –
and increasingly the world – teen scene, their biggest rivals in recent
years have come from the USA: Kevin, Howie, Nick, Brian and AJ,
otherwise known as The Backstreet Boys.

Taking their name from the local 'Backstreet Market' in Orlando,
Florida, the Boys started out as a trio but were spotted by Lou
Pearlman who suggested they recruit a couple of other voices – enter
Kevin and his cousin Brian.

Written by Max Martin and Herbie Crichlow, their worldwide hit 'Quit
Playing Games (With My Heart)' appeared on either the album
Backstreet Boys or *Backstreet's Back*, depending on the territory.

Working lyrics by Max Martin

Raindrops Keep Fallin' on my Head

Lyric: Hal David   Music: Burt Bacharach

Raindrops keep fallin' on my head
And just like the guy whose feet are too big for his bed
Nothin' seems to fit
Those raindrops keep fallin' on my head
They keep fallin'
So I just did me some talkin' to the sun
And I said I didn't like the way he got things done
Sleepin' on the job
Those raindrops are fallin' on my head
They keep fallin'
But there's one thing I know
The blues they send to meet me won't defeat me
It won't be long 'till happiness steps up to greet me
Raindrops keep fallin' on my head
But that doesn't mean my eyes will soon be turning red
Cryin's not for me
I'm never gonna stop the rain by complainin'
Because I'm free -- nothin's worrying me

RAINDROPS KEEP FALLIN' ON MY HEAD

SACHA DISTEL

COMPOSED BY BURT BACHARACH/HAL DAVID

SACHA DISTEL, DESPITE HIS latter-day middle of the road image, was working as a professional jazz guitarist from the age of 16, making his debut single at the age of 23. A better guitarist than singer, his success in his native France was difficult to repeat in Britain, but during 1970 his version of Burt Bacharach and Hal David's 'Raindrops Keep Fallin' On My Head' charted four times, peaking at Number Ten.

"'Raindrops' was written for the film *Butch Cassidy And The Sundance Kid*," Hal David explains. "The music was written first by Burt Bacharach and I then added the lyric. The basis of the lyric came from the scene in which Butch (Paul Newman) was riding on a bicycle with Katherine Ross on the handlebars. They were riding around having a great old time and he was sort of whistling, the sun was shining and it looked like the world was his and everything was great, but underneath it all you knew that everything turned out wrong for Butch Cassidy.

"Looking for the hook in the lyric, I decided the way to write it was not to go with the way the scene looked, all bright and happy and fun, but write it more the way Butch Cassidy really felt underneath, and the way everything just went wrong for him, which was rather different – 'nothing's worrying me' it goes, but you know it is really.

"We thought the song had a hell of a shot and could be a big hit but we had no idea of the impact it would eventually have. We recorded it for the movie with BJ Thomas, and while we love to hear other people's interpretations, both Burt and I think that the original remains the definitive version."

On the back of the film, Thomas's version reached Number One in the US in 1969. ▣

RELAX

FRANKIE GOES TO HOLLYWOOD

COMPOSED BY PETER GILL/ HOLLY JOHNSON/MARK O'TOOLE

FORMED IN LIVERPOOL IN 1980, FRANKIE GOES TO Hollywood was the first act since Gerry And The Pacemakers to hit Number One in the UK with their first three releases ('Relax', 'Two Tribes' and 'The Power Of Love'). Produced by Trevor Horn, not only did Frankie dominate the charts between 1983 and '86, they also dominated the T-shirt market with their 'Frankie Says...' slogans.

"I was living in Liverpool in 1982 and I was late for rehearsals, which happened a lot because I never had the bus fare and had to walk," Holly Johnson says. "When I got to Princess Avenue the song suddenly just floated right into my head. I started singing it – it's a wide avenue with not many people around luckily – so I set up a sort of rhythm to walk to and get to rehearsals quicker. When I arrived, they were jamming around one chord and it seemed to fit what I'd had in my mind.

"We tried various middle eights and eventually opted for a simplified one, although there are several versions, like one we did on the John Peel session called 'Relax (In Heaven Everything Is Fine)' – that's the one with the complex middle eight – and then there was 'Relax' as everyone knows it. We did the earlier version on *The Tube* although at that stage we didn't even have a record deal.

"Then we got signed and the song got techno'd by our producer Trevor Horn, and caught up with the Fairlight stuff – it was the sound of the Eighties and made everything else sound a little old fashioned. It opened the world of sampling, and multiple remixes. It was groundbreaking in that it created the single remix as a whole new marketing tool.

"It got to Number Six in the charts before it got banned, or rather taken off the playlist for possibly dubious lyrics (!), but we'd already performed it on *Top Of The Pops*, which helped to push it up to Number One for a few weeks. For me, the song sums up my youth, all the energy. Actually, I don't see it as a classic song, more as a classic record and I can't imagine anyone else singing it convincingly. And of course it spawned all the 'Frankie Says...' T-shirts too, using the Kathryn Hamnett lettering."

Saddled by history as the man who 'banned' 'Relax', former Radio One DJ Mike Read says: "Without wishing to explode any myths, I wasn't actually responsible for banning 'Relax'. I didn't have the power to ban anything. I believe, as Holly points out in his autobiography, that my producer caught his two young daughters rewinding a potentially unsavoury part of the accompanying video. Always happy to take my punishment (however unjust) I was pilloried for it, but you can't re-write folklore." ▣

'T-shirt' lyrics by Holly Johnson

FRANKIE SAYS USE CONDOMS

RELAX DON'T DO IT
WHEN YOU WANT TO
SUCK IT. CHEW IT
RELAX DON'T DO IT
WHEN YOU WANT TO COME...

Holly Johnson

ST ELMO'S FIRE (MAN IN MOTION)

JOHN PARR

COMPOSED BY **DAVID FOSTER/JOHN PARR**

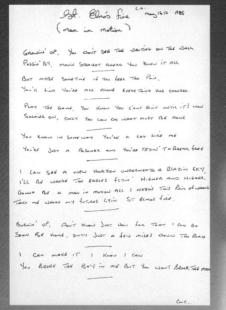

Handwritten lyrics by John Parr

'ST ELMO'S FIRE (MAN IN MOTION)' WAS the title song of the motion picture *St Elmo's Fire*, which starred, among others, Rob Lowe, Demi Moore and Andie MacDowell. David Foster was the musical supervisor for the film, and scored the music, including the title track which was written with Doncaster-born singer/songwriter John Parr.

"In 1985 I was on tour with Toto when I got a call from Doug Morris, the MD of Atlantic Records," Parr recalls. "He asked me to co-write a song for a movie with David Foster, who quite honestly I hadn't heard of. Toto, it turned out, had done a lot of work with him and I was soon boned up on him. At that time he was probably the world's top producer so I was very apprehensive about the whole situation. When we finally got together in the studio I found this guy who was completely shattered and exhausted. He'd got involved in doing the soundtrack for *St Elmo's Fire*, but was also doing the incidental music as well, which is unheard of. He had to produce twelve different tracks with twelve different people and score the film. He first played me something that I really didn't like, and I was then faced with the problem: should I go ahead and sing this awful song or stand my ground?

"So I suggested that we should try writing something together, take a couple of days and see what we could come up with. David felt he couldn't but I managed to persuade him to give it a blast. The third song we wrote was 'St Elmo's Fire'; we had the music and the top line, but we didn't have a lyric. I kept singing 'St Elmo's Fire' but David didn't want it, I guess being as he had lived with the film title for so long he was burnt out on it. I went away that night to try and write the lyrics, but I was really struggling.

"That day I'd also met the film's director, Joel Schumacher, and he had given me a synopsis of the film which turned me off completely. It was about yuppies, before the term was invented, and as I said to David, we had everything but I had nothing to hang it on. He said, 'This is nothing to do with the movie, but let me just show you this video of this paraplegic guy who came in the studio last week.' So I watched this amateur video of this young, good looking guy in a wheelchair, named Rick Hansen, who had broken his back in a car accident. He was about to set off around the world in his wheelchair, to raise public awareness about disability.

"On the video there was a scene of these kids running out to ice hockey player Wayne Gretski as he passed and this little lad thrusts his fist in the air – and boof, I got it straight away. I went back to my hotel room and wrote the lyric that night. It was about Rick Hansen, what it's like to break your back at 18 when you've everything to live for. I finished his story, he was going to be successful. This was two years before it actually happened, he had only just set off and he'd passed through Los Angeles three months into his journey.

"I didn't tell David that I had written the song about Rick as I figured that the lyric would suggest what was also going on in the film, this gang going around in a jeep. Nobody sussed it. The producers and director loved it and we got the go-ahead to record it. We laid the track down in 24 hours, using a Linn drum and David played bass. I can't remember who played guitar but Jerry Hay

came in with his team and put a whole arrangement down on the track. Then I did my vocals and that was it. Four months later it was released, and ended up at Number One in the USA, and helped the film gross $60m dollars there.

"The next thing was that the song was nominated for an Oscar and stood a good chance of winning. The only drawback was that if we went public on the real meaning of the lyrics it would knock the song out of the running as the rules state that the song has to be written about the movie. Rick Hansen was struggling at the time and wasn't getting any publicity, so he wasn't making any money for his cause. On top of that he'd torn his shoulder muscles. So we went public and everywhere I went I told people about Rick. My career had taken off on the back of the song and I was touring with Tina Turner so every night I was playing to 25,000 people and I would dedicate 'St Elmo's Fire' to him and tell his story. It took Rick two years to achieve his dream and I was there in Vancouver to welcome him back. David and I played in the stadium there, to 80,000 people. To this day people ask me what the song is about, as they get inspiration from it without knowing why. The song for me was a gift, almost as if I had no part in writing it. It was complete inspiration." ▪

MICK JAGGER
Five Church Row
Wandsworth Plain
London SW18 1ES
Tel: (0181) 877 3100
Fax: (0181) 877 3077

SAINT OF ME

1. Saint Paul the persecutor
was a cruel & sinful man
Jesus hit him with a blinding light
And then his life began
I said yeah

2. Augustin knew temptation, he loved
women, wine & song
& all the special pleasures of doing
something wrong
I said yeah.

2 MICK JAGGER
Five Church Row
Wandsworth Plain
London SW18 1ES
Tel: (0181) 877 3100
Fax: (0181) 877 3077

I said yeah, oh yeah, oh yeah
you'll never make a saint of me

3. And could you stand the torture
and could you stand the pain
Could you put your faith in Jesus
when you're burning in the flames
I said yeah

4. I do believe in miracles
And I wanna save my soul
I know that I'm a sinner
I'm going to die here in the cold
I said yeah

Handwritten lyrics by Mick Jagger

MICK JAGGER
Five Church Row
Wandsworth Plain
London SW18 1ES
Tel: (0181) 877 3100
Fax: (0181) 877 3077

I thought I heard an angel cry
I thought I saw a teardrop falling
from his eye.

5. John the Baptist was a martyr & he
stirred up Herod's hate
But Salome got her wish to
have him served up on a plate!
I said yeah.

I said yeah
oh yeah
oh yea
You'll never make a saint of me.

Mick Jagger 1998

SAINT OF ME

THE ROLLING STONES

COMPOSED BY **MICK JAGGER/KEITH RICHARDS**

DURING THE 1960S THE ROLLING STONES CLOCKED UP AN
amazing nine Number Ones in Britain charting 17 titles, while in
the States they had five Number Ones and charted 23 titles. The
Seventies saw a bit of a reversal, with eleven hits in Britain and 16
in the States, three of those topping the US chart. The hits
continued during the Eighties and Nineties, although their chart
positions in both countries were lower than in the previous two
decades. Album-wise, the Stones have had more Top Ten albums in
Britain and America than any other group in the history of popular
music. The world's most durable rock group have also had their
share of casualties, with the deaths of Brian Jones and Iain
Stewart ('The Sixth Stone') and the shock departure of bass player
Bill Wyman in the Nineties.

Although the group's writers and 'twin towers', Mick Jagger and
Keith Richards, occasionally undertake solo ventures, the Stones
continue to roll. 'Saint Of Me' was taken from The Rolling Stones'
1997 album *Bridges To Babylon* which went to Number Six in the
UK and Number Three in the States and gave their 1999 tour its
title. 'Saint Of Me' was a Top 30 hit in Britain early in 1998.

music: "SHE" Lyrics:
Aznavour. Herbert Kretzmer

She may be the face I can't forget
A trace of pleasure or regret
May be my treasure, or the price I have to pay
She may be the song that summer sings
May be the chill that autumn brings
May be a hundred different things
Within the measure of a day
She may be the beauty or the beast
May be the famine or the feast
May turn each day into a heaven or a hell
She may be the mirror of my dream
A smile reflected in a stream
She may not be what she may seem
Inside her shell...

She, who always seems so happy in a crowd
Whose eyes can be so private and so proud
No-one's allowed to see them when they cry
She may be the love that cannot hope to last
May come to me from shadows of the past
That I'll remember till the day I die
She may be the reason I survive
The why and wherefore I'm alive
The one I'll care for through the rough and ready years
Me, I'll take her laughter and her tears
And make them all my souvenirs
For where she goes I've got to be
The meaning of my life is she!

Handwritten lyrics by Herbert Kretzmer

"She"
Aznavour Herbert Kretzmer

She may be the face I can't forget
A trace of pleasure or regret
May be my treasure, or the price I have to pay
She may be the song that summer sings
May be the chill that autumn brings
May be a hundred different things
Within the measure of a day

She may be the beauty or the beast
May be the famine or the feast
May turn each day into a heaven or a hell
She may be the mirror of my dream
A smile reflected in a stream
She may not be what she may seem
Inside her shell...

She, who always seemed so happy in a crowd
Whose eyes can be so private and so proud
No-one's allowed to see them when they cry.
She may be the love that cannot hope to last
May come to me from shadows of the past
That I'll remember till the day I die

She may be the reason I survive
The why and wherefore I'm alive
The one I'll care for
Through the rough and ready years
Me, I'll take her laughter and her tears
And make them all my souvenirs
For where she goes I've got to be
The meaning of my life is she!

Music by Charles Aznavour. Lyrics by Herbert Kretzmer

SHE

CHARLES AZNAVOUR

COMPOSED BY **CHARLES AZNAVOUR/HERBERT KRETZMER**

CHARLES AZNAVOUR WAS born in Paris in 1924 and began writing and performing songs in 1950. He starred in many films but it is as a singer he is largely thought of. In 1974 he took 'She' to Number One in the UK, a song he co-wrote with Herbert Kretzmer.

"The story of 'She' is really the story of a series of TV plays called *The Seven Faces Of Woman*, produced by London Weekend Television in 1974," Kretzmer explains. "There was no link between the plays, which were written by seven different playwrights, but LWT needed something that would tie them together as a series. I was phoned by the producer, Richard Doubleday, who asked me if I would write a theme song that could act as a suitable link. It had to be about the mystery, the mystique and the agelessness of woman, and he initially wanted a song that could be sung by Marlene Dietrich. I didn't think much of that idea and said that if you were going to write a song about the mystery of woman, it shouldn't be a woman singing. I thought we should go for a voice that represented the romantic male, and I suggested Charles Aznavour, whom Richard then went to France to see.

"Aznavour agreed to do it, and inevitably LWT were in a great hurry and wanted everything to move straight ahead. Charles was going to Africa for some concerts and he said that he would do the song during his trip, and I should meet him the next Friday. Accordingly, I went to Paris and we returned to the Eddie Barclay Studio. Charles sat at the piano and played me his melody, and when I heard that long opening note, the word 'She' immediately jumped into my head, and I thought, 'That's perfect.' If you're going to sing a song about the mystery of woman, the word 'She' is a godsend. Every now and then a word falls out of God's lap into yours, and 'She' was just such a gift: the perfect word for that note. I didn't even know what I was going to call the song until I heard that long note.

"The song was dedicated to a very special lady in my life. I had spent a lot of time with her in the summer of 1973 and it was one of the more important romances of my years, between my two marriages in 1970 and 1988. She was English, a Geordie, and when we broke up I told her, 'There'll be a song in this, and I'll tell you when I write it.' Even though 'She' isn't all about her, some of the lyrics were specifically about this dear lady. I told her that it had been written for and about her before it was released, and when it became a Number One she was thrilled. That was the only song I've actually ever written with a specific person in mind. It also made me realise for the first time just how powerful television is.

"It has not been one of the songs that had a lot of cover versions, possibly because people find it difficult to sing. The difficulty lies in the middle eight, which is very deceptive. It's a far harder song to sing than it appears when Aznavour sings it, because he performs it with such ease, but when others have sung it, you can hear them struggling with the middle eight, and its half notes and semitones."

In 1999 Elvis Costello rose to the challenge and recorded 'She' as the main theme for the film *Notting Hill*. ▤

She's Not There

Well, no one told me about her
   The way she lied
Well, no one told me about her
   How many people cried

But it's too late to say you're sorry
How would I know – why should I care?
Please don't bother trying to find her –
   She's not there

Well, let me tell you 'bout the way she looked,
The way she acted, the colour of her hair
Her voice was soft & cool; her eyes were clear & bright
But she's not there
   —

Well, no one told me about her
What could I do
Well, no one told me about her
Though they all knew
   —

Rod Argent

Handwritten lyrics by
Rod Argent

SHE'S NOT THERE

THE ZOMBIES

COMPOSED BY **ROD ARGENT**

BEATLE GEORGE HARRISON giving the song the 'thumbs up' on *Juke Box Jury* was a good kick start to 'She's Not There' becoming a hit on both sides of the Atlantic. Written by Zombies group member Rod Argent and worked out in bassist Chris White's house in Markyate, it drew a little inspiration from John Lee Hooker's 'No One Told Me'. "If you play that John Lee Hooker song, you'll hear 'no one told me, it was just a feeling I had inside…'," Rod Argent explains. "But there's nothing in the melody or chords that's the same, it was just the way that little phrase tripped off the tongue. In the second section it goes from D to D minor, and the bass is on thirds, F# and F, a little device I'd first heard in 'Sealed With A Kiss', and it really attracted me."

The Zombies' frontman, Colin Blunstone, much admired by other singers for his 'breathy' vocals, has vivid recollections of recording 'She's Not There'. "When The Zombies first started recording, we were in Decca Studios in West Hampstead," he says. "It was our first time in a proper commercial studio, and unfortunately the engineer had had rather a long lunch hour! He was roaring, absolutely roaring, and very aggressive as well. I remember thinking, 'If this is professional recording, it's not for me.' Luckily, he collapsed about an hour into the session, and had to be carried out in a coma. The assistant engineer took over, and that was Gus Dudgeon, who went on to produce many of Elton John's big albums, as well as producing many other major artists. We did three tracks with him on that first session: 'She's Not There', 'You Make Me Feel Good', and the Gershwin classic, 'Summertime', and I think it was all in the can by midnight. 'She's Not There' went on to sell a million copies and went to Number One in *Cashbox* in the States."

Gus Dudgeon remembers that session: "I moved to the engineer's chair for the first time, and had a ball doing it. I just love what the band did, and they were a really nice bunch of guys. I used to look forward to their sessions more than anyone else I worked with."

SIT DOWN

JAMES

COMPOSED BY **TIM BOOTH/ LAWRENCE GOTT/JAMES GLENNIE/GAVAN WHELAN**

FORMED IN
Manchester in 1983, the core of the group comprising Tim Booth, Larry Gott and Jim Glennie, James made their recording debut a year later, on the local Factory label. Although they cut an EP called *Sit Down* in 1986 during their time on the Sire label, the song of that name didn't appear until three years later, when it was released as a single on Rough Trade. It was also available on twelve-inch vinyl – the first 500 with postcards! – and as a three-inch CD.

'Sit Down' didn't become a hit in 1989, but a re-recording in 1991 for Fontana, saw the song fly up the UK charts to Number Two. During the next seven years, James had another twelve hits, before returning a re-mixed version of 'Sit Down' to the Top Ten. ▤

'Chair' lyrics by Tim Booth

'Moon' lyrics by Tasmin Archer

SLEEPING SATELLITE

TASMIN ARCHER

COMPOSED BY **TASMIN ARCHER/JOHN BECK/JOHN HUGHES**

BRADFORD-BORN TASMIN ARCHER WORKED FOR SEVERAL YEARS WITH
John Hughes as The Archers before signing to EMI and releasing 'Sleeping Satellite'. The single went to Number One in the UK (32 in the States), displacing The Shamen's 'Ebeneezer Good'.

"Although this song wasn't released until September 1992, it was written in the early summer of 1989 around the time of the 20th anniversary of the first moon landing," Archer says. "It occurred to me at the time that in the 20 years since then, there had been very little progress in the field of space exploration. Although there had been a few 'spin-off' applications from technology developed for the moon missions, the whole space exploration thing had virtually ground to a halt without having achieved any real lasting benefit to the planet Earth or mankind.

"It seemed that there had been an almighty race to achieve this goal and once it was achieved we weren't in a position to take advantage of the achievement. It was as if there hadn't even been any plans in place to take the adventure any further and that the whole point to America was just to get there first and nothing else. Remarkable as it was at the time, the magnitude of the achievement seemed to have been diminished over the following 20 years because there had been no real continuation or further progress in the field. These thoughts became the basis for the lyric of the song." ▤

Stay
by Lisa Loeb

You say I only hear what I want to.
You say I talk so all the time - so ..

And I thought what I felt was simple
and I thought that I don't belong
and now that I am leaving,
now I know that I did something wrong
cause I missed you. yeah. I missed you.

You say I only hear what I want to.
I don't listen hard and I don't pay attention
to the distance that you're running or to anyone anywhere.
I don't understand if you really care
I'm only hearing negative. "No. no. no. bad."

So I turned the radio on, turned the radio up-
and this woman was singing my song-
Lover's in love and the other's run away
Lover is crying cause the other won't stay.

Some of us hover and we weep for the other,
who was dying since the day they were born-
Well, this is not that, I think that I'm throwing, but I'm thrown.

And I thought I'd live forever, but now I'm not so sure
You try to tell me that I'm clever, but that won't take me anyhow-
or anywhere with you

And you said that I was naive, and I thought that I was strong.
I thought. "Hey I can leave, I can leave."
But now I know that I was wrong cause I missed you-
Yeah- I missed you.

You say you caught me cause you want me, and one day you'll let me go.
You try to give away a keeper, or keep me cause you know you're just so
scared to lose.
And you say, "Stay."
You say. I only hear what I want to.

3-18-98

STOP THE CAVALRY

JONA LEWIE

COMPOSED BY **JONA LEWIE**

AS TERRY DACTYL, JOHN LEWIS HAD A
Number Two hit with 'Seaside Shuffle', but it was as Jona Lewie that he had his biggest successes, scoring with 'You'll Always Find Me In The Kitchen At Parties' and 'Stop The Cavalry' in 1980.

"Stop The Cavalry' was released in 1980, but it was actually conceived around four or five years before that," Lewie recalls. "I started tinkering around with the melody in 1976 and went back to it in 1977, and finally ended up with what seemed like a decent melody from beginning to end, and a decent arrangement. Then I had to start thinking about a lyric. The first idea I came up with was 'can you end the gallantry', then I changed 'gallantry' to 'cavalry', and that gave me the idea of the Crimean war and the stupidity of the Charge of the Light Brigade.

"I then started thinking about other war scenarios – hence there's a line which goes on about Mary Bradley still at home in the nuclear fallout zone, while I'm in the trenches in France. There's also a line that goes 'wish I was at home at Christmas', because all the generals and field marshals would be while the privates on the front were cold and hungry. I suppose it was that line that led to it becoming a Christmas number in the UK, although it was never intended to be.

"Things were going badly with Stiff Records. The powers that be weren't keen at all on 'Cavalry', and more or less said, 'It's an anti-war song, let's leave it out.' But I was very keen on the number so I went back to do an eight-track version. I fleshed it out, did all the backing tracks and musical bits on my Polymoog which had some good brass and trumpet sounds. I then took it back in again, and they said, 'Okay let's do something with it.' Bob Andrews and I went into the studio and co-produced it. I actually insisted that there should be a brass band on it – luckily by this time 'Kitchen' was out and was having some success, so Stiff agreed to fork out quite a lot of money for a real brass band. I also transferred some of what I'd played on my eight-track to the 24-track as we couldn't get the same feel.

"I went on holiday to Spain with my girlfriend for three weeks, but I was pondering whether to stay another week. So at the airport I decided to ring Stiff and they said, 'Come home straight away, it's gone in at Number 64 and we need you here to promote it!'

"So I went back and it did very well, rocketing from 64 to Twelve the next week, and then up to Number Three. It was selling 250,000 copies a week and stayed at Number Three for five weeks into the New Year, for two reasons: firstly EMI were pulling all the stops out to make St Winifred's School Choir Number One; and then of course John Lennon was killed and his records took over the Number One and Two spots. Actually St Winifred's dropped to Number Four while 'Cavalry' stayed at Three, which I was quite pleased about." ▤

STAY (I MISSED YOU)

LISA LOEB

COMPOSED BY **LISA LOEB**

LISA LOEB'S BIG BREAK
came in 1994 when her song 'Stay (I Missed You)' was used as the theme to the film *Reality Bites*, a comedy about young, post-graduation love set in the 1990s.

Reality Bites, produced by Danny DeVito and Michael Shamberg, starred Ben Stiller, Winona Ryder and Ethan Hawke amongst others, with Karl Wallinger being responsible for the score. The inclusion of 'Stay' in the Stiller-directed movie gave it a wide audience, resulting in an American Number One and a Top Ten record in Britain, where it stayed on the chart for 15 weeks. Following her big hit, Lisa Loeb was signed in the States by Geffen Records, and she set about making her debut album with her group Nine Stories and producer Juan Patino, for which she was able to draw on songs she'd written over the previous ten years. ▤

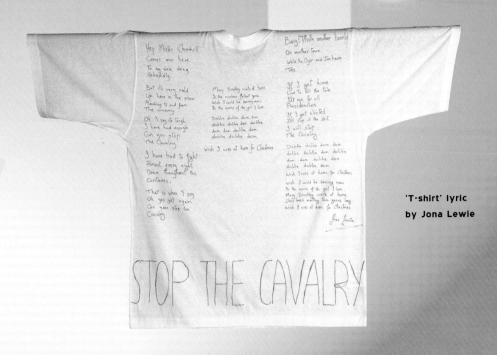

'T-shirt' lyric
by Jona Lewie

SUMMER HOLIDAY

CLIFF RICHARD

COMPOSED BY
BRUCE WELCH/BRIAN BENNETT

THERE HAD BEEN AN EARLIER FILM of the same name back in 1948, but Cliff Richard, then an eight-year Harry Webb, was to make the definitive *Summer Holiday*. Released in 1962 it was directed by Pete Yates and starred Cliff and Laurie Peters along with Melvyn Hayes, Una Stubbs, Ron Moody and The Shadows. As Sir Cliff comments, "There was a real buzz around the studio while we were making the film. Everyone knew that it was going to be very special." It needed a title song, though – step forward Brian Bennett and Bruce Welch.

"'Summer Holiday' was written by Brian Bennett and myself in the pit of the Globe Theatre, Stockton-on-Tees in the depths of winter of January 1962," Welch recalls. "The Shadows were starring in pantomime and I'd get in at 8.30 am to tune my guitar in time for the 2.30 pm performance! Brian was there early too, he was taking a postal music course and used this time to learn arranging. By then *The Young Ones* had been out and was a smash, and the next idea was that a team named Myers and Cass, who'd written the production numbers for *The Young Ones*, intended to write all the songs for the second film. However, Cliff didn't want that, so The Shadows were going to write some pop songs for it.

"The brief came through, and the song was to be about four guys hiring a bus and taking it on a summer holiday. Once the brief had arrived, I just picked my guitar up and went, 'We're all going on a summer holiday, no more working for a week or two, fun and laughter on our summer holiday...' and Brian liked it. He wrote the middle eight immediately, then I came back with the last verses and it was all done in half an hour before curtain up! We taped it on Brian's Starlight plastic tape recorder before the afternoon matinee.

"Cliff liked it and Hank put on the famous guitar intro and it became Number One! The actual film *Summer Holiday* was good to us, because we had three million sellers from it, 'Summer Holiday', 'Bachelor Boy' and 'Foot Tapper' which Hank and I wrote."

Recorded on 5 May 1962 between 7.00 and 10.45pm at Abbey Road studios the single went to Number One around the world. By February 1963 Cliff had become the first artist to get four songs from the same film into the chart at the same time: 'Summer Holiday', 'Bachelor Boy', 'The Next Time' and 'Dancing Shoes'.

Handwritten lyrics by Bruce Welch, signed by Welch, Sir Cliff and Bennett

SWEET DREAMS (ARE MADE OF THIS)

EURYTHMICS

COMPOSED BY **ANNIE LENNOX/DAVE STEWART**

ABERDONIAN, ANNIE LENNOX AND DAVE STEWART FROM Sunderland met while Dave was a member of the group Longdancer and Annie was at the Royal College of Music. They played together in The Tourists before forming The Eurythmics from the ashes of their former outfit. After a couple of minor hits, 'Sweet Dreams (Are Made Of This)' shot up the chart on both sides of the Atlantic, reaching Number One in the US and Number Two in the UK. They never looked back, having a string of successful singles and albums throughout the Eighties and into the Nineties, with Annie also having many hits under her own name. She also made her film debut alongside Al Pacino and Donald Sutherland in *Revolution*, while Stewart produced for such acclaimed artists as Mick Jagger, Bob Dylan, Tom Petty, Daryl Hall and Bob Geldof, amongst others.

A remix of 'Sweet Dreams' just scraped into the chart in 1991 while in 1997 it was successfully, and bizarrely, covered by heavy metal outfit Marilyn Manson.

Handwritten lyrics by Annie Lennox

Sweet dreams are
made of this —
Who am I to disagree?
I travel the world
and Seven Seas,
Everybody's looking for
something ....
Some of them want
to use you
Some of them want to get
used by you
Some of them want to
abuse you
Some of them want to
be abused ....
(Hold your head up —
Keep your head up ....)

Annie Lennox. 5th March '96.

the sweetest thing ♡ Bono age 26

my love she throws me like a rubber ball
oh oh the sweetest thing
but she wont catch me or break my fall
oh oh the sweetest thing.
Babys got blue skies up ahead
but in this I'm a rain cloud...
she wants a dry kind o love
I'm losing you.
I'm losing you.
aint love the sweetest thing.

oh oh the sweetest thing
with a tongue of fire she turns me to straw
oh oh the sweetest thing
now I got black eyes but they burn
so brightly for her.
I guess its a blind kind of love—
I'm losing you
I'm losing you.
aint love the sweetest thing
aint love the sweetest thing (dont give up on new)

blue eyed boy meets a brown eyed girl ♡
oh oh the sweetest thing
you can sow it up, but you can still see the tear
oh oh the sweetest thing.
Babys got blue skies up ahead
and in this I'm a rain cloud...
I guess we got a stormy kind o love

Do Do Do Do Do Do Do the funky gibbon.....

SWEETEST THING

U2

COMPOSED BY **BONO/THE EDGE/ADAM CLAYTON/LARRY MULLEN JR**

DURING THE 1990S U2 CHALKED UP TEN UK TOP TEN hits, the decade having begun with the *Rolling Stone* magazine readers' poll putting Bono as Best Songwriter and Sexiest Male Rock Artist and Adam Clayton as Best Bassist. In the same year, 1990, drummer Larry Mullen wrote the official Eire World Cup song for their football team, and The Edge wrote the theme to the Royal Shakespeare Company's production of *A Clockwork Orange 2004*. The Nineties saw them have two UK Number Ones with 'Discotheque' and 'The Fly'.

1998 brought a compilation of hits of the Eighties twinned with single B-sides. To mark the event the former B-side 'Sweetest Thing' was remixed as an A-side, reaching Number Three in its own right. Bono recalls its origins:

"We were working on it in a house on the outskirts of Dublin called Danesmoat in 1986," he says, "and as well as recording we had a studio up there to paint in; it was like a little commune. Sometimes we would forget to go home, working until the early hours. It was my missus Ali's birthday at the time which I'd actually forgotten about, so I thought whilst I'm here I can paint her picture and write her a song as I didn't have time to get a gift. It was supposed to be a really sweet song but it turned out a bit bitter. So anyway I gave it to her and she said, 'It's not really that sweet is it, but I'll take it,' and fuck me, she did!

"We recorded it as a very obscure B-side from the *Joshua Tree* album, but lots of people wanted to record it. Carole King's daughter Louise Goffin wanted to do a version, and so did Boyzone, which is why they're in the video, as is my missus. When it came to be released in 1998, Ali said, 'I own that.' I said, 'What do you mean?' and she replied, 'Well, remember you gave that song to me.' I said, 'What are you getting at?' She said, 'Publishing, actually!' So she then wrote off to Edge and Adam and Larry, and they all had to agree because she was giving the publishing rights to this Russian charity project she's involved with. She drives with a convoy of aid workers from Dublin to Chernobyl every year, ambulances and trucks full of goodies for orphanages and children's homes, so it's all in a good cause, like the Hits Under The Hammer charity auction.

"I think people like U2 as a pop group sometimes, as if they're saying, 'Get on, do your job, be pop stars and get in the pop charts!' Actually it's a nice feeling, it's a clear melody, there's nothing cloudy about it. It's great for us, we were just giggling away. We probably spent just two days on it, all in all. The first day was when it was written and demo'd and put out as a B-side, and the second time round when we brought in producer Steve Lillywhite to fix it up. It turned out a great gift to us, although it might not have been the gift my missus was after." ▤

Handwritten lyrics by Bono

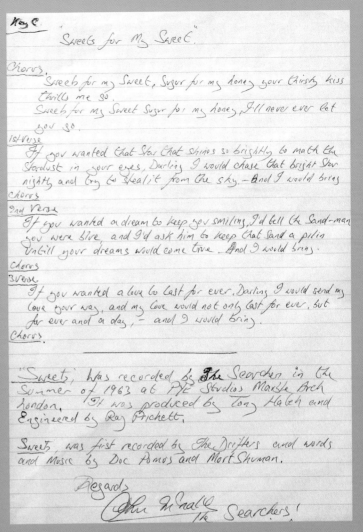

Handwritten lyrics by John McNally

SWEETS FOR MY SWEET

THE SEARCHERS

COMPOSED BY **DOC POMUS/MORT SHUMAN**

'SWEETS FOR MY SWEET', THE FIRST OF THREE NUMBER ONES for The Searchers, was originally a Top Ten hit in America for The Drifters in 1961, and was written by Doc Pomus and Mort Shuman. Pomus and Shuman were prolific songwriters, their litany of classics including 'Save The Last Dance For Me', 'His Latest Flame', 'She's Not You', 'Suspicion', 'Little Sister', 'Spanish Lace', 'I Count The Tears', 'Viva Las Vegas' and, of course, 'Sweets For My Sweet'.

Founder member of The Searchers, John McNally, recalls the speed with which their version was laid down: "It was recorded on the way to our second visit to The Star Club, Hamburg. In fact we got a train from Liverpool Lime Street down to London, Euston, got all our gear round to Pye Studios at Marble Arch and recorded it at the request of Tony Hatch. The gear that we had to record 'Sweets' on, was a home-made bass amplifier and a home-made valve amplifier…and we recorded it all round two mikes, one for the lead vocal and the other for the harmonies. About three takes and it was done, we packed the gear up and caught the boat train to Hamburg." ▤

Thank U

how bout getting off of these antibiotics
how bout stopping eating when I'm full up
how bout them transparent dangling carrots
how bout that ever elusive kudo
thank you india
thank you terror
thank you disillusionment
thank you frailty
thank you consequence
thank you thank you silence

how bout me not blaming you for everything
how bout me enjoying the moment for once
how bout how good it feels to finally forgive you
how bout grieving it all one at a time
thank you india....
the moment I let go of it was the moment I got more.
than I could handle the moment I jumped off of it
 was the moment I touched down.
how bout no longer being masochistic
how bout remembering your divinity
how bout unabashedly bawling your eyes out
how bout not equating death with stopping
thank you india
thank you providence
thank you disillusionment
thank you nothingness
thank you clarity
thank you thank you silence

Alanis Morissette

THANK U

ALANIS MORISSETTE

COMPOSED BY **ALANIS MORISSETTE/GLEN BALLARD**

BORN IN OTTAWA, CANADA ALANIS MOVED TO GERMANY WITH her family at the age of three, her father having taken a job with NATO. She returned to Canada three years later, landing a part on the children's TV comedy show *You Can't Do That On Television*. Her first single release, albeit on her own label, showed the determination of the 13-year-old whose sights were set on a career in music. Although 'Fate Stay With Me', which she co-wrote, didn't chart, it eventually led to her being signed by MCA Records, and releasing the album *Alanis* in Canada. It sold well, and she was voted Canada's Most Promising Female Artist.

After searching for a musical direction for a year or two, she ended up in a songwriting collaboration with Glen Ballard, signing with Madonna's label, Maverick, and releasing the album *Jagged Little Pill* in 1995. It sold over 20 million copies worldwide and went to Number One in the States. During 1996 she won five Grammy awards, and in Canada, five Juno awards.

'Thank U', from the album *Supposed Former Infatuation Junkie*, was a Top Five hit for Alanis in the UK in the autumn of 1998.

Handwritten lyrics by Alanis Morissette

THANK YOU FOR BEING A FRIEND

ANDREW GOLD

COMPOSED BY **ANDREW GOLD**

ANDREW GOLD CAME FROM GOOD musical stock, his father having won an Oscar and a Song Of The Year award for the theme of *Exodus* and his mother providing the singing voices for the characters played by Audrey Hepburn and Natalie Wood in *My Fair Lady* and *West Side Story*. Gold played with various Los Angeles groups and backed Linda Ronstadt for some time. His solo career took off in 1977 when 'Lonely Boy' went to Number Eleven in the UK and Number Seven in the States. 'Thank You For Being A Friend', while a hit in its own right in 1978 on both sides of the Atlantic, became a household favourite when it was used as the theme to an American comedy show...

"*The Golden Girls* used it and I was thrilled, especially when it became the Number One show," Gold says. "This was my most financially successful release, a sort of 'one size fits all' type of song. Everybody's got a friend that they can think of that it applies to, and it seems to fit all middle-of-the-road commercials too. Every couple of weeks I get enquiries from people wanting to use it for dog food commercials or whatever! That's what I like about this business, you can write a thousand songs and earn nothing, and then one song earns you ridiculous amounts of money.

"When I write I'm much better if I let fly and not try to plan too much," he says. "I sort it all out afterwards and that's the secret to my most successful songs. If I struggle it usually means there's basic flaws. 'Thank You For Being A Friend' was the fastest song I ever wrote, it was done in two bits and both of them took around 20 minutes, words and music.

"It began because I was waiting for a couple of friends who were coming over to pick me up and take me to the airport. I began writing the song because I really liked them, I was grateful for the favour they were doing me. We used to hang out and take the odd illegal substance together and called them 'cadillacs' – born from the film where Steve Martin sang, 'It's impossible – to put a cadillac up your nose, it's just impossible.' We thought that was hilarious and so the most irresponsible line in the song, 'If it's a car you lack, I'll surely buy you a cadillac,' was penned with them in mind!

"I prefer to write on piano although I play guitar and drums too, but the piano is a little

Handwritten lyrics by Andrew Gold

more complete for me. I was never afraid to be twee in my writing, I was more concerned in writing stuff that I liked. My parents are writers and musicians so I think that's why my songs are well structured despite not reading music myself. I have a good ear and can pick things out so I enjoy doing most of the stuff myself in the studio – perhaps that's why some of it is a little idiosyncratic."

Gold later formed Wax with 10cc's Graham Gouldman having two hits during 1986-7 including the Top 20 'Bridge To Your Heart'.

THE BARTENDER AND THE THIEF

THE STEREOPHONICS

COMPOSED BY **KELLY JONES/RICHARD JONES/RICHARD CABLE**

'Glass' lyrics by Kelly Jones

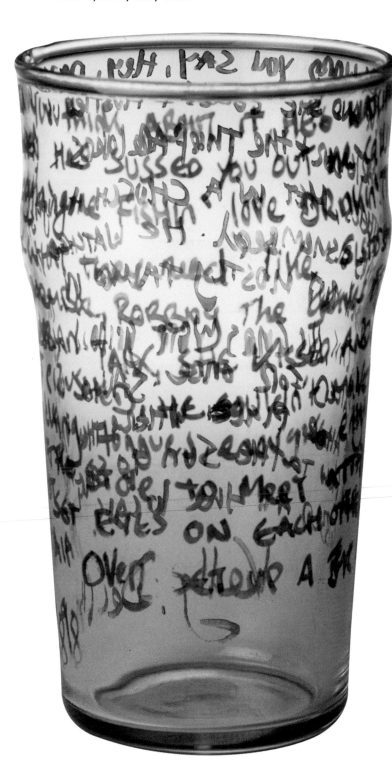

THE STEREOPHONICS, FROM ABERDARE, MID

Glamorgan in Wales, first charted in 1997, notching up four hits that year, including the brilliant 'A Thousand Trees' and the Top 20 hit 'Traffic'. During 1998 their re-released 'Local Boy In The Photograph' became a hit for the second time, peaking at Number 14. Their album *Word Gets Around* went silver in the UK and they were voted Best Newcomer at the Brit awards.

Written by all three band members – Kelly Jones (vocals/guitar), Richard Cable (drums) and Richard Jones (bass) – 'The Bartender And The Thief' reached Number Three in the UK in November 1998.

"The title comes from an idea I had when I was in a small bar in New Zealand at the end of our Australasian tour," Kelly Jones recalls. "It was full of sailors and all these surreal things were going on, so that's where the idea came from, just all the things that a bartender gets to see. About five months later I started writing for our next album, and wanted something with a long title like 'The Cook, The Thief, The Wife And His Lover' or 'Frankie And Johnny Were Lovers', and that's when the idea came up again.

"It's basically about this bartender working in a really seedy bar. He looks around the room and finds out who the drunkest guy is and the most gullible, and he calls out to his missus and she comes in and flirts with him and then they pickpocket him and split the takings. But by the end of the song he gets a guilty conscience and decides they can't rob all these people, and she's a head-case, she'll go out with lesbians and do anything to get a bit of money and they decide that they're going to fly off to a hot country and do a Ronnie Biggs and leave it all behind. But of course the last line is they get there, they set up a bar and rob all the locals, and it just goes on and on really.

"I've never done like a purely fictional kind of thing before, but that's the closest I've got. It's more of a Quentin Tarantino film than a song. We needed a fast track for the album as everything was quite mid-tempo, so I just tuned the guitar down and did some riffs which we don't usually do; it was one of those happy accidents I think. And then everybody decided that it was going to be the single. I found the melody on an old dictaphone tape which I always put ideas down on, and which I realised that I hadn't listened to, so it came from a while ago probably."

The song's success as a single caught the band by surprise. "We made it to Number Three which was a real shock," Jones admits, "what with all the references to lesbians and other stuff and considering that everything else in the charts was really pop at the time. It was probably to our advantage as there were no rock records on the radio and it did really well."

Handwritten lyrics by Geoff Stephens

THE CRYING GAME

BOY GEORGE

COMPOSED BY **GEOFF STEPHENS**

A RADIO FAVOURITE FOR 35 YEARS, 'THE CRYING GAME' WAS A Number Five hit in Britain in 1964 for Sheffield's Dave Berry, who took his stage name from rock 'n' roller Chuck Berry. The song was written by prolific songwriter Geoff Stephens. "I wrote 'The Crying Game' around the end of 1963," he recalls. "In those days, as with most of my peers, the accent for writing songs nearly always revolved around getting a good title. I just don't know how this title arose, except that it was during a concentrated writing session when my mind was fully engaged in coming up with something special title-wise. Of course, there was the lovely 'September Song' which carried the line referring to "the waiting game", so perhaps subconsciously I may have got some inspiration from there.

"Having demo'd the song, it didn't grab any record companies' immediate interest but we all felt that it was going to happen sometime. Eventually, Mike Smith who was then the A&R man at Decca Records, said to me one day in the pub at the end of Denmark Street that his wife kept telling him that he should cut it, so he produced it with Dave Berry. This recording featured the inimitable sound of Big Jim Sullivan, using the revolutionary 'wah-wah' guitar sound."

Dave Berry wasn't initially sure that the song was suitable for him, having a preference for R&B music. "I had the acetate from Geoff Stephens," he says. "He gave me 'The Crying Game' at the *Ready Steady Go* studios, but I didn't really think it was me. About 18 months went by and my guitarist, Alan, kept harping back to it, so I called Mike Smith at Decca and we arranged to record it, with those marvellous guitar parts from Big Jim Sullivan and Jimmy Page. They didn't have any problems switching their musical style, so that was a good influence on me."

Interest in the title of the song brought a surprise communique for Geoff Stephens. "Shortly after it became a hit in the UK, I received a nice letter from the novelist, John Braine, who'd had great success with his novel *Room At The Top*," he says. "He wanted to use 'The Crying Game' as the title of the book he was then working on, and I was very naturally happy to agree. The opening verse was printed on the flyleaf." The song has been recorded by many other artists including Peters And Lee, Freddie Starr and Barbara Dickson. Boy George had a hit with it in 1992, produced by The Pet Shop Boys, when it was featured in the Neil Jordan Oscar-winning movie which used 'The Crying Game' as its title. ▤

The Downtown Lights

sometimes I walk away, when all I really want to do
is love and hold you right, there is just one thing i can say. —
nobody loves you this way
it's alright,
can't you see
the downtown lights

mi love were all the same
we're walking down an empty street
and with nobody call your name
empty streets
empty nights,
the downtown lights

how do i know you feel it ?
how do i know it's true ?

tonight and every night,
let's go walking down this empty street
let's walk in the cool evening light
wrong or right, be at my side. —
The downtown lights.
it will be alright
it will be alright,
the downtown lights

how do i know you feel it ?
how do i know its true ?

it's alright,
it's alright,
the downtown lights.

the neons and the cigarettes, the rented rooms, the
                                                rented cars,
The crowded streets, the empty bars.
the chimney-tops, the trumpets, the golden lights,
                                    the loving prayers
the coloured shoes, the empty trains
              instead of crying on the stairs
                          the downtown lights.

Paul Buchanan.

THE DOWNTOWN LIGHTS

THE BLUE NILE

COMPOSED BY **PAUL BUCHANAN/ROBERT BELL/PAUL MOORE**

FORMED IN 1981 BY PAUL Buchanan, The Blue Nile were a Scots trio comprising Buchanan, Robert Bell and Paul Joseph Moore. Their debut single was 'I Love This Life', but a more permanent record label situation arose when hi-fi specialists Linn used the group's demos for testing their equipment. This led to Linn forming their own label, and releasing The Blue Nile's first album, *Walk Across The Rooftops*, in 1984, and their first single for the company, 'Stay'. The second single, the wonderfully atmospheric 'Tinseltown In The Rain', didn't chart in Britain despite healthy airplay, although it became a massive hit in Holland.

The record company's publicity blurb with the re-released 'Stay' in the autumn of 1984 proclaimed that The Blue Nile were "hard at work on the second album". In reality, their second album, *Hats*, was five years in coming.

'Downtown Lights' from that album gave them their first of three small hits when it went to Number 67 in the UK chart in September 1989. Their third album, *Peace At Last*, was even longer in arriving, eventually being released in 1996. ▤

Handwritten lyrics by Richard Ashcroft, photographed with a selection of Ashcroft's favourite albums

THE DRUGS DON'T WORK

THE VERVE

COMPOSED BY **RICHARD ASHCROFT**

'THE DRUGS DON'T WORK' WAS RECORDED BY WIGAN-BASED band The Verve, who added the 'The' in 1994 after the record label of the same name threatened legal action.

The line-up on 'The Drugs Don't Work' was Richard Ashcroft (vocals/guitar), Nick McCabe (guitar), Simon Jones (bass), Simon Tong (guitar/keyboards) and Peter Salisbury (drums). In spring 1999 Ashcroft, the leader, announced that the band was splitting up as he was going to concentrate on a solo career. However, he has dramatically left the group on more than one occasion in the past, only to make a triumphant return with even better material. For example, after an acrimonious, and seemingly irrevocable, split in 1995 they re-

formed early the following year with Simon Tong joining on guitar.

Having been cited by Oasis as the best band in Britain, in the summer of 1997 The Verve arguably proved it with the release of the album *Urban Hymns*. The first single was 'Bitter Sweet Symphony', based on an instrumental version of The Rolling Stones' hit 'The Last Time' performed by The Andrew Loog Oldham Orchestra, but with Ashcroft's lyrics. It reached Number Two in the UK, but the follow-up, Ashcroft's classic 'The Drugs Don't Work', went all the way to Number One.

The song and the album brought the group many accolades, including prestigious Brit and Ivor Novello awards. 🗎

THE LAST WALTZ

ENGELBERT HUMPERDINCK

COMPOSED BY **LES REED/BARRY MASON**

BORN GERRY DORSEY, ENGELBERT Humperdinck's career as a household name began when he reached Number One with his first hit, the record-breaking 'Release Me'. 'There Goes My Everything' missed the top slot by one place, but his third release, Les Reed and Barry Mason's 'The Last Waltz', emulated his first by topping the UK charts.

"Les Reed and I always used to meet at Les's house in Woking, Surrey," Barry Mason says. "We were originally introduced by a publisher named Stuart Reid, who thought we would work well together. I'd already had a couple of hits while Les was an arranger. Stuart put us together and we had a hit pretty quickly with The Fortunes' 'Here It Comes Again' in October 1965, and thought, 'We've cracked it, we're gonna make a million pounds!' Of course we then wrote around a song a week for the following year, without having any hits whatsoever, which was really frustrating.

"So there we were on a dark winter afternoon at Les's house, and we were in the middle of writing 'Everybody Knows' which was to become a hit for The Dave Clark Five. We were actually trying to a get middle eight for it, and couldn't so we eventually finished it without one. However, after about the tenth cup of tea when we'd dried up of ideas, we were just chatting, and Les started talking about when he was a young lad. He mentioned his parents would go to a village on a Saturday night, and that he would always know when they were coming back because he could hear the MC over at the village hall saying, 'Take your partners please for the last waltz.'

"There was then a long pause, and I then asked Les, 'Has anybody ever written a song called '"The Last Waltz"?' – which was a million dollar moment, just a piece of luck that the conversation had turned that way. And then we wrote the song, or rather it wrote itself once we had that title – just 20 minutes' work and it was finished. When we did the demo it was in the middle of flower power – sex, drugs and rock 'n' roll – and we were in the studio and some hip disc jockey, who was probably half stoned on a joint, asked us, 'What's the title of the song?' When we told him, he burst out laughing, and said, 'No guys, tell me the real title' – he didn't believe it! You wouldn't have got four pence on that idea selling at the time, what with all the uppers and downers and tripping going on then.

"However I knew Engelbert Humperdinck's manager Gordon Mills very well so we gave the demo to Gordon and crossed our fingers. A while later I was over in Malta doing a broadcast on local radio – with no air conditioning and with the biggest hangover in living memory – when somebody showed me a copy of the *New Musical Express* which said that the follow-up to Engelbert's 'There Goes My Everything' would be 'The Last Waltz'. As you can imagine, that was one of the best moments of my life, despite the way I was feeling. The record was released on 23 August 1967 and took just two weeks to reach Number One and stayed there for five weeks."

Working score by Barry Mason and Les Reed

FOR ENGELBERT HUMPERDINCK "THE LAST WALTZ" BY. LES REED/BARRY MASON.

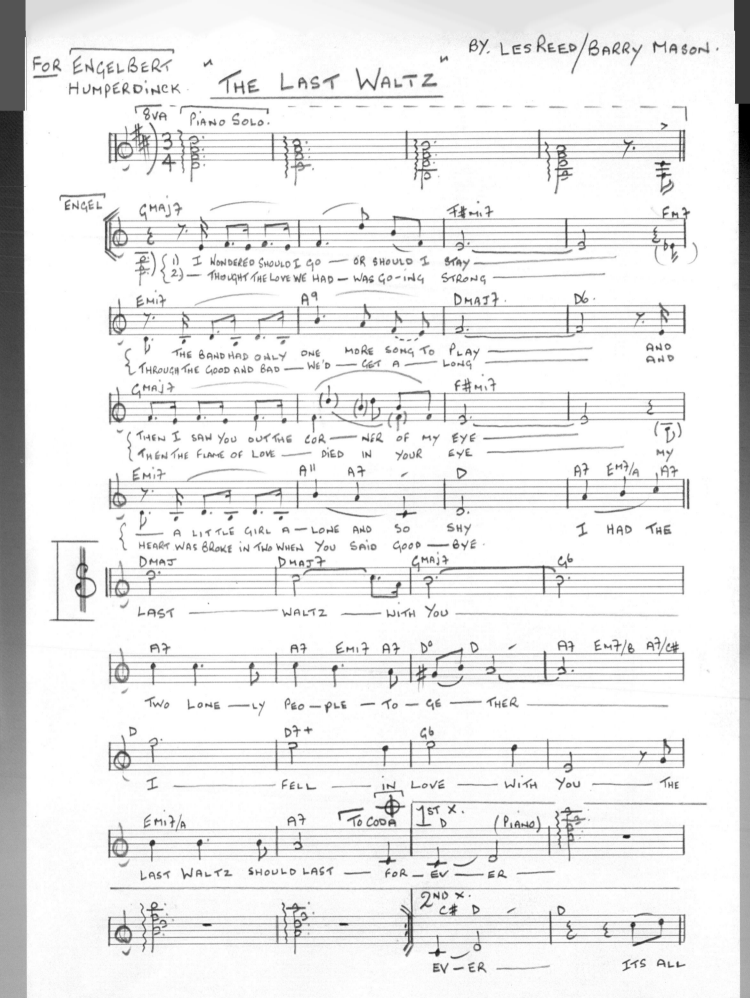

ORDER REF: 12674

"The More You Ignore Me, The Closer I Get"
by MORRISSEY

I will be
in The bar
with my head
on The bar
I am now a central
part
of your minds
landscape.
wheTher you
care / or do not
I'VE MADE UP
YOUR MIND

The More you
ignore me — The
clos___
I ge___

BEWARE!
I bear more grudges
Than lonely High
Court Judges
When you sleep
I will creep
o your ThoughTs
like a bad debT That you cant pay
la-de-dah-dah
CLUNK

THE MORE YOU IGNORE ME THE CLOSER I GET

MORRISSEY

COMPOSED BY MORRISSEY

THE SMITHS WERE FORMED IN Manchester in 1982 by Stephen Morrissey and guitarist Johnny Marr, with local musicians Andy Rourke and Mike Joyce coming in on bass and drums respectively. Morrissey's wonderfully gloomy vocals and his passion for such diverse characters as Oscar Wilde, Johnnie Ray and Billy Fury, made him a fascinating frontman for the group. Their debut chart single, 'This Charming Man', began a four-year run of hit singles, 16 in all, and six major albums, including four that got to Number Two and the chart topping *Meat Is Murder*. The group folded in 1987 as Morrissey appeared to be upset at Marr playing with other artists like Bryan Ferry and Billy Bragg, although Rourke and Joyce had been playing as a sideline with The Adult Net for two years.

Morrissey's solo career has brought him ten more years of success, his singles usually having intriguing titles, such as 'You're The One For Me, Fatty', 'November Spawned A Monster', 'Ouija Board Ouija Board' and 'We Hate It When Our Friends Become Successful'. Refreshingly, Morrissey doesn't disguise his lyrics, dress them up or give them more acceptable titles. The 15th of his two dozen solo hits, was the 1994 single, 'The More You Ignore Me The Closer I Get', his final Top Ten record to date.

NAGOYA HILTON

GUEST STATIONERY

The Number Of the Beast

I left alone, my mind was blank
I needed time to get the memories from my mind
What did I see, Can I believe,
That what I saw that night
was real and not just fantasy

Just what I saw, in my old dreams
Were they reflections of my warped mind
Staring back at me
'cause in my dreams, it's always there
the evil face that twists my mind and
Brings me to despair

the Night was black was no use holding back
'cause I just had to see was someone watching me
In the mist dark figures move and twist
was all this for real or just some kind of hell
666 the Number of the beast
Hell and fire was spawned to be released

Torches blazed and sacred chants were praised
As they start to cry hands held to the sky
In the night the fires burning bright
the ritual has begun Satan's work is done
666 the Number of the beast
Sacrifice is going on tonight

Handwritten lyrics by Steve Harris

THE NUMBER OF THE BEAST

IRON MAIDEN

COMPOSED BY STEVE HARRIS

IRON MAIDEN'S FIRST TWO ALBUMS, *IRON MAIDEN* **AND** *KILLERS,* featured Paul Di'Anno on lead vocals. The only short-haired member of the outfit, he was replaced by former Samson frontman Bruce Dickinson for the third album, *The Number Of The Beast*. "For us it was our best album yet," Iron Maiden founder, Steve Harris recalls with pride. "My personal favourites are 'Number Of The Beast' and 'Hallowed Be Thy Name', both of which are still exciting to play live, even now. Calling it *Number Of The Beast* got us into a big press ballyhoo in America – 'agents of the devil', and all that – but we didn't play it up as much as we could have."

The album went to Number One in the UK while the single scored in the charts on both sides of the Atlantic.

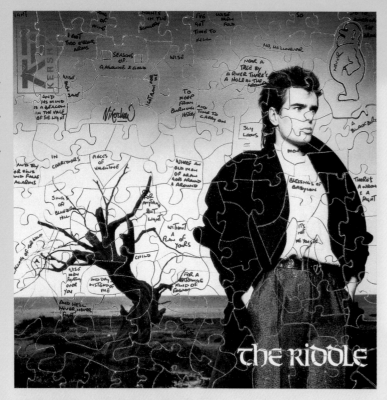

THE RIDDLE

COMPOSED BY **NIK KERSHAW**

'YOUR SONG', WHICH ALSO features in this book, was the first single that Nik Kershaw bought, a little later forming a group called Half Pint Hog with schoolfriends. After leaving school, in 1976, he formed Fusion, who had a short recording career before splitting in 1982. Multi-instrumentalist Kershaw's solo career was launched in 1983 with 'I Won't Let The Sun Go Down On Me', which would make Number Two when re-released the following year. By the time Nik released 'The Riddle', late in 1984, he'd had two Top Ten and two Top 20 hits.

'The Riddle', from the album of the same name, was the subject of much speculation as to its meaning. Fifteen years on, Nik explains, "My producer, Peter Collins came to my house before the second album to listen to my new songs, and although he thought they were okay, he didn't hear a hit single. When he'd gone I went straight upstairs and wrote 'The Riddle' in ten minutes, with a rough lyric that was just gibberish. When I came to demo the song I still only had the temporary words, as I just couldn't come up with any lyrics that sounded as good, so I left them in! When the single came out, still with the original, and meaningless, words I found myself in a position where people were constantly asking me what it meant. It didn't help when the record company, MCA, decided to set up a competition around the meaning of the lyric! I remember going to appear on Bruno Brookes' show on Radio One, and he'd been running a competition on it all week. At the time I just couldn't own up!"

'The Riddle' was the fifth of Nik's eleven hit singles in Britain. 🗎

THESE ARE THE DAYS OF OUR LIVES

COMPOSED BY **QUEEN**

IN 1989, WHEN _THE MIRACLE_ WAS released, many Queen fans wondered if the four members of Queen would begin to concentrate mainly on solo projects. Freddie Mercury refuted this: "I think we know each other quite instinctively now after all these years, and there wasn't anything like, 'Oh, I want to go and further my career without you…it wasn't that sort of thing. We've been together now 18 years, I would say, and if egos came into it they would have done that a long time ago, and we'd have gone our separate ways. I think it's just that after a while we get bored with each other and we need a bit of space."

In 1991, though, they were back in grand style with a new album. 'These Are The Days Of Our Lives' was taken from _Innuendo_, the last album Queen made during Freddie Mercury's lifetime. Although credited to Queen, the song was largely written by drummer Roger Taylor, previously responsible for the hits 'Radio Ga Ga' and 'A Kind Of Magic'. The album was recorded at Metropolis Studios in Chiswick, London and Mountain Studios, Montreux, Switzerland, and the promotional interviews for around the world recorded at the former studio with broadcaster Mike Read.

By the end of 1991, the chart topping album had supplied four hit singles: 'Innuendo', 'I'm Going Slightly Mad', 'Headlong' and 'The Show Must Go On'. To commemorate Mercury's death a month earlier, the December 1991 single 'These Are The Days Of Our Lives' was coupled with a re-release of 'Bohemian Rhapsody'. The double A-side went to Number One in the UK, staying at the top for five weeks, with all profits going to AIDS charities.

In the spring of 1993 'These Are The Days Of Our Lives', performed by George Michael and Queen with Lisa Stansfield, featured on George Michael's _Five Live_ EP. The chart topping EP also contained Michael's duet with the band on 'Somebody To Love'. 🗎

Working lyrics by Roger Taylor

V1   Sometimes I get to feelin'
         I was back in the old days – long ago .
When we were kids – when we were young –
         things seemed so perfect – you know
The days were endless – we were crazy // – we were young
The sun was always shining – ~~the fish were jumping~~ we just lived for fun ~~slow~~
Sometimes it seems like lately – I just don't know
The rest of my life's ~~has~~ been just a show .

Ch.   These were the days of our lives —
The bad things in life ~~were~~ so few seemed .
These days ~~were~~ all are gone now (but one thing's still true) is
      When I look, + I find, that I ^ love you .
                        still

V2   You can't turn back the clock – you can't turn back the tide
         Ain't that a shame .
I'd like to go back one time on a rollercoaster ride
         When life's just a game .
?!   No use in sitting and a thinkin' on what you did .
     When you can **lay** back and enjoy it through your kids
Sometimes it seems like lately – I just don't know
?!   I'd better ~~sit~~ sit back and go – with the flow .

'Cos, these are the days of our lives, time
They've gone in the ~~tick~~ swiftness of ~~time~~
These days are all gone now but some things ~~they're~~ remain,
      When I look, + I find ~~the~~
                no change .

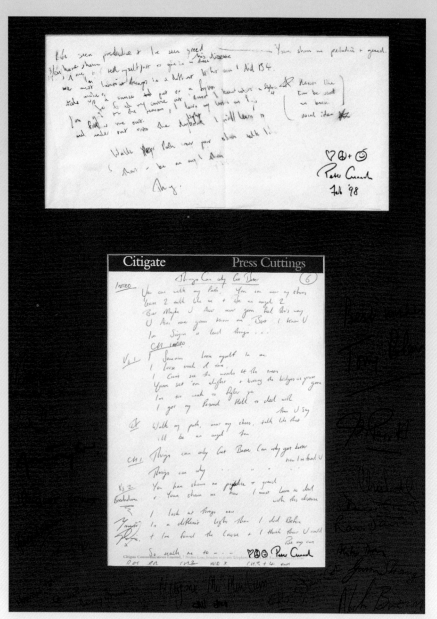

THINGS CAN ONLY GET BETTER

D:REAM

COMPOSED BY **PETER CUNNAH/JAMIE PETRIE**

AS D:REAM PETE CUNNAH AND JAMIE Petrie began having hits in 1992 when 'U R The Best Thing' just sneaked into the chart. Their second single, 'Things Can Only Get Better', first charted in 1993 but again fared better on its re-release in 1994 when a remixed version reached Number One. Three years later it was a hit again as Tony Blair's Labour Party adopted it as their theme song for their victorious election campaign.

"Getting the song taken up by the Labour Party was the latest in a line of events for us," Cunnah says. "I think what happened was that at the party conference in Brighton, where Tony Blair was the newly-elected leader of the opposition, they used it to close the conference with. The next thing I knew they were on the phone to me saying, 'It's gone down so well we want to use it for our next conference,' and then it just catapulted from there. The election night when Labour won in May 1997 was incredible. I'll never forget that experience of having our song bringing in what was really a new era in British history."

"It was written from dreams and hope, so maybe that's why the Labour Party chose to use it," Petrie suggests. "We'd been suffering from over ten years of the Conservative Party and the country needed a change. We would never have thought five years before what would have happened to the song, and it's possibly the first time there's been that marriage between politics and music in this country. It still feels good.

"The song began when my wife said she was carrying our first child," he continues. "We didn't know if we wanted to hang out together for the rest of our lives, so I sat down and wrote the lyric starting 'you can walk my path, you can wear my shoes...' Peter and I were working together in a duo called Jordan. I used to go over to his bedsit and we used to co-write songs. Peter heard the idea and said, 'Great,' and basically took the idea and made it what it is today. The song was written out of a belief and hope. We were both skint, we were making our own prospects."

"I remember at the time I was working in a fairly miserable office job, where I was sitting opposite Roland Gift's sister in an open plan office," Cunnah recalls. "It was my idea of hell, where lots of quick-fire comments about people's attempts at success would be levelled around the room. I remember her firing something at me like 'things can only get better' or something like that, and I went into the toilet with my Walkman and put it down on tape. I'm not sure if I had that melody or the lyrics. Anyway, when I got together with Jamie we already had that chorus 'walk my path...' and the intro to the current tune was the verse. When I later started D:Ream we had this big saxophone riff rolling underneath it, and I started jamming the chorus. Now the intro and chorus would work, but the other stuff didn't, it was too rocky when this was a very soulful tune. So I ended up re-writing a whole verse section, and that's more or less the shape it held then after three or four versions until we released it. Its evolution was over a long period of time from late '89 until early '92.

"The first time it came out we got lucky with a release date of 27 December 1992, which is a great window for a new band. Then we made it to Number 24 without any effort, and thought that was fine and then followed it up with the next single 'U R The Best Thing' in the spring. It wasn't until a year later and after a tour with Take That when we re-released it, that it hit the psyche of the country and stayed at Number One for four weeks. Actually most people don't realise it had been around the year before."

COMPOSED BY **ANDY HILL/PETE SINFIELD**

DESPITE ONLY SEVEN YEARS OF HITS, Celine Dion is already one of the Top 50 artists of all time in the UK charts. Like Elton John, Aretha Franklin, Cliff Richard and George Michael, many of her hits have come as duets with other singers – among them Barbra Streisand, The Bee Gees, R Kelly and Peabo Bryson. In 1994, though, she was on her own as she took the Andy Hill/Pete Sinfield track 'Think Twice' to Number One all round the world.

"'Think Twice' was part of a session of one of the last two songs Andy Hill and I wrote," Sinfield recalls, "the other being 'Call The Man', ironically enough also recorded by Celine Dion. It was written at Andy's place in Surrey, and also in Abbey Road where I used to live. Andy really is a genius for melodies, he's quite extraordinary, and he's annoying sometimes that he will take on production gigs and so I would have to wait around until he finished something. In this case he had come back from a trip to Los Angeles to work with a male artist who I wasn't totally convinced about, but Andy asked me to write some lyrics to a tune he'd started.

"I think as much as my lyrics are very autobiographical, Andy's music really does come from his soul, it comes from deep inside, and 'Think Twice' just got both those things at a point in time. It has an awful lot of expression of something, probably desperation. I have thought my everything depended on someone else, I've been that jealous person.

"Oddly enough 'Think Twice' wasn't as autobiographical as some other songs perhaps were, and yet it's full of all these things that make a song work. Even when we finished it we had it sitting around because nothing happened with it, although I thought it was good. The original demo had been around three or four months and was a good professional song but I didn't love it as much as some other numbers. So I actually gave it to another band called Big Blue, who were managed by a friend of mine called Allan James. The girl in the band, Mellie, had this nice sort of husky voice, and they made a demo which was okay.

"In the meantime, the story goes that Allen Jacobs at EMI Music Publishing had also sent a copy to an A&R guy at Epic Records in Canada, who had played it to Celine Dion, as well as to her producer Chris Neil, who likes having a big box of songs because he's that sort of producer.

The next thing we heard was that Celine, this French Canadian singer we'd never really heard of, had recorded it. Apparently she'd done a song of ours before, which was a version of 'Land Of Make Believe' in French. So I think EMI persuaded Big Blue not to put their version out for a year, so that we would have a chance of it as a single with Celine.

"Then Celine's version came out in America, and it sort of went 75, 74, 60 and went down and out. Then it came out in the UK and it was getting quite a lot of play and she was just becoming a little bit known, but she was just this new Canadian girl. The record company couldn't put her previous US hit, 'The Power Of Love', out here because it was a Jennifer Rush hit. However 'Think Twice' started climbing here before it started going down again, and I thought, 'Oh, well, it is obviously going to do the same as it did in America.' But then it went up, which was a big surprise, and got more and more radio plays and eventually took 14 weeks to get to Number Two.

"I was in hospital at the time, having a minor operation. After three weeks at Number Two I thought, 'Well, enough, I can't take anymore.' Then it went to Number One and you think you'd like it to stay there for one more week, but it stayed there for six or seven, which is about as much as you can ask of any song in your career. It was absolutely magic. The first time I ever saw Celine sing it live was at the Cambridge Theatre, the first time she played for the press here, and I was in tears. She's really quite extraordinary."

THINK TWICE
ANDY HILL & PETE SINFIELD

DON'T THINK I CAN'T FEEL THAT THERE'S SOMETHING WRONG
YOU'VE BEEN THE SWEETEST PART OF MY LIFE FOR SO LONG
I LOOK IN YOUR EYES THERE'S A DISTANT LIGHT
AND YOU AND I KNOW THERE'LL BE A STORM TONIGHT
BABY THIS IS SERIOUS
ARE YOU THINKING 'BOUT YOU OR US

DON'T SAY WHAT YOU'RE ABOUT TO SAY
LOOK BACK BEFORE YOU LEAVE MY LIFE
BE SURE BEFORE YOU CLOSE THAT DOOR
BEFORE YOU ROLL. . . . . . . THOSE DICE
BABY THINK TWICE.

BABY THINK TWICE FOR THE SAKE OF OUR LOVE
FOR THE MEMORY
FOR THE FIRE AND THE FAITH THAT WAS YOU AND ME
I KNOW IT AIN'T EASY
WHEN YOUR SOUL CRIES OUT FOR HIGHER GROUND
COS WHEN YOU'RE HALFWAY UP YOU'RE HALFWAY DOWN
BABY THIS IS SERIOUS
ARE YOU THINKING 'BOUT YOU OR US

DON'T SAY WHAT YOU'RE ABOUT TO SAY
LOOK BACK BEFORE YOU LEAVE MY LIFE
BE SURE BEFORE YOU CLOSE THAT DOOR
BEFORE YOU ROLL THOSE DICE
BABY THINK TWICE. . . . .

SOLO

BABY THIS IS SERIOUS
ARE YOU THINKING 'BOUT YOU OR US

DON'T SAY WHAT YOU'RE ABOUT TO SAY
LOOK BACK BEFORE YOU LEAVE MY LIFE
BE SURE BEFORE YOU CLOSE THAT DOOR
BEFORE YOU ROLL THOSE DICE
DON'T DO WHAT YOU'RE ABOUT TO DO
MY EVERYTHING DEPENDS ON YOU
WHATEVER IT TAKES I'LL SACRIFICE
BEFORE YOU ROLL . . . . . . THOSE DICE
BABY THINK TWICE. . . . .

● BIG NOTE MUSIC LTD / EMI MUSIC LTD 1992

Typed lyrics by Pete Sinfield, signed by sinfield, Hill and Celine Dion

3 Lions

It's coming home. It's coming home. It's
coming – football's coming home (repeat)

(Frank)

Everyone seems to know the score
They've seen it all before
They just know. They're so sure
That England gonna throw it away
Gonna blow it away
~~But I know they can play~~
~~They don't know how to play~~

Coz I remember

Chorus – 3 lions on a shirt
Jules Rimet still gleaming
30 years of hurt
Never stopped me dreaming

(Dave)

So many jokes, so many sneers
But all those oh-so-nears
Wear you down through the years
But I still see that tackle by Moore
And when Lineker scored
~~Bobby belting the ball~~
~~Terry Butcher at work~~
And Nobby dancing

Chorus 3 lions etc

– Music + commentary bit
I know that was then but it could be again
– It's coming home + chorus. Fade to end.

THREE LIONS

THE LIGHTNING SEEDS, BADDIEL & SKINNER

COMPOSED BY **IAN BROUDIE/DAVID BADDIEL/FRANK SKINNER**

AS THE PERENNIAL QUIZ question runs, "Which act had a Number One in 1970, and another Number One in 1990 with a completely different group line-up?" – the answer, of course, is the England World Cup Squad!

They first charted in 1970 when 'Back Home' went to Number One, a song written for them by Bill Martin and Phil Coulter; unfortunately it didn't help the lads down Mexico way. 'This Time (We'll Get It Right)' from the pen of Smokie's Chris Norman and Pete Spencer, proved sadly unprophetic in Spain in 1982. The record fared better than the football, as Kevin Keegan led his team up the chart to Number Two. In 1986 the squad's song 'We've Got The Whole World At Our Feet' contained those classic lines, "You'll hear the Lions roar…" and "There's not a single team that we can't beat" – ah, not strictly true, but if the Argentinians had recorded it…

The England team released a single in 1988 to support their campaign in the European Championship finals, with the help of those three strikers Stock, Aitken And Waterman. On the pitch the honours went to Holland, and the single fell a little flat too, peaking at Number 54. New Order took the team in hand two years later, helping them to a Number One with 'World In Motion', but on the field most of the motion went Germany's way. In the Nineties, comedians turned lyricists David Baddiel and Frank Skinner linked up with The Lightning Seeds and struck the top of the UK charts twice with their 'Three Lions', to help make football songs 'cool' again. It went to Number One in the summer of 1996, reaching the top for a second time in 1998, as 'Three Lions '98'. ▣

'Gravestone' lyrics engraved by Rod Temperton

THRILLER

MICHAEL JACKSON

COMPOSED BY **ROD TEMPERTON**

THE PROBLEM WITH SOMETHING AS SUCCESSFUL as 'Thriller' is trying to follow it, as Michael Jackson is constantly aware. "No matter what you do, you're competing against your previous product and everybody's expecting more," he complains. "You really have to top yourself all the time, and it's hard. You should grow, you should get better. It's like that saying, 'I'm not getting older, I'm getting better.'"

The song 'Thriller' was written by former Heatwave member, Rod Temperton, who also wrote Jackson's 'Rock With You' and 'Off The Wall'. The album of the same name was produced by Quincy Jones and sold three million copies in the UK alone.

The single was showcased in a 14-minute, million-dollar video choreographed by Jackson himself, and featured a monologue from horror actor Vincent Price. ▣

TIE ME KANGAROO DOWN SPORT

ROLF HARRIS

COMPOSED BY **ROLF HARRIS**

BORN OF WELSH PARENTS IN PERTH, AUSTRALIA IN 1930, THE multi-talented Rolf Harris is not only an artist, songwriter and performer but a pianist and sculptor. Rolf got his break after coming to Britain, auditioning for TV producer Jo Douglas and drawing cartoons on children's television. Over a 37-year period Rolf has had eight hit singles, including the Number One 'Two Little Boys' and an offbeat version of Led Zeppelin's 'Stairway To Heaven'. His first taste of chart success came, though, with 'Tie Me Kangaroo Down Sport'.

"In the mid Fifties when I first came to England, I was entertaining at a club for Australians and New Zealanders called the Down Under Club," Harris says. "I was getting everybody to sing along with me and my piano accordion on stuff like 'Waltzing Matilda'. Of course with that kind of act you're always on the lookout for songs with a good chorus.

"Around that time a chap called Harry Belafonte was sweeping the world with his calypso music, and it was the first time anyone had heard that kind of stuff, it was absolutely amazing and everybody loved it. I went to a party one night and friends were playing an album, there was one with a chorus that said, 'tie me donkey down there, let him bray let him bray, everybody...' I thought it was a great song, I could turn it into an Australian calypso and make it a kangaroo instead of a donkey. When I tried to do it, it didn't fit, kangaroo has one syllable too many. However, I couldn't get the idea out of my head, 'tie me kangaroo down there'. I thought 'there' was too insignificant for such an important place in the

musical construction of the song, so I tried 'mate' and that didn't sound right. So then I tried 'sport' and knew I had it! The tune seemed to write itself – almost as if it had been handed out of mid-air to me.

"Sometime later I was painting a portrait on a sheet of hardboard and was trying to dry it off and suddenly found the piece of board was red hot. I picked it up and fanned it to cool it down and it made this amazing noise, 'bluh blub bluh'. It fitted beautifully to the song! Obviously, had I found this out before the song it would never have happened but because the song was in existence I could see where it would fit – it was a magical combination!

"I started writing the rest of the words – silly things, anything Australian that would fit – and then I started singing it at the club. It went down really well so I did it for about three years before it was actually recorded. By then I really knew how it should be performed for maximum effect and I think that helped it go straight to Number One in four weeks Australia-wide in 1960. Then it came out in 1962 on an album and got to Number Three in the States in 1963. Apparently even Pat Boone had wanted to record it. Since then it's been covered in German, Dutch, Japanese and Swedish. Not a bad return for something originally recorded on one microphone suspended from the ceiling with everyone standing around it!"

The song reached Number Nine in the UK in 1960. ▨

TUBTHUMPING

COMPOSED BY **CHUMBAWAMBA**

FIRST PERFORMING IN 1983, A DECADE BEFORE THEY'D HAVE their first hit single, the eight-strong Chumbawamba released their debut album in 1986 independently. The anarchic octet put out *Never Mind The Ballots Here's The Rest Of Your Life* and *English Rebel Songs 1381-1914* in 1987 and 1989 respectively. The second half of the 1990s saw their attitude shift slightly as the more pop-orientated 'Tubthumping' got to Number Two in Britain and Number Six in the States.

"The song came about because of a couple of areas in Leeds called Chapel Town and Harehills," reveals the band's Danbert 'Nobacon' Bruce. "Quite a few of us lived round that area and the council put no money into it at all. The only high spot there is a pub called the Fforde Greene which was our local – in fact it was the only pub for miles in quite a big multi-cultural area. It had a great atmosphere and is the sort of place where people go out to really enjoy themselves and forget about their terrible lives and join in the great atmosphere.

"'Tubthumping' is a song for the underdog really, it's all about resiliance and people having dignity in the face of it all. The original version was quite different and it wasn't immediately obvious that we had such a catchy song, but once we'd taken out some of the ideas and simplified it, things sounded much better. The refrain was probably one by ['Frank'] Boff who's a real football fan, so that would account for the 'chant' style element to it. The bit of 'Danny Boy' in the song was inspired by a guy who went to the pub every night and always went home singing it.

"We produced the song ourselves and it was the first thing we'd done that went mainstream and caught the imagination worldwide. Our original record company had rejected it and our other ideas so we went to EMI Records in Germany. It was easier to get a deal outside of Britain. We'd run our own label before, been independent and decided with this one to go one stage further, make a go of it and it was a total shock for it to be such a success."

Chumbawamba followed 'Tubthumping' with 'Amnesia' (Number Ten) and 'Top Of The World (Ole Ole Ole)' (Number 21). 📄

'Cymbal' lyrics by
Danbert Nobacon

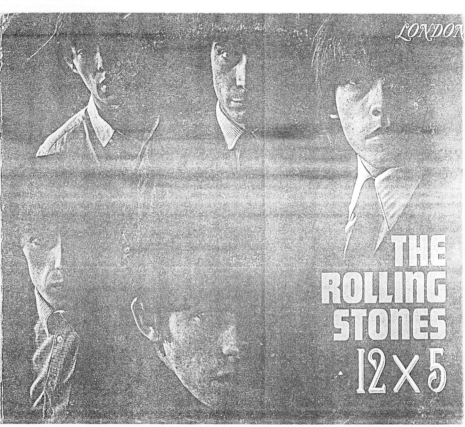

When the sun beats down and burns the tar up on the roof and your shoes get so hot you wish your tired feet were fireproof

Under the Boardwalk down by the sea on a blanket with my baby is where I'll be

Under The Boardwalk out of the sun
UTB – we'll be havin' some fun
UTB – people walkin above
UTB – we'll be makin love
UNDER The Boardwalk
Boardwalk...

Love, Kenny Young

UNDER THE BOARDWALK

THE DRIFTERS

COMPOSED BY **ART RESNICK/KENNY YOUNG**

ORIGINALLY FORMED IN NEW YORK IN 1953, THE DRIFTERS have had an extraordinary career over 47 years, during which time they've had four main lead singers: Clyde McPhatter, Ben E King, Rudi Lewis and Johnny Moore, the latter passing away in December 1998. Their sixth UK hit single, 'Under The Boardwalk', was first heard by many British teenagers via The Rolling Stones' cover version of the Art Resnick/Kenny Young song, begging the question: "What is a boardwalk?"

"My mother lived in Brooklyn right near Coney Island and I used to wander down there, literally under the boardwalk," Young says. "It was a weekend sub-culture hang-out place. There was all these things going on, there were people under blankets making out and having a great time, you could see through the cracks as girls walked by. Being 'under the boardwalk' seemed like an obvious thing to write about, and I remember wondering why hadn't anybody thought of that before.

"I was writing songs with Arty Resnick, who also wrote 'Yummy, Yummy, Yummy' and 'Good Loving'. We wrote 'Under The Boardwalk' in the Brill Building, where we used to work out of the office of Jeff Barry and Ellie Greenwich, with Motown and Leiber and Stoller next door. I had written a few things with Arty before that but they weren't successful. This was to be our first major hit.

"'Under The Boardwalk' was written pretty quick one afternoon," Young explains. "We took the song to Jerry Wexler of Atlantic who took it to producer Bert Burns, who took it to The Drifters, who had a recording session booked. The lead singer at the time was Rudi Lewis who had sung on all The Drifters' hits like 'On Broadway' and 'Up On The Roof'. However, the day the session was booked to do 'Under The Boardwalk', Rudi died – a terrible thing to happen. So we got the news that the session had been cancelled, and thought that was that.

"However, Johnny Moore, who used to do backing vocals, was then brought in as new lead singer of The Drifters and he did the vocals with 'Under The Boardwalk' as his first lead. It turned out great, and it just took off, like they did in those days – you put a record out, it gets played, and The Drifters would get plays automatically, they were pretty big then. I didn't play close attention in those days about records breaking in different territories or different states, but it was a big summer hit in July 1964.

"There have been many cover versions, probably over 100, maybe more. The major ones were by The Rolling Stones, and Bruce Willis who did a version which made Number Two in the UK, along with others by Tom Tom Club, Ricky Lee Jones, Bette Midler, Sam And Dave and many others. It's been good to us over the years – I'm glad my mother lived right near that boardwalk..." ▣

VALOTTE

JULIAN LENNON

COMPOSED BY JULIAN LENNON/JUSTIN CLAYTON

BORN IN LIVERPOOL IN 1963, JULIAN LENNON'S RECORDING career as a singer/songwriter was blighted by comparisons with his famous father, John. After playing in groups like The Lennon Drops, solo success came with 'Too Late For Goodbyes' from the album *Valotte*. The title track itself became Lennon's second hit in December 1984 (Number Five in the US).

"When I signed up with Charisma Records, Tony Stratton-Smith suggested that I go away to France and do some writing," Lennon explains. "So I took this long coach ride with Justin Clayton and Carlos Morales and we found ourselves in the middle of nowhere in a little beaten up old chateau called Valotte. There was a moat and some land and a few outhouses, and after a bit of deliberation we set up in one of the old barns. It took a while, but eventually we relaxed and lost the noise and dirt and general madness of London. The scene couldn't have been more different, it was so quiet we could hardly get a telephone line out. We ate beautiful food, rowed out to the outhouses and saw beautiful sunsets. After we'd adjusted to this life, being close to nature, I found an inner calm and the song was born from that. It was a co-write with Justin and it's basically about longing for a place to live with the love of your life. It was the first time I'd been back to the country since my late teens and I loved it.

"We had a little eight-track reel-to-reel with us to throw the ideas down. When our producer, Phil Ramone, heard our stuff he got straight on the phone and the next thing I knew I was in Alabama at the famous Muscle Shoals studios. It was a nerve-racking experience working with all these great musos in the studio until I relaxed and got a bit of confidence. Then the track started coming together.

"In the studio it was important for me to capture the moment and the reason why the track was originally written, and keeping the visualisation of the chateau and the sunsets in mind. I tried to link it as closely as possible with my vocals, trying to achieve a feeling of time and place, which was hard being in southern America with all these people in the studio! It was the first song that I did final vocals on for the album, so it helped guide me for the rest of the album.

"It was my first single in the States, but strangely enough I didn't feel like I was just waiting for the reaction. Writing, recording and singing to me is so natural that I feel like, 'Well folks – there it is, *que sera*,' and all that. I just hope for the best and if not, well that's okay too. It didn't feel important and still doesn't, it's not why I write songs in the first place. Looking back at the album I feel sometimes that it's a naïve attempt at life but not a bad first shot at all."

Handwritten lyrics by Julian Lennon

VIENNA

ULTRAVOX

COMPOSED BY **WILLIAM CURRIE/CHRISTOPHER CROSS/WARREN CANN/MIDGE URE**

ULTRAVOX TRANSMOGRIFIED FROM THE GROUP TIGER LILY IN 1976, singer John Foxx later going solo. Former Slik/Rich Kids/Thin Lizzy member Midge Ure joined in 1979 with the group first charting in 1980. It was their third hit, 'Vienna', which really put them on the map, racing up to Number Two and staying there for a month behind Joe Dolce's 'Shaddap You Face', a comedy record that Ultravox have never seen the humour of.

"I had just joined Ultravox who'd lost their singer and guitarist and been dropped by their record company," Midge Ure recounts, ignoring the ignominy. "In the first couple of weeks of rehearsing and writing, I got the chorus line 'it means nothing to me' going round in my head. The seed of 'Vienna' was sown when our old manager kept mispronouncing the title of the Fleetwood Mac song 'Rhiannon' as 'Vienna'. It seemed to link up with the hook I was hearing in my head, so I went off and read up about the city, especially about the turn of the century people and events that happened there.

"I used the city as a purely romantic imagery point to write a holiday romance, and that's basically what the song is about. The idea of being somewhere special where you're not doing the daily grind and you have a different attitude. You meet someone in this romantic city and think it's all going to continue when you go home, but of course in the cold light of day it's not the same. That's why the song harks back to the line 'it means nothing to me' – 'now' is nothing, 'then' was how I preferred it, so give me that time back again."

The holiday romance of the lyrics is as misplaced as that of the recording, Ure recalls. "It was a logistical nightmare," he says. "We were using a lot of synthesisers and drum machines and because we didn't have MIDI in those days, we couldn't synchronise all the parts of the song. It ended up as a complicated mix of live performances being recorded, pre-set tapes and drum machines, lots of stopping and starting in-between and finally cutting and joining several master tapes and then re-recording over these. It was the third single off the album and originally the record company wanted us to edit the song down. We said it had to be like that or nothing and were proved right.

"Once it was a hit, the album sales went crazy, but the record was at Number Two before we made a video. We had to finance it ourselves and shot it on 16mm because we wanted it to be like a film, not a video and because we pulled so many favours it only ended up costing us £16,000. The director was Russell Mulcahy, who was only an editor at the time. He's since gone on to make features but it was his big chance to prove himself. We went to Vienna for the day for the first time ever but a few of the scenes were shot around Covent Garden and Kilburn too – maybe not quite as romantic, but quite appropriate in an odd way, as 'Vienna' can be whatever you make it."

Until their initial demise in 1985 Ultravox had 15 UK hit singles, reuniting briefly for another two in 1986. Tony Fennelle replaced Midge Ure in 1993 and that same year 'Vienna' recharted at Number 13.

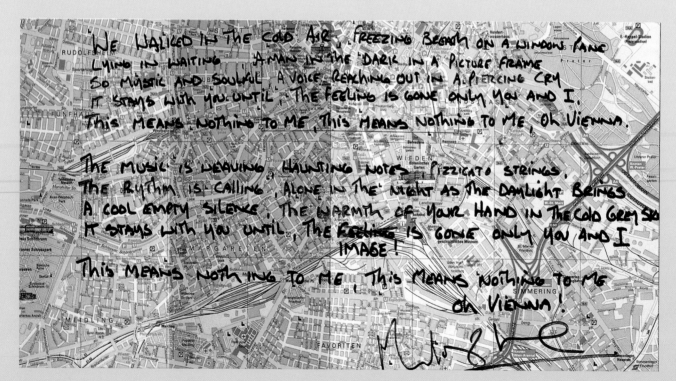

'Map' lyrics by Midge Ure

WAKE UP BOO!

THE BOO RADLEYS

COMPOSED BY **MARTIN CARR**

TAKING THEIR NAME FROM HARPER LEE'S PULITZER
Prize-winning novel *To Kill A Mockingbird*, The Boo Radleys came into existence as a group in 1988. Previously signed to Rough Trade, the hits started coming when the band joined Creation Records.

"'Wake Up Boo!' was our eleventh single and it sold more than the previous ten put together," the band's Martin Carr admits, "although all of them charted. I normally write at night, but this one was written in the day watching telly, which is unusual for me – which is probably why it sounds different, and which is why I remember it because I took so much time over it. It usually takes me an hour or two to write a song, but this took me a couple of days just to make sure everything was right. I've never worked on a song so much before or since – maybe I should!

"I wanted to write about how much I loved autumn and I particularly liked 'Autumn Almanac' by The Kinks. October is my favourite month, so I thought I'd write a song about how much I hate summer and like autumn. Ironically, the record was released in April and is now forever associated with summer. I'm surprised by the lyric sheet I found, because it actually says 'Wake Up Boo!' on it, which makes me think it's not the very first draft because I was playing with all sorts of autumny kind of words and titles. Then it just came, you write a few words and then you start to get a theme.

"Originally, I was just going to call it 'Wake Up' but I knew there was an XTC song of that title, so the obvious thing to put in was 'Boo', which meant it was one of ours – a good job because the same week we released it, Elastica released one called 'Waking Up' or something.

"Not only did I spend ages writing it, we spent a long time recording it as well. It originally had loads of big guitars on it, it just sounded like one of our songs but a bit better. We recorded four songs for an EP, in the summer of 1994, and Creation loved it, it was gonna be a single although I had doubts that it was a bit too indie. The first version was rather a cop-out, but we decided to redo it which was quite brave for us because we never released anything without big guitars on before. So we re-did it with some of Tom Jones' brass section at Rockfield studios in Wales, as one of them had played with us before. We'd written out what we wanted them to play which was based on this minor-key flamenco guitar thing I'd written and I was asking, 'Can you get it like the Stax sound?', but they were bouncing along more like Tom Jones, so I changed it and it became more of a very major happy thing. Oh, and the piano is the same one that was played on 'Bohemian Rhapsody' – we didn't tune it either, which maybe we should have..."

'Wake Up Boo!' reached Number Nine in the UK in 1985.

Working lyrics by Martin Carr

Walking Down Madison.

Walking Down Madison
Swear I never had a gun
No I never shot no-one
Wouldn't do it just for fun
Walking Down Madison
Swear I never had a gun
I was philosophising some —
Checking out the bums
See you give 'em your nickels
pennies & dimes but you
can't give 'em hope in these
Mercenary times
And you feel real guilty 'bout the
coat on your back
& the sandwich you had
Chorus: from an uptown apt to a knife
on the A train – it's not that far
from the Charles intep arthouse to the rats
in the basement, it's not that far
to the bag lady frozen asleep in
the park – ohno its not that far
would you like to see some more – I can show you if you'd like to.

WALKING DOWN MADISON

KIRSTY MACCOLL

COMPOSED BY **KIRSTY MACCOLL/JOHNNY MARR**

THE DAUGHTER OF FOLK SINGER EWAN MACCOLL, KIRSTY BEGAN releasing singles during the latter half of the Seventies, her first hit 'There's A Guy Works Down The Chip Shop Swears He's Elvis' reaching Number 14 in 1981. Kirsty's biggest successes have been collaborations (including marriage to producer Steve Lillywhite): Billy Bragg's 'A New England', 'Fairytale Of New York' with The Pogues and 'Walking Down Madison', written with former Smiths guitarist Johnny Marr.

"I was in New York when I wrote it," MacColl says. "In fact I actually thought of it while I was walking down Columbus Avenue, but that didn't scan as well! It was weird because I was thinking about Bob Marley's song 'I Shot The Sheriff' as I was walking along, but I'd also been spending a lot of time in New York, which had a lot of impact on me – the immense wealth and the third-world poverty all mixed up, which is what the song is all about really.

"I wrote the lyrics with a brisk walking speed in mind as the rhythmic basis of the song, and had them sitting in my notebook for ages but didn't have any music for them. I tried out writing a few ideas musically for it, but I wasn't very happy with any of them. I think it was about a year later that I got a tape through the post from Johnny Marr with a few ideas he'd been working on for us to write together, and one of those tunes was to become the music to 'Madison'. The minute I heard the guitar riff I thought, 'Well, that's perfect,' because it needed to have a very urban feel to it, it wouldn't have worked as a country song, for instance.

"We recorded it partly in England and at Electric Ladyland studios in New York, the one that Jimi Hendrix owned, which is why the album was titled *Electric Landlady*. On the session were Elliott Randall, who had previously played with Steely Dan among others, Johnny Marr on some guitar and keyboards, Guy Pratt on bass, David Palmer on drums, George Chandler and Jimmy Chambers from London Beat singing backing vocals, and a rap by a guy in Manchester named Aniff Cousins. It was a bit of a hit and I still enjoy performing it."

WALK LIKE AN EGYPTIAN

THE BANGLES

COMPOSED BY **LIAM STERNBERG**

IN 1986 ALL-FEMALE ROCK GROUP THE BANGLES TOOK THE international charts by storm with their version of Prince's 'Manic Monday'. Speculation about the Purple One's relationship with the band's frontwoman, Susanna Hoffs, didn't harm sales as The Bangles scored another three UK hits that year, including the Number Three (US Number One) hit 'Walk Like An Egyptian', written by Liam Sternberg.

"I was in Los Angeles across the road from the Capitol Records building in a studio called Eldorado," Sternberg says, "and I was looking at my notebook which was full of ideas. In it I'd noted down the title 'Walk Like An Egyptian', which I'd written during some drunken revelry during a journey on the Dover to Calais ferry. So I left the office, walked down to a magic shop on Hollywood Boulevard and bought a picture of Queen Nefertiti, which I put on my wall and said, 'Make this song a Number One in America and I'll go see you in Egypt!'

"I actually sat down to write the song intending it to be popular, so when I heard that The Bangles were going to do it I was thrilled. I loved their version because they'd virtually reproduced the demo but done everything better. Originally Debbie the drummer was going to sing it, but in the studio they thought it would be fun if everyone had a verse.

"However, it almost didn't get to be a single because of the Middle East conflict before the release. They chose something else first, but finally it came out and, hey, it went to Number One. So I bought that ticket for Egypt and off I went, although I didn't get to see Nefertiti because they don't know where she's buried! The song reached Number One in seven countries and fortunately the Egyptians liked it too, so nobody took offence."

Working lyrics by Liam Sternberg

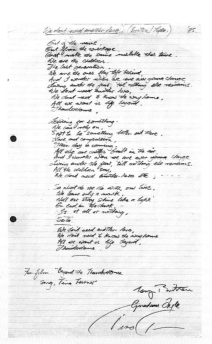

WE DON'T NEED ANOTHER HERO

TINA TURNER

COMPOSED BY **TERRY BRITTEN/GRAHAM LYLE**

ON THE DAY THAT TINA TURNER'S single 'What's Love Got To Do With It?' went to Number One in the States, Australian director George Miller signed her to appear in his new film, *Mad Max: Beyond Thunderdome*. Miller had already co-directed *The Twilight Zone* with Steven Spielberg and John Landis, as well as having directed *Mad Max* in 1979 and *Mad Max 2* two years later. In the third 'Max' film Tina played the part of Aunt Entity to rave notices, her song, 'We Don't Need Another Hero (Thunderdome)' from the film soundtrack reaching Number Two in the UK and Number Three in the US. A follow-up single, 'Out Of The Living', also from the soundtrack, charted in Britain and the States.

At the end of 1985 Tina Turner won the NAACP award as best actress for her performance in the film, while George Miller went on to direct films such as *The Aviator*, *Spooner* and *The Witches Of Eastwick*. ▨

WHEN WILL I BE FAMOUS

BROS

COMPOSED BY **NICKY GRAHAM/TOM WATKINS**

TWINS MATT AND LUKE GOSS WERE born on 29 September 1968 and began their career as Gloss in 1984. After adding bass player Craig Logan they signed a record deal in 1987, making their chart debut with 'When Will I Be Famous', written by the group's manager Tom Watkins and Nicky Graham.

"It was probably around 1985 or '86 that Tom and I hooked up after I bumped into him in my lawyer's office," Graham says. "He told me he had a group called The Hudsons with a singles deal with EMI, who'd had a minor gay club hit with a song 'One Man's Meat Is Another Man's Poison'. It turned out that The Hudsons were Tom himself and someone in his office, so it was all a bit of a joke really. However he was looking for a follow-up, based on the title that he'd thought of called 'When Will I Be Famous'.

"Tom wrote the lyrics on the paper and I shut myself away in the studio and came up with the song, after juggling a few things around. Tom came down to try it but he can't really sing and it had some quite stretching musical notation. The song was put on the shelf, but we knew it was obviously too good to leave. I then told Tom about these three kids I'd found in Lightwater called Gloss and suggested that he saw them. In the meantime he was auditioning for singers to sing the track. I remember one guy was actually very good and thought it was a fantastic song but not right for him, so we were no further on.

"In the meantime, we eventually signed Gloss, changed their name to Bros and started recording an album. Tom kept on saying, 'We've got to get them to do that song,' but when I played it to Matt, Luke and Craig, I remember Matt in particular thought it was too commercial and too high energy and not really his cup of tea. However, Tom phoned them up one day and said, 'Look guys, the American management of CBS have heard this song and say you have to do it,' so they all went, 'Oh, all right.' I'd virtually finished the album and it was the last song to go on and made in a real rush, recording vocals as we were mixing. Of course it ended up being the biggest hit off the album worldwide, even though it only reached Number Two over here.

"I think the song was definitely of its time, ie the Eighties," Graham admits. "Lyrically it was originally supposed to be sung by a man about himself, but when we did it with Bros we turned the lyrics around as if it was a girl asking the question, and Matt was responding to her. Basically it was all about the hook and the general vibe of the track – and of course the group themselves – that made it so successful."

Bros went on to have eight Top Ten hits and a Number One ('I Owe You Nothing') and individually have all had minor success. ▨

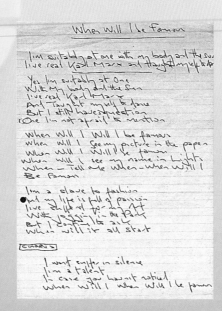

Handwritten lyrics by Nicky Graham

"When You Walk In The Room"

I can see a new expression on my face
I can feel a glowing sensation taking place
I can hear the guitars playing lovely tunes
Every time that you walk In The Room

I close my eyes for a second and pretend its me you want
Meanwhile I try to act so nonchalant.
I see a summer's night with a magic moon
Every time that you walk in the room.

Baby it's a dream come true
Walking right alongside of you.
Wish I could tell you how much I care
But I only have the nerve to stare

I can feel a something pounding in my brain
Just anytime that someone speaks your name.
Trumpets sound and I hear thunder boom.
Every time that you walk in the room.

Words and music by Jackie De Shannon.

Sadly we didn't write our big hits but this one was a bit
special to me as it was my first recording with
the group after my joining on August 3rd 1964 and I took
one half of the dual unison lead line. It's still the strongest
of our hits performance wise and my own particular favourite.
Regards,
Frank Allen

STILL LEADING THE PACK AFTER MORE THAN THREE DECADES
JOHN MCNALLY, FRANK ALLEN, BILLY ADAMSON AND SPENCER JAMES

Alan Field Ltd, 3 The Spinney, Bakers Hill, Hadley Common, Herts, EN5 5QJ
0181 441 1137, 0181 447 0657 (fax)

WHEN YOU WALK IN THE ROOM

THE SEARCHERS

COMPOSED BY **JACKIE DESHANNON**

'WHEN YOU WALK IN THE ROOM' WAS WRITTEN BY EMINENT US songwriter Jackie DeShannon (born Sharon Myers), who first recorded as Sherry Lee Myers at the age of 16, in 1959. Her songs were covered by such artists as The Kalin Twins, Brenda Lee, The Byrds, Kim Carnes, Van Morrison and The Searchers. Searchers bass guitarist and vocalist Frank Allen remembers 'When You Walk In The Room' with affection: "It was the first Searchers record I ever played and sang on, soon after joining the group in August 1964. Before that I had been one of Cliff Bennett's Rebel Rousers, an outfit whose repertoire, coincidentally, The Searchers had plundered to get hold of their best-known hit, a Sonny Bono composition called 'Needles And Pins'. We had already purloined that tune from the original artist, Jackie DeShannon who had flopped with her version. She was not best pleased at having her thunder stolen."

The writing style really suited the melodic, jangly, guitar-based sound of The Searchers, and it was therefore quite natural for them to turn again to Miss DeShannon when a new hit was required. Frank was delighted. "We emphasised the twelve-string guitar, and I got to do joint lead vocal," he recalls, "which was a real thrill for a 'new lad'! This time, however, the act of highway robbery brought a grin to Jackie's face, as she was the writer of the song and therefore just about to come into a large amount of money! She deserved every penny. It's still, in my opinion, the strongest of our hits, and over the years has been covered by a vast array of talent, including Bruce Springsteen, Johnny Logan and a host of others. I hope though, that in the years to come, history will remember it as a Searchers song."

History undoubtedly will, but it's worth mentioning other notable artists who've covered it. These include Del Shannon, Bobby Vee, The Ventures, Billy J Kramer And The Dakotas, Bobbie McGee, Paul Carrack and Child.

WILD THING

THE TROGGS

COMPOSED BY **CHIP TAYLOR**

ORIGINALLY FORMED IN ANDOVER, HAMPSHIRE AS THE
Troglodytes, by 1965 the line-up had settled to Reg Ball, Ronnie
Bullis, Chris Britton and Pete Staples. On signing to Kinks manager
Larry Page, Reg changed his name to Presley, Ronnie to Bond and the
group name telescoped to The Troggs. Given the choice of two songs
as potential singles, they opted for 'Wild Thing', written by Chip Taylor.

"Up until 1965, my success as a songwriter had been mainly with my
country stuff," Taylor says. "Chet Atkins was producing for RCA at the
time, he had become a fan and seemed to be cutting almost everything
I sent down there. So I guess you could say he was single-handedly
keeping me alive in this business until the rock 'n' roll stuff kicked in.

"On this particular day, I had a session booked in the late afternoon to
do a demo of another country song. I guess it was mid-afternoon when
I got a call from an A&R person/producer, Jerry Granahan. He had heard
that I was writing some good rock 'n' roll stuff and asked if I would
make an attempt to write something for a group he was producing,
Jordan Christopher And The Wild Ones. The recording session was only
two days away and he was unhappy with the song selection thus far. I
was so flattered that this guy, whom I had never met or spoken to
before, would ask me to write a song, particularly a rock song, since I
had never had any success in this area of music before.

"As soon as I got off the phone I picked up the guitar and the stream of
consciousness thing that I do started kicking in with this 'Wild Thing'

chorus. Obviously, it wasn't much of anything, but sometimes the
simplest thing can be pretty magical and this one felt pretty good right
away. I kept singing the chorus over and over again and pausing to say
something directly to this girl that I was thinking about. I headed over to
my session with the chorus and the first verse pretty much intact.
Before I left I called my engineer, Ron Johnson, and asked him to have
my microphones and my stool set up. Ron started the tape machine as
soon as I walked through the door. I sat down on my stool and sang it
one time through, making up some stuff along the way. I listened back
and said, 'That's it.'

"If you hear the demo, it sounds almost exactly like The Troggs' record,
except that on my version I'm banging on my old Broadway Kay
acoustic instead of the electric they used. The Wild Ones did record it,
but not with the same spirit or feel as the demo. There were horns and
strings booked for the session already, so they incorporated them into
the arrangement. Can you imagine 'Wild Thing' with horns and strings?
Through my publishing company in England (Dick James Music) the
demo got into the hands of The Troggs' producer, Larry Page, and then
to the boys themselves. The story I heard from them was that they
were looking for one more song for their session. They were given a
stack of approximately 30 demos, and evidently Reg Presley said
something like, 'Oh my God, what the hell was that? Let's hear it
again,' and they all agreed that was the one they would record.

"I can't imagine how that song could've been recorded any better.
Larry Page and The Troggs seemed to catch exactly the same spirit
that was there on the demo. They were absolutely the perfect group
for 'Wild Thing'."

'Wild Thing' reached Number One in the US and Number Two in the
UK in 1966.

'Ocarina' lyrics by Chip Taylor

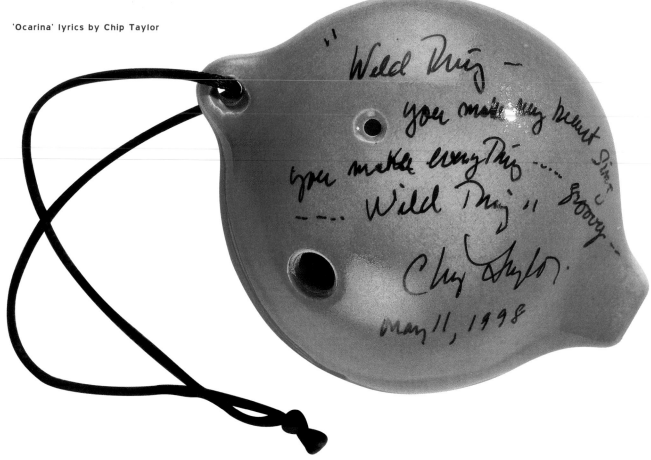

WIND BENEATH MY WINGS

BETTE MIDLER

COMPOSED BY JEFF SILBAR/LARRY HENLEY

'WIND BENEATH MY WINGS' WAS CO- written by Larry Henley, who as the falsetto lead singer with The Newbeats had hits with 'Bread And Butter' and 'Run Baby Run (Back Into My Arms)' in Britain, and seven hits in the States. He also co-wrote 'Am I Not My Brother's Keeper?', the B-side of 'Run Baby Run'. Following a ten-year spell with The Newbeats, Henley left, and from 1974 turned more towards songwriting, penning, amongst other material, 'Wind Beneath My Wings' with Jeff Silbar. The song became a 1983 country hit for Gary Morris in the States, charting in Britain the following year for Lee Greenwood, when it reached Number 49.

In 1988 singer/actress Bette Midler appeared in the Academy award-nominated film *Beaches*, the soundtrack of which included her version of the song, produced by Arif Mardin. The album *Beaches* went gold, as did the single in its own right, the latter going to Number One in the States and Number Five in Britain, giving Midler her first UK hit and winning her a Grammy in 1990 for Best Song.

Henley and Silbar's classic is becoming something of an evergreen, being voted 315th greatest song of all time in a 1992 nationwide UK poll, and becoming British hits for actors Bill Tarmey and Steven Houghton. ▤

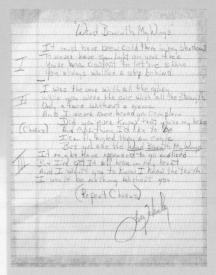

Handwritten lyrics by Larry Henley

WONDERFUL LIFE

BLACK

COMPOSED BY COLIN VEARNCOMBE

LIVERPOOL-BASED BLACK, INITIALLY A trio, was essentially Colin Vearncombe who gigged around Merseyside and released singles on local labels and WEA. After two unsuccessful singles for the latter, Vearncombe's song 'Wonderful Life' was put out on the Ugly Man label for the first of its three releases, eventually reaching Number Eight in the UK (for A&M) in 1987.

"When I write, I wait for the bullet like most people do, wait for the muse to strike and then after that is what makes people's songs individual," Vearncombe says. "I don't think anybody can really say for sure where the ideas come from, but the more open you are to them the easier they come. After that, actually finishing off a song is much harder than getting the idea for one, you've just got to get off your behind and walk about the streets on your own until you find some inspiration. And then eventually they come together, the music and the lyrics go hand over shoulder until they're done.

"'Wonderful Life' was written in about five minutes in late 1985. My wife had given me the words by dumping me and I was descending into self pity and I caught myself just in time. Everything had gone wrong, I was homeless and didn't have anything, I was staying on people's floors, basically. And then

one afternoon I just had that melody line that's in the chorus, 'no need to laugh and cry, it's a wonderful, wonderful life' – bang, it was just there and I just worked backwards from that point. It was absurdly easy.

"The original four-track demo was pretty much unchanged, just embellished later on when I was trying to get a publishing deal but no one would go for it. They said they liked 'Wonderful Life' but they didn't really care much for anything else. So I hung onto it and by then I was with my present manager Steve Baker,

who basically put himself on the line and instead of paying money that was supposed to go to the taxman we sat down and wrote out a schedule of two days recording in a 16-track and two days in an eight-track to do three songs. So we went in and did them, including 'Wonderful Life', and made an independent single. We had met a couple of brothers who had some money and had always had a dream about owning an independent label, so we hooked up with them. Then we managed to get a manufacturing and distribution deal and hired a plugger and press person at a very low-key level, and it made Number 72 in the charts on its own.

"However, we decided to pull it even though the phones were ringing, but because we knew we wanted to re-release it at a later date with a proper chance – because basically an indie record in 1985 just got swamped. So we started negotiations which eventually A&M won because they had one of the only guys with any real ears in the A&R departments, Chris Briggs. After a couple of experiments they let me go off and make it on my own with my ex-partner Dave Dix in the producer's seat. We took the recording that we already had and finished it off as we would have done if we'd had the proper budget, which was basically a remix and a couple of overdubs, and that's the single that sold more than a million copies." ▤

Working lyrics by Colin Vearncombe

WOULD I LIE TO YOU

CHARLES AND EDDIE

COMPOSED BY **MICK LEESON/PETER VALE**

Handwritten lyrics by Mick Leeson

CHARLES PETTIGREW AND EDDIE

Chacon began performing together after meeting in New York, Pettigrew from Philadelphia and Chacon from California having previously played in other outfits. Their debut album, *Duophonic*, spawned their Number One hit (13 in the US). While the duo's roots are firmly in the States – their second hit was 'NYC (Can You Believe This City)' – 'Would I Lie To You' was written by British songwriters Mick Leeson and Peter Vale.

"The song was written in May 1990," Leeson explains. "I'd sent Pete the title, in fact I sent him nearly the whole chorus, and he just put a tune to it. I remember he had the sample of the drum break and that tied us down to a Tamla thing, and it was finished in more or less a day, although we had the hook already. When we finished writing it we really liked it, we both thought it was great. There was no great story behind the lyrics at all, but the verses were deliberately in the style they are. It wasn't meant to be a love song, it was always meant to be ambiguous. When you write a song you're going for that second when the whole relationship is kind of finished or beginning, that crucial moment, and this lady who's being sung to, this is the moment she has to decide whether this guy is telling the truth or not.

"So we wrote it in a day, and took it on our annual trip to Los Angeles where we usually like to play four or five of our new songs. This was in October 1990, and everybody liked it, but nobody knew it would go into the megasphere as it did. Eventually Pete cut the song with an a cappella act from New York called True Image who were signed in the UK, but their A&R man left the company and his successor didn't see the project through, and it was basically dumped. But then they – and we – circulated copies of their album around the business, which is how Josh Deutsch the producer got to hear the song. Josh took basically everything that was good, added some things and made what was there better: I mean, that's what you dream about. But he didn't invent the way it sounds, he refined it from Pete's original ideas. If you're going to write a Whitney Houston song, a ballad or something, then you don't have to be that inventive on your demo because David Foster or someone is going to come along and spend weeks and hundreds and thousands of dollars making it sound absolutely magnificent.

"Anyway, Josh identified the song as the one which would break Charles And Eddie. To break an act you need to be twice as good as everybody else, because you're coming from nowhere. So he identified it as the breakthrough single and worked a long time, and spent a lot of money just going back and getting it better and better. He did a fantastic version, and what we loved best of all is that basically he married it with Tamla, especially the chorus, while the verses are very reminiscent of early Aretha Franklin.

"I remember the first time it was on the radio, the mother of a friend of my little lad said, 'That sounds like a Tamla Motown song, I'm going out to buy it,' which was the first intimation I had that it was a bit special. That's what you're trying to achieve the whole time, trying to write songs that do that to people, and this one seems to have done it. We never thought we would ever have a British Number One, we thought our songs were too complicated, which a lot of them are. However, it made Number One in ten or twelve countries, and as in the USA and Britain it hung around in every territory." 📖

WRONG NUMBER

THE CURE

COMPOSED BY **ROBERT SMITH/ REEVES GABRELS/MARK PLATI**

CRAWLEY BAND THE CURE CAME together in 1976 as The Easy Cure, comprising Robert Smith, Lawrence Tolhurst and Michael Dempsey. Several line-ups later, they achieved a hit in every year of the Eighties in the UK and became stadium superstars in the US towards the end of the decade. 'Wrong Number' is one of the few Cure songs not written entirely by the band.

"In fact this is the only time it's ever happened," singer Robert Smith reveals. "It was a collaboration with an outside writer. In January 1997 I was invited to sing at David Bowie's 50th birthday concert in New York and I'd gone over a couple of days early to rehearse and spend some time with the people there. I got talking to his guitarist Reeves Gabrels and David's producer Mark Plati. Co-incidentally Mark was a big Cure fan and during the week I spent in New York we spent time together and agreed it would be good to do something musically.

"The Cure were just about to bring out the second volume of singles from the last ten years – *Galore* – and I wanted to put a new single on there. I'd written something I thought would work so I went to the studio with Reeves and Mark and that's how 'Wrong Number' came about. I had the music but lyrically, it was based on a phone call I had in New York and the conversation that formed the song took place in the course of me getting to know Reeves and Mark, which is why I wanted to do it with them. Time and place all just seemed to tie in together.

"It was the last single we released. It did well in America and made the Top Ten in European countries. The voice at the end saying, 'Sorry wrong number,' is the wife of a friend that we rang out of the blue. We purposely asked for the wrong name and she said, 'Sorry wrong number,' right on cue." 📖

WRONG NUMBER (13/8/97 VERSION)

LIME GREEN
LIME GREEN AND TANGERINE
ME SICKLY SWEET COLOURS OF THE SNAKES I'M SEEING
LIME GREEN AND TANGERINE
ME SICKLY SWEET COLOURS OF THE DEVIL ~~HAS~~ *IN MY DREAMS*

FRIDAY   *I*   *YOU*
IT GETS TO T~~UES~~DAY AND ~~YOU~~ GIVE ~~ME~~ A CALL
"YOU KNOW I'M GETTING KIND OF WORRIED
~~NO~~ SHE DOESN'T SEEM HERSELF AT ALL...
LIME GREEN AND A SICKLY KIND OF ORANGE
NEVER SEEN HER LIKE THIS BEFORE... "

*JOIN DOTS
TO DISCOVER
MISSING
WORDS.*

✱?

I HAD THE BEST LAID PLANS THIS SIDE OF AMERICA
STARTED OUT IN ~~CHAINS~~ *CHURCH*
△ *+ FINISHED WITH ANGELICA? ✱*
RED ~~WHITE~~ AND BLUE SOUL WITH A SNOW ~~BLIND~~ SMILE
"CAN YOU DIG IT?"   *WHITE*
YEAH I DIG IT IN THE DIRT
AND ~~I'M DOWN HERE FOR SOMETIME~~...
   I'LL BE DOWN HERE FOR A WHILE...

SO PL~~EASE~~ MAKE UP YOUR MIND AND MAKE IT SOON
IS THERE ROOM IN YOUR LIFE
FOR ONE MORE TRIP TO THE MOON?
   O MAMA ?
solo _____ *("is there room etc."*

*try
DOUBLES
NORMS
SALOON ?
telephone
voice bx ?*

BURN ~~BLOOD~~ RED AND GOLD
ME DEEP DARK COLOURS OF THE SNAKES I HOLD
~~BLOOD~~ RED AND GOLD
ME DEEP DARK COLOURS OF THE DEVIL AT HOME
"SHE PULLS ME DOWN JUST AS I'M TRYING TO HIDE
GRABS ME BY THE HAIR AND DRAGS ME OUTSIDE
AND STARTS DIGGING IN THE DIRT...
" FOR A NOT-SO-EARLY-BIRD IT'S THE ONLY WAY
FOR HER TO GET THE WORM..." " *? (DIFFERENT VOICES ?)*

I HAD THE BEST LAID PLANS THIS SIDE OF AMERICA
STARTED OUT IN ~~CHAINS~~
△ *AND FINISHED WITH* *CHURCH* *ANGELICA ?*
RED ~~WHITE~~ AND BLUE SOUL WITH A SNOW ~~BLIND~~ SMILE *WIDE?*
"CAN YOU DIG IT?"   *WHITE*
I HAD THE BEST LAID PLANS THIS SIDE OF AMERICA
STARTED OUT IN ~~CHAINS~~ *(OR KEEP CHAINS — try it ?)*
AND FINISHED _____ *? HARMONICA — FANTASTICA ?! AAGH!*
"CAN YOU DIG IT?"
YEAH I DIG IT IN THE DIRT AND I'LL BE DOWN HERE FOR S~~OMETIME~~...
   A WHILE

*Telephone
bit at "hello — hello is anyone there...
end —
/ other voice?*   *tap.
"sorry. wrong number!!*

YOU AIN'T SEEN NOTHING YET

BACHMAN-TURNER OVERDRIVE

COMPOSED BY **RANDY BACHMAN**

IN THE EARLY SEVENTIES, FORMER GUESS WHO MEMBERS Randy Bachman and Chad Allan, along with Randy's brother Robbie and CF (Fred) Turner, performed as Brave Belt before Tim Bachman replaced Allan and they became Bachman-Turner Overdrive, the latter part of the name borrowed from a trucking magazine. In 1973 they signed to Mercury Records, released their debut eponymous album and saw Blair Thornton replace Tim Bachman. The line-up was now set for their biggest success.

"Bachman-Turner Overdrive had been hugely successful with 'Let It Ride' and 'Takin' Care Of Business'," Randy Bachman explains. "It was coming up to our third album, and we needed a monster to go beyond 'Takin' Care Of Business'. I had this work song that didn't have a title, and I was kind of playing a riff like Dave Mason's 'Only You Know And I Know', but in my song I always had a heavy rhythm part and a light part, so I could use it as a 'test' track to hear how the band sounded playing loud and quiet. Anyway, I was playing these riffs and thought, 'Gee this could be really interesting.' At the same time my brother Gary had decided to stop being our manager, and I was ticked off at him, because we'd decided to move from Winnipeg to Vancouver because we couldn't get any work, but he didn't want to move with us. Gary spoke with a bit of a stutter, so I thought right, I'll get him, I'm going to stutter through this song, I'm going to mix it and send it to him. He'll have a fright that it's on our album, when in fact it wasn't supposed to be, it was really meant just as a joke.

"So I did this track and I was stuttering this 'b-b-b-baby...' kind of thing, it was really done without any thinking, I was singing any old lyrics. It was almost like me rapping with myself, I'd throw in a line and I'd think, 'Gee, two lines later I've got to make this rhyme,' and I did the whole song that way, and – boom! It was literally written in the instant that it was being played, and when I tried to change it, it just didn't work. I don't even know what it means, it seems this song means something different to everybody, as most things do. But I didn't sit there and say, 'I'm gonna write a song about whatever,' I was just playing this Dave Mason rhythm and out came 'I met a devil woman, she took my heart away', and the rest followed.

"I think we did two takes of it and it was over, and I put it away. We then did the album, with one or two attempts at each song, until I had all the tracks over-dubbed. Then a guy named Charlie Fach, who was the head of our label, flew in to Seattle where we were recording, and listened to the album and said, 'Oh, it's great, it's just what they need

for FM radio, but where's the pop masterpiece, the single?' I said, 'We don't have one, and in two days we're back on the road, I can't write one, we can't do it, this is the album.' The engineer then digged me in the elbow and said, 'Play him the work track, you know, the one with all the yelling.' I said, 'You've gotta be kidding,' and he said, 'No, play him that track, it's great.' So I played it for Charlie, who jumps up saying, 'It's a monster, it's a smash,' and I'm saying, 'It can't be, you're crazy – but at least let me re-sing it.'

"This was all about two o'clock in the morning, and I came back the next day about eleven and tried to sing it again, but it just sounded terrible, like I was doing Tony Bennett or something. However Charlie then persuaded me to put the original on the album and that was our first one that had nine tracks. I put the four longest songs on one side and the four shorter songs on the other and added this fifth song, I buried it somewhere near the end of the second side, putting it on just to make Charlie happy. However, I was still embarrassed whenever I heard the track, and then the album came out and Fach phoned me every single day saying, 'This song is a monster, it's Number Two in Detroit on phones, it's Number One in Portland, it's Number Three in Dallas – you've got to release it as a single.' I had approval because I was the producer, and I kept saying, 'No, no, no, I'm embarrassed, I'm singing flat,' I mean, I'm not even a singer to begin with.

"However, Charlie persisted and said, 'Look there's magic there,' and I eventually said, 'Okay, release it as a single, but you'll be sorry, it'll be the end of BTO.' Boy, was I wrong! It came out as a single and it did unbelievably, I think it went to Number One in 16 or 18 countries, and it's been re-recorded several times since then, four, five, six times in different languages. I've got it in Austrian, in Finnish, even in some sort of Egyptian language. The funny thing is that every time we see each other, my brother Gary has never mentioned it. I'm sure he's read this because I've told the story before, but he's never said, 'Why the **** did you do that to me?' But it was never meant meanly, I have nothing against people who stutter but you know when you're an older brother and you have a younger one, it's a kind of a brotherly jab so to speak. However, from that point on he stopped stuttering and stammering, so whatever it did, it achieved something therapeutic at least."

The song reached Number One in the US and Number Two in the UK in 1974. A version by Bus Stop featuring Randy Bachman hit Number 22 in the UK in October 1998. ▤

Handwritten lyrics by Randy Bachman

YOUAI
NTSEEN
NOTHINGYET
RANDYBACHMAN

I MET A DEVIL WOMAN
SHE TOOK MY HEART AWAY
SHE SAID I HAD IT COMIN TO ME
BUT I WANTED IT THAT WAY
SHE SAID THAT ANY LOVE WAS GOOD LOVE
SO I TOOK WHAT I COULD GET
SHE LOOKED AT ME WITH HER BIG BROWN EYES
AND SAID —

* YOU AIN'T SEEN NOTHIN' YET
B-B-BABY, YOU AIN'T SEEN NOTHIN YET
HERE'S SOMETHING THAT YOU'RE NEVER
GONNA FORGET
B-B-BABY, YOU AIN'T SEEN N-N-NOTHIN YET.

AND NOW IM FEELIN' BETTER
COS I FOUND OUT FOR SURE
SHE TOOK ME TO HER DOCTOR
AND HE TOLD ME I WAS CURED
I KNOW THAT ANY LOVE IS GOOD LOVE
SO I TOOK WHAT I COULD GET
SHE LOOKED AT ME WITH HER BIG BROWN EYES
AND SAID —

Randy Bachman

YOUR LATEST TRICK

DIRE STRAITS

COMPOSED BY MARK KNOPFLER

DIRE STRAITS' DEBUT SINGLE, 'SULTANS OF SWING', SET THE
group on the road to success with its release in 1978, although it
didn't chart until the following year, when it reached the Top Ten in
Britain and America.

Between 1979 and 1984 they released five albums, but it was the
sixth, *Brothers In Arms* that was, for many, their finest hour. Produced
by frontman Mark Knopfler and Neil Dorfsman, the album topped the
charts in the UK for three weeks and in the US for nine. While the
album was at the top in Britain, the group received the 1985 Silver
Clef award from the Nordoff-Robbins Music Therapy Charity for
Outstanding Services To British Music. The album brought them a
whole clutch of awards, including Best British Group at the 1985 Brit
awards, another Brit award the following year, and three Grammys.
Spin-off single 'Money For Nothing' also took trophies at the MTV
awards. The fourth single from the album, after 'So Far Away', 'Money
For Nothing' and 'Walk Of Life', was 'Your Latest Trick', which peaked
at Number 26 in Britain. By November 1987, *Brothers In Arms* had sold
a record breaking three million copies in the UK alone.

Working lyrics by Mark Knopfler

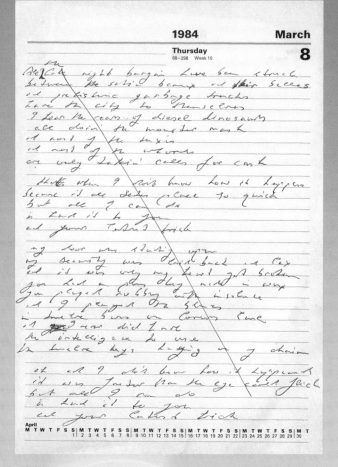

YOUR SONG

ELTON JOHN

COMPOSED BY ELTON JOHN/BERNIE TAUPIN

WRITTEN BY ELTON JOHN AND BERNIE TAUPIN, 'YOUR
Song' came from Elton's debut album and, following his
performance of it on *Top Of The Pops* on 14 January 1971, it
became his first hit single.

The two writers met after answering an advertisement
placed in the *New Musical Express* by Liberty Records. Says
Taupin, "It's always a case of me writing a set of lyrics, then
passing them on to Elton who, after studying them, fits a
tune around them. It's as simple as that." On the meaning of
'Your Song', he says, "That song was meant to have been
written by somebody who hadn't written a song before, and
didn't know how to write. Though it's a basic love song, it's
not meant to be naive…I suppose it's very personal."

Billy Paul covered the song on his 1972 album, *360 Degrees
Of Billy Paul*, having a UK Top 40 hit single with it five years
later. It has also been recorded by Al Jarreau and Cissy
Houston.

Left: sheet music signed by Sir Elton John
Opposite: handwritten lyrics by Bernie Taupin

Its A Little Bit funny This feeling Inside
Im not One of those who can easily Hide
I Dont have much Money But 🙂 if I did
I'd Buy a Big 🏠 where we both could Live

If I was A Sculptor But then again No
or a 😊 who sells ⚗ in a travelling show
I know its Not much but its the Best I can Do
My 🎁 is my 🎵 and this ones for YOU !

And you can tell everybody
THIS IS YOUR SONG IT MAY BE QUITE SIMPLE
BUT NOW THAT ITS DONE I HOPE YOU DONT MIND
I HOPE YOU DONT MIND
THAT I PUT DOWN IN WORDS HOW WONDERFUL LIFE
IS WHILE YOUR IN THE WORLD

I Sat on the △ and kicked off the mess
A FEW OF THE WORDS HAVE GOT ME QUITE ☹
But The ☀ 's Been quite Kind while I wrote this 🎵
Its for people like you that keep it turned On

So excuse me forgetting But these things I do
But you see I've forgotten if their green or their Blue
ANYWAY THE THING IS WHAT I REALLY MEAN
YOURS ARE THE SWEETEST 👁 👁 I'VE EVER SEEN

'Boots' lyrics by Errol Brown

YOU SEXY THING

HOT CHOCOLATE

COMPOSED BY **ERROL BROWN**

IN 1969 ERROL BROWN AND TONY WILSON MADE THEIR
recording debut on the Apple label with a version of John Lennon's
'Give Peace A Chance'. As Hot Chocolate, their hits began in 1970
with 'Love Is Life', and ran unbroken until 1984, the group being only
one of three acts to chart every year of the Seventies. Released three
times in the UK, the song hit Number Two in 1975 and Number Six 22
years later when it was used in the hit film about male strippers *The
Full Monty*.

"We receive requests quite often for songs to be used in TV and
films, which our publisher Brenda Brooker at Rak Music always
deals with," Errol Brown explains. "When a request for its use in this

low-budget unknown British film called *The Full Monty* came in, Brenda stipulated that it could be used as long as it was also used on the closing credits, which is maybe why it had its second chance in the charts.

"I started writing the song because I wanted to get the word 'sex' in a title without being too obvious and 'You Sexy Thing' seemed to be a clever way round it. As it turned out, it was a very good title to use and one that has been kind to me. I wrote it for a very special lady who since became my wife over the last 20 years, and I guess it's one of those songs that people remember in lots of situations. The song seemed to come quite naturally once I'd got the riff and the title,

and the rest came fairly easily.

"I'm happy it's been so popular, both first time round and recently, although a lot of people think that Hot Chocolate had a Number One hit with it over here. It never actually was though: we went in at Number Six in the charts, then up to Number Two at exactly the same time that Queen came in at Number Nine with 'Bohemian Rhapsody' which then went straight to the top. They stayed up there for nine weeks, so there was no way we were going to catch them. But I don't mind that, I respect the fact that we were second place to such a classic song. However, we did reach Number One in the States in some charts, which of course was fantastic." ▤